MODELLING SPATIAL HOUSING MARKETS
Theory, Analysis and Policy

Advances in Urban and Regional Economics

VOLUME 2

Series Editors:
Richard Arnott, Boston College, U.S.A.
Peter Englund, Uppsala University, Sweden

Also in the series:
Papageorgiou, Y. and Pines, D.: AN ESSAY ON URBAN ECONOMIC THEORY

MODELLING SPATIAL HOUSING MARKETS
Theory, Analysis and Policy

by

Geoffrey Meen
The University of Reading, UK

KLUWER ACADEMIC PUBLISHERS
Boston / Dordrecht / London

Distributors for North, Central and South America:
Kluwer Academic Publishers
101 Philip Drive
Assinippi Park
Norwell, Massachusetts 02061 USA
Telephone (781) 871-6600
Fax (781) 871-6528
E-Mail <kluwer@wkap.com>

Distributors for all other countries:
Kluwer Academic Publishers Group
Distribution Centre
Post Office Box 322
3300 AH Dordrecht, THE NETHERLANDS
Telephone 31 78 6392 392
Fax 31 78 6546 474
E-Mail <services@wkap.nl>

Electronic Services <http://www.wkap.nl>

Library of Congress Cataloging-in-Publication Data

Meen, Geoffrey P.
Modelling spatial housing markets : theory, analysis and policy / by Geoffrey Meen.
p. cm. -- (Advances in urban and regional economics ; v.2)
Includes bibliographical references and index.
ISBN 0-7923-7307-3 (alk. paper)
1. Housing--Location--Mathematical models. 2. Regional planning--Mathematical models. 3. Housing policy--Mathematical models. 4. Space in economics--Mathematical Models. 5. Housing--Location--Great Britain--Mathematical models 6. Regional Planning--Great Britain--Mathematical.models 7. Housing policy--Great Britain--Mathematical models I. Title. II. Series.

HD7287 .M43 2001
363.5'01'5118--dc21 **00-140182**

Printed on acid-free paper. Printed in the United States of America

For Cathy, David and Julia

Contents

Preface

The origins of this book lie in a report on regional house price models, produced in 1998 for the UK Department of the Environment, Transport and the Regions (Meen and Andrew 1998a). The report argued that regional models represented a rather uncomfortable compromise between national and urban models and, in themselves, were a rather small part of the overall housing literature. But, if the rationale for regional models was to be considered properly, then the other spatial dimensions also had to be surveyed. Therefore, the final report surveyed the range of models from national to regional to urban that have appeared in the international literature. One theme of the report was that a single integrated framework for all spatial dimensions together is not possible, given the current state of knowledge, although progress can be made.

In fact, rather little of the original report remains in this book, having been extended in a number of directions. A second major influence has been a project entitled *The Role of Housing in City Economic Performance*, conducted under the Economic and Social Research Council's (ESRC) integrated programme of work into the competitiveness and cohesion of cities. Almost all the urban modelling work appearing in Chapters 5 and 8 comes from this project.

The final influence comes from a growing unease with aggregate, macroeconomic models of housing markets. In the UK, concern with house prices has become almost a national obsession and economists are not immune. This is reflected in the large number of time-series models of house prices that have been estimated. But the UK, in common with many other countries, has undergone important structural changes, particularly in the labour market, which affect the income distribution. These changes in the income distribution have fundamental effects on the nature of aggregate relationships. In some cases we may be able to take account of these changes at the aggregate level, but more usually we need to place greater emphasis on microeconomic analysis. For example, there have been important changes in desired tenure amongst younger households during the nineties, which are difficult to incorporate into aggregate models. Therefore, rather than relying purely on macro models, the book tries to integrate both micro and macro analysis as far as possible.

The book also attempts to take an international perspective. Perhaps, inevitably, given the location of the author, more weight has been given to UK research. But I have also attempted to relate the work to findings in the much more extensive US literature. Further examples are also often taken from the Australian literature. Although models of the Australian market are more limited, there are often useful parallels. Other examples come from around Europe; Scandinavia is particularly strong in the standard of its analysis, aided by the high quality of its data. By contrast, many of the larger European countries suffer from a shortage of high quality housing time-series. Therefore, there are few empirical models for Germany, France, Italy or Spain on which we can draw.

Finally, industrial and commercial property shares many of the characteristics of housing and, yet, empirical research on housing has a much longer history. Although the book does not explicitly consider the industrial and commercial sectors (except in Chapter 8), hopefully, someone might consider the relevance of the ideas put forward in this book to these sectors.

The ideas in this book have developed over a long period of time and I am very grateful to the many colleagues with whom I have discussed my views over the years. Mark Andrew is joint author of the results presented particularly in Chapter 8, arising from the ESRC project mentioned above. I am grateful to the ESRC for funding under award number L/130/25/1045. Peter Englund provided very valuable comments on the first draft of the book. I am indebted to the hospitality of Mike Berry at RMIT University in Melbourne during the summer of 2000, where the Australian elements were developed. Finally, thanks are due to the Centre for Spatial and Real Estate Economics at The University of Reading, directed by Alan Evans, for the excellent research climate, which allowed the work to be completed.

Geoff Meen
The University of Reading

October 2000

Chapter 1

INTRODUCTION

1.1 Introduction

It is often argued that the need for a housing market analysis, which differs from that used for other goods and services, arises from a number of distinctive features that characterise housing markets and, indeed, property in general. The most commonly cited characteristics are the longevity of the housing stock, its heterogeneity, the frictions that operate in the market, the existence of non-neutralities (particularly through the tax and planning systems) and, finally, the spatial fixity of housing. Although we shall have something to say on each of these issues, this book is primarily concerned with the last - the theoretical and empirical analysis of housing markets at different spatial scales. This has been broadly interpreted. At one extreme, we consider international differences in housing markets; at the other extreme, the book deals with urban markets. In between, we look at regional analysis. Each spatial dimension gives rise to a distinct set of analytical and policy problems. For example, European differences in housing market structures have given rise to an increasing literature on the implications of housing for monetary union. Urban housing analysis is intimately tied up with equally topical issues of economic polarisation and social exclusion. Regional housing differences have been highlighted as a factor in explaining regional growth variations.

Analysis at different spatial scales is one form of disaggregation. However a further theme of this book is disaggregation between different types of household. Primarily because of labour market reforms, it has increasingly been recognised – notably in the USA, UK and Australia – that some concept of an "average household" has become less and less relevant over the course of time for housing analysis. The most obvious manifestation of these labour market changes has been a widening of the income distribution. The wage gaps between skilled and unskilled workers and between young and older workers have increased significantly. Furthermore, an increasing proportion of new jobs have been fixed-term appointments, offering less security. As we shall see, formally, changes in the income distribution affect the parameters of any aggregate housing demand (or price) function, so that market trends become less predictable. Moreover, in some countries, tenure patterns have been affected markedly. Rather than continuing to increase, home-ownership rates have fallen at different times in each of the above three countries. A higher proportion of newly forming households have chosen the private rental sector – at least temporarily.

The concentration on different spatial scales also gives rise in the literature to different analytical frameworks. A framework that integrates all the distinctive features of housing noted above at each of the different spatial scales currently does not exist. For example, the longevity of the housing stock has given rise to an extensive literature on investment, which adopts a similar framework to financial market analysis. This literature, typically, pays little attention to spatial issues and much of the work is conducted on time-series data. By contrast spatial issues are central in urban housing analysis, much of which still relies on extensions to standard residential location theory; theory and estimation are typically microeconomic in orientation.

1.2 The Scope of the Book

The book deals with both economic theory and empirical analysis. Some of the book surveys the existing literature and attempts a synthesis, but the majority reflects the author's own research programme over the past ten years. The book has four components representing, data and definitional issues, the theory of housing markets at different spatial scales, empirical findings and policy.

1.2.1 Data and Definitions

At first sight, a chapter on data and definitions does not appear very exciting; however these are at the heart of housing analysis. First, a huge amount of housing work is concerned with data measurement problems. Whereas macroeconomists, for example, often take measures of GDP or consumers' expenditure as given from official sources, without questioning too much their quality, this is not true for housing economists. The difference arises from the heterogeneity of housing. Therefore, measured changes in house prices across time (and location) may confound quality changes with pure price changes. This problem has given rise to the vast literature on quality-adjusted price measures and to the extensive estimation of hedonic and repeat sales models. Such estimates can be found for many industrialised countries. For those interested in investment, the concentration on price measurement is unsurprising, since capital gains represent the major element of the return on housing. Policy makers have also paid increasing attention to house price measurement, since house prices may be a forward indicator of the future general rate of inflation.

Second, the time-series properties of house price data at different spatial scales turn out to be crucial to analysis. We shall find that, in some countries, real house prices are less trended than in others. But basic theoretical models would suggest that stationarity should be the norm. Why should this be violated and what are the implications?

At the regional level, the time-series properties of *relative* house prices have been a particularly important issue in the United Kingdom. This has generated a large number of tests, based on cointegration methods, designed to look at the long-run relationship between prices, in particular whether price differentials have widened over time between the South and North of the country. In the USA, tests of regional house price convergence have been conducted, related to the literature on growth convergence.

At the urban level, time-series tests on the properties of local house prices are less common, primarily because long time series are rarely available. Estimation work has been conducted mainly on cross-section or panel data sets. Consequently, rather little is known about any tendency of house prices to converge or otherwise at the local level.

Third, a further strand of statistical tests concerns unit root processes in house prices. In particular, since houses are a form of asset, do their prices follow a random walk as appears to occur in financial markets? Alternatively, do prices exhibit short-run autocorrelation and mean reversion in the long run? A large literature has tested these propositions on international data and, to a limited extent, on regional data. These tests are generally conducted in a univariate framework, but recent research has extended the tests to bivariate models of house prices and property transactions.

Finally, we have to define what we mean by housing market areas at different spatial scales. This might be straightforward at the international level, but regional and urban markets are usually defined in empirical work by administrative boundaries, which have only limited significance for households. For example inter-regional migration, which is often considered as a measure of long-distance population movement, may, in practice, represent only short distance flows as individuals cross either side of arbitrary administrative boundaries. A substantial literature has now addressed the problem of appropriate methods for delineating housing submarkets. These methods are typically based on finding areas in which the coefficients of hedonic price equations are similar and, hence, represent close substitutes.

1.2.2 Economic Theory and Housing

Overall, these issues can be seen as the background to the theoretical and empirical models considered in the remaining chapters of the book.

The second component concerns the theory underlying spatial housing models. Although most of the discussion deals with *economic* theory, some useful techniques are introduced from the spatial econometrics literature, which have proved useful in regional and urban housing modelling. We show that the housing literature takes strands from both macroeconomic and urban economic theory. Although, in an ideal world, housing models should synthesise the two, in practice, this has not been the case. National and international aggregate time-series housing models have typically been derived from extensions to the standard life-cycle consumer model, whereas urban housing models are still closely allied to residential location theory. Regional models, rather uneasily, are still more closely related to the macroeconomic than the urban tradition. Therefore Chapter 3, which is the first of the theoretical chapters, discusses life-cycle models of housing demand, both partial models and set in a general equilibrium framework. As a part of this, the impact of credit market constraints is considered. These models are directly related to housing investment and arbitrage conditions and can be used to account for the existence of lags and autocorrelation in house price movements.

The chapter then considers extensions to the life-cycle model and its emphasis on housing demand. Stock-flow models of housing demand and new construction are built. Then, at the national level, joint models of prices and transactions are discussed. Finally, the chapter embeds the housing model within a broader general equilibrium two-sector growth model, allowing us to consider such issues as crowding out. Overall, therefore, the chapter starts with the derivation of a single equation and ends with a full general equilibrium model.

Regional housing theory is discussed in Chapter 4. All the issues from the previous chapter remain relevant, but additional questions arise. However, this is perhaps the most disappointing area of research in the literature from a theoretical perspective. Quantitative housing research has generally concentrated on regions because of expediency. Frequently it is the lowest spatial scale for which consistent, time-series data exist for a country as a whole. Often empirical research has adopted the basic national, life-cycle paradigm with spatial structure added as an afterthought. Nevertheless, there are important theoretical issues. In particular if, as we observe, housing markets are linked across regions, what are the transmission mechanisms? Are markets linked through search, migration or spatial arbitrage? Alternatively, are the spatial dependencies spurious arising from inappropriate definitions of local housing market areas? In the British literature, the idea of a "ripple" effect has attracted considerable comment, where prices rise initially in the south of the country and gradually spread northwards over the course of time. We also discuss the question of whether the differences in behaviour between regions arise from structural differences in population and in housing markets rather than from differences in underlying regional economic conditions.

Although this is not an econometrics book, there are a number of useful methods – some of which are quite new – that can be utilised in both urban and, particularly, in regional analysis. These are taken partly from the spatial econometrics literature, where the concepts of spatial dependence and spatial heterogeneity are central. Methods of spatial dependence provide ways of allowing us to model the spatial interlinkages between regional and local housing markets. Furthermore, models of heterogeneity permit us to consider structural differences between housing markets. In addition, recent developments in the mainstream econometrics literature, concerning dynamic heterogeneous panel models, are relevant. The effects on housing demand of both an increasing dispersion of household incomes and of regional growth rates can be examined using this framework in terms of aggregation conditions; the existence of common stochastic trends is shown to be particularly important. We show how spatial coefficient heterogeneity and dependence can be modelled, using a new approach, which can contribute to explaining the ripple effect observed in Britain.

The idea that housing spatial structure depends on the characteristics of the resident population is taken further in Chapter 5, which deals with urban markets. The chapter begins with a brief review of some aspects of location theory and its extensions. Location theory predicts that, under certain conditions, households with common characteristics (notably similar incomes) will tend to congregate in similar locations. However there are some drawbacks in using this approach to explain economic polarisation between different locations. Instead we argue that spatial structure arises from the location decisions of different types of households at different stages in their housing careers. Young single-person households are likely to live in different locations from families with children. Both demographic and economic changes over time generate the moving patterns that we observe between cities and suburbs. Economic polarisation will be reinforced if high and low income groups have differential access to credit markets. Therefore, the chapter traces the housing careers of individuals from new household formation, through moving, to retirement. We suggest that environmental conditions are particularly important in determining the choice of neighbourhood. We show how urban/rural population drift in London and South East England is consistent with this view.

1.2.3 Empirical Analysis

The third element of the book, which comprises Chapters 6 to 9, covers empirical findings at each of the three spatial scales. The organisation and topics are similar to those in the corresponding theoretical chapters.

At the national level, in Chapter 6, we begin by providing empirical estimates of the most important elasticities from house price equations, initially from UK studies. These include both long-run elasticities and the nature of lags. We also discuss the consistency of the results with microeconomic evidence on price and income elasticities of housing demand. We, then, consider findings for other countries, which turn out to be very different and which, in principle, could account for the stronger real price trends in the UK. However a part of the difference in results comes from different methodological approaches to house price modelling around the world. Perhaps, the most glaring differences occur between the US and UK traditions. These reflect, partly, alternative approaches adopted towards econometrics as a whole. But, in addition, policy concerns have differed, which have been reflected in the type of analysis conducted. To complete the single equation discussion, we model the impact of increasing income dispersion on aggregate house prices and show how this can account for the poor performance of "traditional" house price models in the UK during the nineties.

The chapter, then, considers joint models of prices and construction (including construction costs) in the stock-flow tradition. These variables are modelled as a vector error correction model (VECM). In simulation, the model can be used to demonstrate the nature of cycles. However, the main point is to show how different real house price trends depend on the size of the price elasticity of supply, which varies considerably between countries. We also show that the rate of change of prices has an effect on supply independently of the level. This is a form of credit market influence and, in fact, is quantitatively more important than the level of prices; furthermore it is a major contributor to construction cycles.

The chapter, then, constructs a joint model of prices and property transactions, designed to explain the observed positive correlation between the two variables. Both are modelled as functions of estimated housing market disequilibrium. Finally, the chapter discusses the results from full econometric models of housing markets and the macroeconomy.

Chapter 7 presents empirical results at the regional level; it attempts to explain the ripple effect in the UK and examines the extent to which a similar regional phenomenon exists in other countries. US evidence on spatial diffusion processes or positive feed-backs is particularly relevant, where recent strength in one local sub-market feeds into other sub-markets. Perhaps surprisingly, there is little evidence that investors have attempted to exploit the spatial differences in the rates of return on housing. But the main emphasis of Chapter 7 is on explaining spatial interactions between regional housing markets and the ripple effect. There are a number of contributory factors but, perhaps, the most innovative aspect concerns heterogeneity in the coefficients that have distinct spatial patterns.

Chapter 8 uses qualitative response models to examine household formation, moving decisions and location choice. A complete model is constructed which, in combination with a model of the labour market, can be used to examine issues in increasing income dispersion and urban/rural drift. The model has a number of additional implications, for example, concerning crowding out. We show that housing and industrial location may be positively correlated under some circumstances, rather than the more usual crowding out result.

1.2.4 Housing Policy

The final part, comprising Chapters 9 and 10, is concerned with policy. We certainly do not attempt to be comprehensive over the vast range of policy issues that arise in housing. Rather we select a number of topics that arise from the models. Chapter 9 deals with the national and international dimensions and Chapter 10 with regional and urban issues. Amongst the topics covered in Chapter 9 are the effects of international differences in housing market structure on monetary union. The differences occur in both housing tenure and in mortgage markets. One strand of the literature suggests that the differences hinder macroeconomic convergence. Housing also raises inflation, through consumers' expenditure, in some countries but not others. Furthermore some research has suggested that international unemployment variations are strongly correlated with owner-occupancy rates. However, an opposing school disputes any distinctive role for housing in macroeconomic policy. The chapter also considers the effects of inflation targets on housing market stability. We argue that general inflation targets, where interest rates are the main policy instrument, can exacerbate housing cycles. However the chapter also shows that volatility is enhanced by the nature of credit markets and the requirement for deposits. The chapter ends on a different note by looking at the nature of government household projections, which historically have been based on expected demographic trends rather than on economic behaviour. But once economic trends are taken into account, the downturn in owner-occupancy rates in recent years is less surprising and uninterrupted increases in rates over the future cannot be taken for granted. In the UK, at least, we speculate that further increases are likely to take place only slowly.

Chapter 10 is concerned with the role of housing in policy at the regional and urban levels. At the regional level, our main concern is with the effects of housing on regional economic convergence. A series of papers by John Muellbauer suggests that, in the UK, housing has hindered convergence and contributed to inflation and unemployment. Planning constraints play an important part in the story. At the urban level, the three issues raised are, first, whether population loss from cities is inevitable; second, whether halting urban/rural drift, in fact, solves the problems of low-income households and, third, how cumulative processes of urban decline can arise.

Chapter 2

ISSUES IN HOUSING DATA ANALYSIS

2.1 Introduction

Consider figures 2.1 to 2.4; between them these graphs illustrate many of the core analytical problems of housing economics. Figures 2.1a-2.1d show movements in real house prices across an illustrative sample of three countries, the USA, Japan and the UK. Although more formal tests will be presented later, casual observation suggests that neither the cycles nor the underlying trends are identical. The second graph shows differences between measures of national house prices in the USA and the UK. The diversity *within* the countries of measures that are supposed to capture the same variable is striking and is worrying; we might imagine that there are *short-run* differences between house price measures that are eliminated over time, but the differences appear to widen. Figure 2.3 graphs the ratio of house prices in South East England relative to the North. Again casual observation suggests that any long-run tendency for sub-national prices, at this spatial scale, to drift apart over time has been limited. Finally, figure 2.4 plots cycles in residential construction across a selection of European economies. It appears that cycles differ both in amplitude and in terms of timing. These features of the data give rise to the following key time-series issues:

- the stationarity of real prices,
- measurement errors and biases arising from different data construction methods,
- the extent of spatial convergence,
- cyclical co-ordination.

Each is considered in the following sections. Throughout, the three main variables with which we will be concerned are house prices, housing construction and the volume of property transactions.

2.2 Time-Series Properties of International House Prices, Construction and Transactions

One of the basic building blocs of theoretical housing economics (see Chapter 3) suggests that any demand shock will lead to a temporary change in real house prices, due to short-run inelastic housing supply, but prices will overshoot and, in the long run, prices will change in line with construction costs. If construction costs rise with general prices in the economy, then long-run real house prices would be expected to be constant or, in a stochastic environment, stationary. If, therefore, real prices are found to be non-stationary (and measurement errors can be excluded), then this simple empirical finding would at least indicate that a modification or extension is required to a major element of housing economic theory[1]. A prime candidate concerns the land market. Since a significant component of house prices comprises the cost of land, clearly land markets play a central role in any explanation of housing market behaviour. Differences in land market conditions – both in terms of price and availability – contribute to house price variations at both international and regional levels. Malpezzi (1999), for example, demonstrates for the US how the strength of planning controls raises the ratio of house prices to incomes. In the presence of planning controls, house prices and land prices may cointegrate, but this does not necessarily imply that house prices can be *explained* by land prices since causality may run in the opposite direction. Under "residual valuation" methods, changes in land prices are caused by changes in house prices.

Time-series properties, therefore, need to be thoroughly tested. However international comparisons of house price trends have been dogged by data problems. Although Ball and Wood (1999) construct price measures, in some cases dating back to the nineteenth century, these are residential investment deflators and exclude land values. Work by Holmans (1990) on true house prices illustrated the difficulties – data across most of Europe are surprisingly poor, although the UK, Ireland and Scandinavia are major exceptions. This partly explains why so many house price studies in Europe have been conducted on these countries. Time-series data for the major

[1] Amongst the other candidates is the possibility of non-stationary real construction costs (arising, perhaps, from differences in productivity between industries), Ball and Wood (1999).

European economies of Germany, France and Italy, for example, are much weaker[2]. Nevertheless, a study by the Bank for International Settlements (BIS), Kennedy and Andersen (1994), has attempted to construct international house price information from the early seventies onwards in order to model the relationship between house prices and savings (an issue considered further in Chapter 9). Only limited evidence exists on trends before the seventies, although Eichholtz (1997) constructs an index for the Herengracht canal area of Amsterdam, dating back to 1628. Both Holmans (1990) and Holly and Jones (1997) have constructed long-run data for the UK. These data suggest that the time-series properties of prices were very different prior to the Second World War. Internationally, Ball and Wood's (1999) data appear to come to the same conclusion. Real house prices were closer to stationarity than they have been since the seventies.

The BIS data have been used by Englund and Ioannides (1997) in the most comprehensive international study of time-series properties, covering fifteen countries. Following the work for the USA of Case and Shiller (1989, 1990) on housing market efficiency, Englund and Ioannides use similar methods to test whether real house price inflation exhibits short-run positive autocorrelation, but longer-term mean reversion. Further detailed work for Sweden, across a panel of urban areas, was conducted by Hort (1997).

The basic equation used to test the efficiency hypothesis is given by (2.1):

$$\Delta \ln(g_{it}) = \alpha_i + \sum_{j=1}^{n} \beta_j \Delta \ln(g_{it-j}) + \varepsilon_{it} \tag{2.1}$$

where:

g_{it} = real house prices in location (i) at time (t)
ε_{it} = error term
Δ = first difference operator
ln = natural logarithm of the variable

As specified, the parameters of interest, (β_j), are assumed in (2.1) not to vary by location, although "fixed effects" are allowed in panel estimation through the (α_i s). However, since coefficient heterogeneity across locations will typically generate biased estimates (see Pesaran and Smith 1995), the spatial homogeneity of (β_j) is typically tested. Note further, that the variables are tested entirely in terms of differences – no levels effects are allowed.

[2] Although the European Mortgage Federation now publishes data for EU countries going back to 1988.

This eliminates any form of error correction from the model. We return to this point in the next chapter.

If housing markets are fully efficient, then no autocorrelation in price inflation is expected, $(\beta_j)=0$, for all (j) so that house prices follow a random walk. In Case and Shiller's original work, strong positive autocorrelation was found at the first (annual) lag, but only weak evidence of mean reversion, i.e. negative coefficients, at longer lags. Englund and Ioannides, estimating a panel model across the fifteen countries found a very similar pattern, with little evidence of coefficient heterogeneity between the countries. Furthermore house prices were predictable by lagged income growth and real interest rates. Hort's study of Swedish urban areas also produces similar patterns of autocorrelation. Overall, the similarity of autocorrelation structures, both across and within countries, is striking. Nevertheless, as we shall see, this does *not* imply that the trends in real house prices in *levels* are the same internationally. Furthermore, neither does it imply that there is a consensus about the factors that cause changes in house prices – models used in the USA differ considerably from those used in the UK. Even within the USA, there are competing theoretical explanations of price movements.

To show this more clearly, we concentrate on three countries – the USA, UK and Japan. Real price trends are shown in figures 2.1a-2.1d. In the case of the USA, data are derived from repeat sales, taken from the Freddie Mac database. Data are presented quarterly from 1975. For the UK, Department of the Environment, Transport and the Regions (DETR) mix-adjusted prices are used quarterly from 1968. Figures for Japan, since 1960, are annual and refer to urban residential land prices. For each country, residential prices are deflated by a general measure of consumer prices.

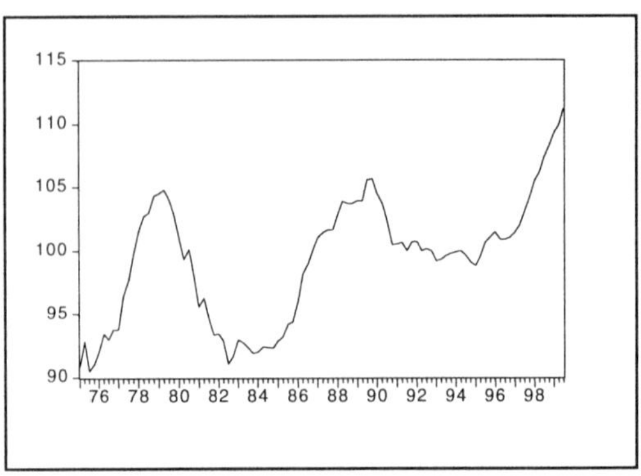

Figure 2.1a. Real House Prices - USA (1995=100)

Source: Freddie Mac Conventional Mortgage House Price Index

Visually, figures 2.1a-2.1c all suggest that real prices are trended, but note that the vertical scales are not identical. Furthermore pronounced cycles occur in all. In figure 2.1a, the cycles for the US appear strong, but when plotted together with the UK in figure 2.1d, both the trends and cycles in the latter are far more dramatic. A recurring theme in this book will be the question of why this is the case and the implications for both theoretical and empirical models.

Estimates of price fluctuations over relatively short periods, taken from Stephens (2000), are set out in table 2.1. Similar information is presented in Boelhouwer (2000).

Table 2.1. Volatility in International House Prices (standard deviation of annual percentage changes in real house prices, 1986-97)

Country	**Standard Deviation**
Austria	1.7
Belgium	2.2
Denmark	6.6
Finland	15.0
France	7.0
Germany	1.8
Greece	3.1
Ireland	5.1
Italy	7.7/11.6*
Luxembourg	2.0
Netherlands	2.6
Portugal	3.5
Spain	9.4
Sweden	8.2
UK	10.0

Source: Stephens (2000) : *depends on the index used.

Although the time periods are short, the table confirms that the volatility shown in figures 2.1a-2.1c holds over a wider spectrum of European economies with Germany exhibiting the smallest fluctuations. Although not clear from the table, Boelhouwer (2000) documents the particularly strong rises in Dutch prices in recent years.

With the arrival of monetary union, co-ordination of business cycles across Europe has become an important issue and the role of housing has attracted particular attention. We look at this in more detail in Chapter 9 but, using rather different methodologies (based on equation 2.1), Englund and Ioannides (1997) suggest that there is little evidence of common house price movements across their fifteen sample countries.

Table 2.2 conducts both Augmented Dickey-Fuller (ADF) and Phillips-Perron tests for stationarity of real house prices. Tests are carried out both with and without trends; the figures in brackets are the MacKinnon critical values at the 5% level for the rejection of the hypothesis of a unit root. In all countries, unit roots in real prices cannot generally be rejected and real prices appear to be difference stationary. An exception is the possibility that real prices in the UK could be trend stationary, at least on the basis of the ADF tests. In fact, this is unlikely as we show in Chapter 6.

Table 2.3 shows the results of estimating the simple univariate model, given as equation (2.1) above, for our three countries. Variables are expressed in terms of annual growth rates. In line with the Englund and Ioannides results, the pattern of initial positive autocorrelation is observed in each country (noting that the tests for Japan are conducted on annual data). All countries also exhibit mean reversion.

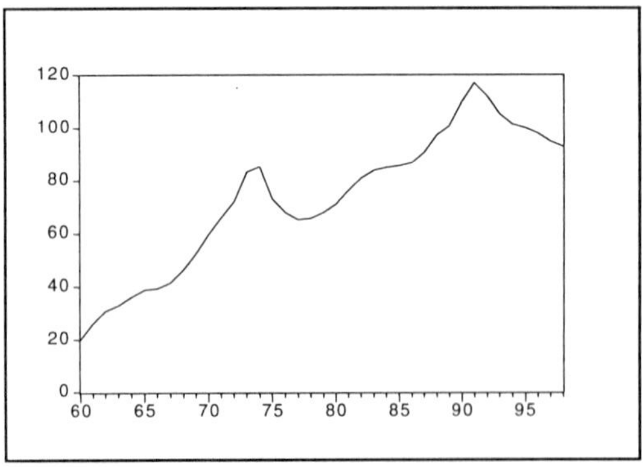

Figure 2.1b. Real Urban Residential Land Prices – Japan (1995=100), Source: Japan Year Book

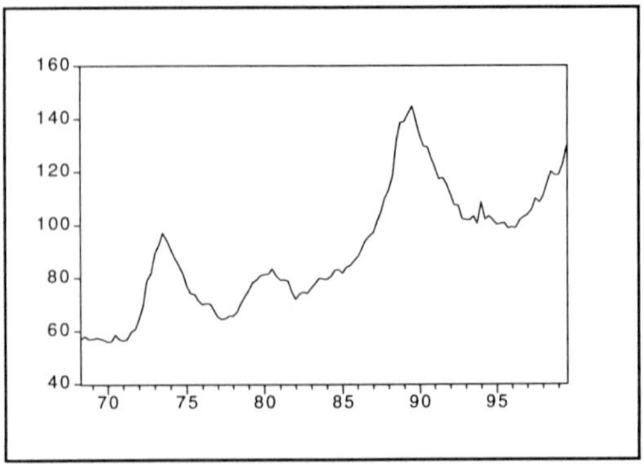

Figure 2.1c. Real House Prices - UK (1995=100), Source: DETR

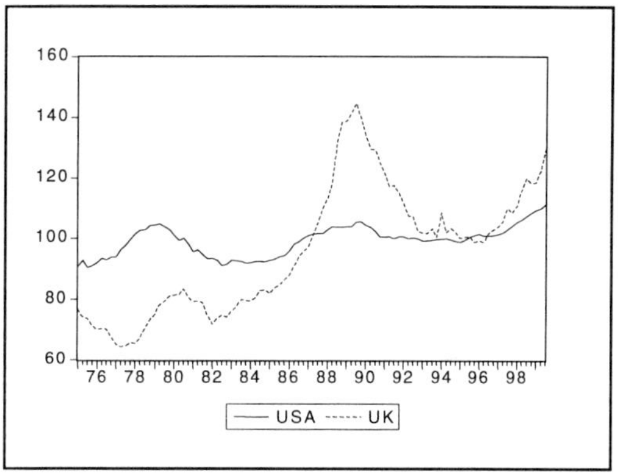

Figure 2.1d. Real House Prices - USA & UK (1995=100)

Table 2.2. Stationarity Tests for Real House Prices

	ADF		Phillips - Perron
	Intercept	Intercept & trend	Intercept
USA: 1976Q2-1999Q3			
Levels	-2.27 (-2.89)	-3.17 (-3.46)	-0.95 (-2.89)
First difference	-2.86 (-2.89)	-2.89 (-3.45)	-7.18 (-2.89)
UK: 1969Q3-1999Q3			
Levels	-2.05 (-2.89)	-4.20 (-3.45)	-1.10 (-2.88)
First difference	-3.52 (-2.89)	-3.50 (-3.44)	-6.80 (-2.88)
Japan: 1962-1998			
Levels	-1.77 (-2.94)	-2.62 (-3.53)	-2.03 (-2.93)
First difference	-3.65 (-2.94)	-3.94 (-3.53)	-3.13 (-2.94)

NB: ADF tests for USA and UK are fourth order and first order for Japan

Table 2.3. Univariate Models of Annual Real House Price Growth

	α	β_1	β_2	β_3	β_4
USA 78Q2-98Q4	0.0003 (0.3)	1.072 (10.4)	-0.274 (1.8)	0.377 (2.5)	-0.356 (3.5)
UK 70Q2-99Q3	0.004 (1.7)	1.105 (12.3)	0.033 (0.2)	-0.066 (0.04)	-0.300 (3.3)
Japan 65-98	0.013 (1.3)	1.003 (5.7)	-0.610 (2.6)	0.412 (1.8)	-0.242 (1.6)

t-values in brackets

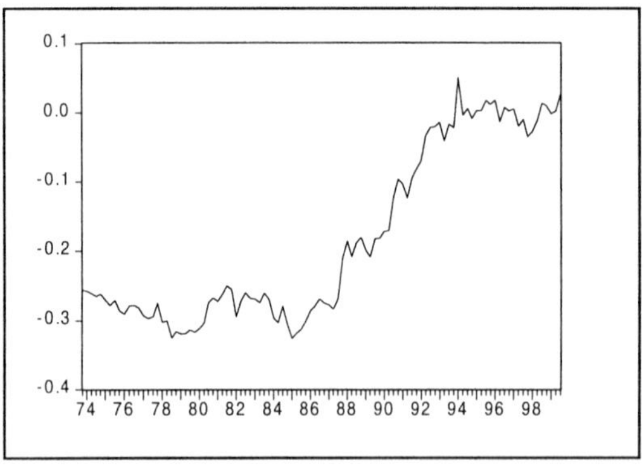

Figure 2.2a. Differences in House Prices - UK

Source: DETR and Nationwide Building Society

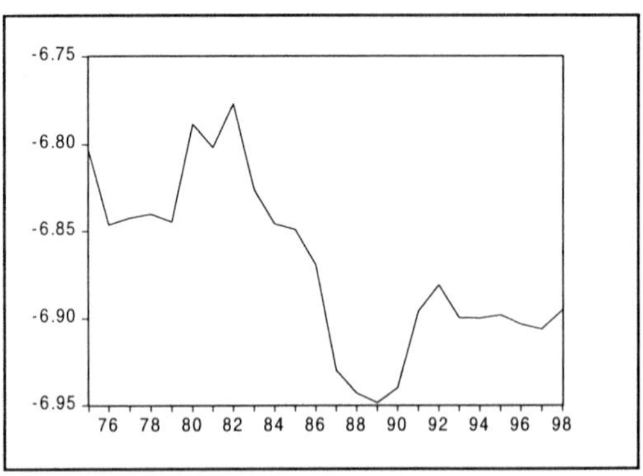

Figure 2.2b. Differences in House Prices - USA

Source: Freddie Mac CMHPI and US Bureau of the Census

The second variable is housing construction. A comparative study by Ball and Wood (1999) tracks housing construction across a sample of industrialised countries from the mid-nineteenth century and decomposes trend changes from the cycle. However, the paper shows that time-series properties are sensitive to the choice of activity measure. As shown in figure 2.5, which graphs the ratio of private sector housing starts to investment, in both the UK and the USA housing starts have moved over time in a different manner from investment. The inclusion of improvement work in investment accounts for a proportion of the difference[3]. However the trend in the ratio appears stronger in the US. ADF(4) tests for the US yield a value of -1.71 over the period 1974 to 1998 (critical value = -3.5) and a value of -3.2 for the UK.

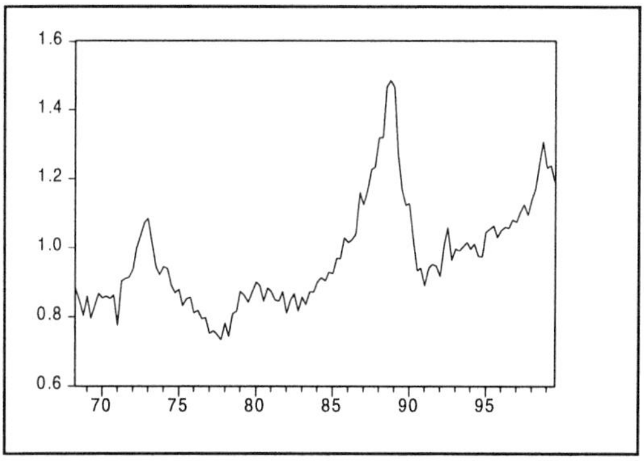

Figure 2.3. UK House Prices: South East/North 1990=1.0, Source: DETR

Ball and Wood conclude:

- internationally, housing has been subject to long cycles since the nineteenth century;
- but, since the seventies, *trends* in housing investment have been broadly flat;
- again since the seventies, the share of housing in GDP has fallen, but over longer periods, the share has fluctuated considerably;
- between 1950 and 1970, there was a weak positive correlation between construction cycles across countries and evidence of negative correlation in some cases. But between 1970 and 1992, much stronger positive correlations occur.

[3] In the UK, the comparison is also affected by the inclusion of housing association activity in investment, but not in starts. See Meen (1996) for a wider range of comparisons.

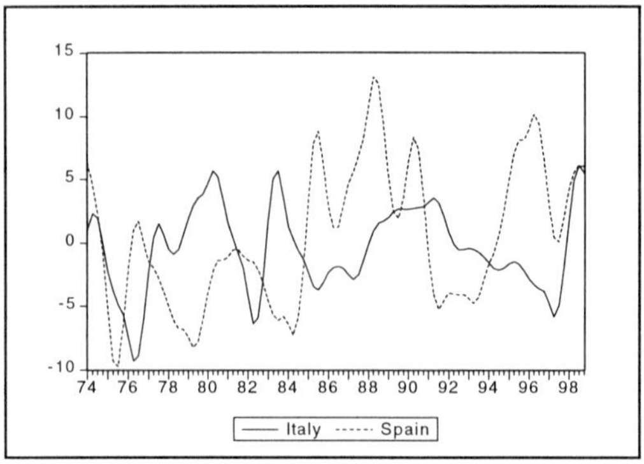

Figure 2.4a. Housing Investment (annual percentage change) - Spain, Italy

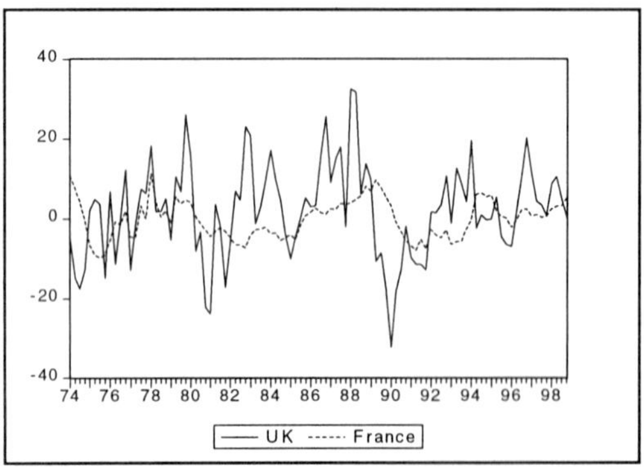

Figure 2.4b. Housing Investment (annual percentage change) - UK, France

As an illustration, figure 2.4b shows that France exhibits only limited fluctuations relative to the UK. In figure 2.4a, visually, the cycles in Italy and Spain appear to show little co-ordination[4]. More substantively, table 2.4 sets out the standard deviations of the annual percentage changes in residential investment, taken from Ball and Wood.

The first part of the table looks at volatility using long-term data and shows that the standard deviation is notably higher in the UK than elsewhere, with Japan exhibiting the lowest degree of volatility. The shorter sample period in the second part of the table allows extra countries to be added. Overall, from 1950, volatility noticeably lessens (although the longer period is heavily influenced by war episodes) and the standard deviation is no longer the greatest in the UK.

[4] Note that the vertical scales in the two graphs differ.

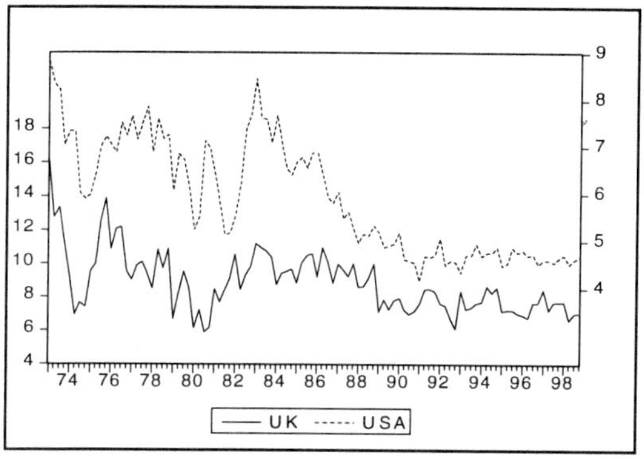

Figure 2.5. Ratio of Housing Starts to Investment – USA & UK

Table 2.4. Housing Volatility (standard deviation of the annual percentage change in housing investment)

Country	Period	Standard Deviation
UK	1856-1992	25.9
Germany	1850-1992	17.8
Sweden	1861-1992	13.9
Finland	1860-1992	17.2
USA	1929-1992	18.3
Canada	1890-1992	16.6
Japan	1885-1992	9.4
UK	1950-1992	9.6
Germany	1950-1992	10.1
France	1950-1992	7.0
Netherlands	1950-1992	8.9
Belgium	1950-1992	15.3
Sweden	1950-1992	6.8
Finland	1950-1992	10.5
USA	1950-1992	13.7
Canada	1950-1992	11.1
Japan	1950-1992	8.9
Australia	1950-1992	10.2

Source: Ball and Wood (1999)[5]

The final variable to be considered is housing transactions. Our interest stems from a recent strand of the literature, which suggests that, in an

[5] The figures in this table are copyright of Taylor & Francis Ltd., PO Box 25, Abingdon, Oxon, OX14 3EU.

efficient market, price movements and transactions should be uncorrelated. Demand shocks, for example, will lead to an immediate change in prices with no effect on the volume of property transactions. However, in the USA, it has been observed that, in fact, the two are correlated particularly in the short run. Although there is limited evidence for other countries (see an exception for Sweden in Hort 2000), figure 2.6 suggests that the same has been true in the UK. The simple correlation between the rate of increase of real house prices and the level of transactions is approximately 0.62.

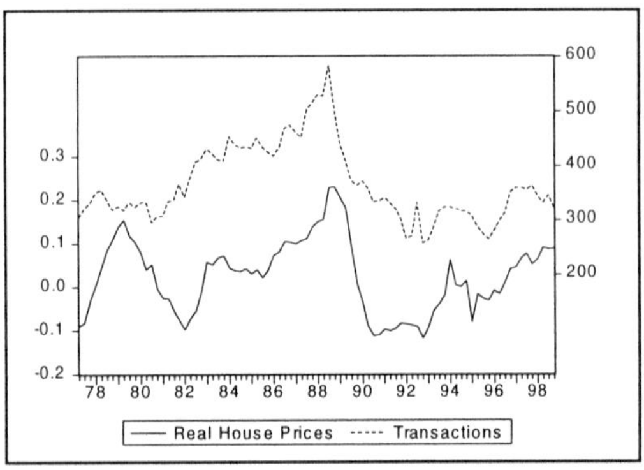

Figure 2.6. Real House Prices (annual percentage change) and Transactions (000s) in the UK

Just as a univariate model for prices is given in equation (2.1), a bivariate equivalent can be constructed as (2.2).

$$\begin{bmatrix} \gamma_{11}(L) & \gamma_{12}(L) \\ \gamma_{21}(L) & \gamma_{22}(L) \end{bmatrix} \begin{bmatrix} \Delta \ln(g) \\ \ln(TR) \end{bmatrix} = \begin{bmatrix} \varepsilon_1 \\ \varepsilon_2 \end{bmatrix} \tag{2.2}$$

where, TR = number of transactions, ε_i are error terms and $\gamma_{ij}(L)$ are lag polynomials.

Later we shall consider the theoretical relationship between these two variables in more detail – in particular the response of each to housing market disequilibrium. But, for the moment, we limit ourselves to estimating a fourth-order vector autoregressive (VAR) model for the two variables.

The results are shown in table 2.5. In this model, although both prices and transactions exhibit strong autocorrelation (with evidence of mean reversion in prices), there is little evidence that either transactions affect prices or *vice versa*. This is a conclusion that will need to be revised when more structural models are estimated. For the moment, simply note that the standard error of the price equation is 2.6%. This is very high compared with most estimated models of UK house prices.

Table 2.5. VAR for UK House Prices and Transactions

	$\Delta \ln g$	$\ln TR$
$\ln TR_{-1}$	0.058 (1.3)	0.950 (7.9)
$\ln TR_{-2}$	0.046 (0.7)	-0.038 (0.2)
$\ln TR_{-3}$	0.011 (0.2)	0.075 (0.5)
$\ln TR_{-4}$	-0.071 (1.5)	-0.034 (0.3)
$\Delta \ln g_{-1}$	0.846 (8.1)	0.200 (0.7)
$\Delta \ln g_{-2}$	0.161 (1.1)	-0.314 (0.8)
$\Delta \ln g_{-3}$	0.176 (1.2)	0.051 (0.1)
$\Delta \ln g_{-4}$	-0.409 (4.1)	-0.006 (0.02)
constant	-0.256 (2.1)	0.275 (0.8)
Adj. R-squared	0.909	0.865
Equation standard error	0.026	0.068

Sample: 1978:2 1998:4
t-statistics in parentheses
Note that, compared with table 2.3, the price equation is specified in terms of *quarterly* changes.

2.3 The Sub-National (Regional) Level

The most appropriate spatial scale for housing analysis is a thorny issue. The literature on methods for estimating appropriate spatial housing sub-markets is discussed in the next section where the issue is particularly relevant but, in this section, we concentrate on regional movements, where the spatial delineations are determined by administrative boundaries, rather than by economic structure. Almost inevitably, these regions will not correspond with any recognisable housing market area. The literature arises partly from data availability – for some countries, this is the lowest spatial scale at which consistent data can be obtained over the whole country[6]. Precise definitions, therefore, vary by country. In the USA, we consider Census Divisions in this section, in the UK the Standard Statistical Regions (or the more recent Government Office Regions) and, in Australia, the states.

The key statistical question with which we are concerned is the extent to which regional housing markets move together over time. Do they converge

[6] This is not true for the USA. Note that for empirical work it is not only data on housing variables that are required, but also the independent variables.

or diverge between areas? The majority of the literature looks at prices rather than construction activity and the relative lengths of the sub-sections below reflect this emphasis. But the regional relationships for prices and construction do not have to be the same. The presence of national builders operating in all markets, for example, might suggest that cyclical variations in construction will be more co-ordinated than in prices. The absence of long time series for property transactions at the regional level, prevent a similar analysis for our third variable.

2.3.1 Regional Prices

Because labour is relatively immobile between regions (since each generally constitutes a distinct labour market area), there is no necessary reason to believe that migration will cause prices to move together, particularly in the short run. Cyclical differences in economic conditions between regions may generate cyclical variations in house prices that are eliminated only slowly. By contrast, in the next section, where metropolitan housing markets are considered, prices might be expected to move together in both the short run and long run, (although the issue is complicated by the appropriate housing market area definition and the existence of housing sub-markets). If metropolitan areas constitute markets within which households are highly mobile, *relative* changes in house prices can rarely persist for long. As DiPasquale and Wheaton (1996) indicate, arbitrage will eliminate the variations. Therefore, prices *within* the urban area will all move together over time in line with the economic fortunes of the area. Absolute differences in property values will reflect only land prices, the individual attributes of the properties and their valuation by households. If any changes in relative prices, in fact, occur within the urban area they should reflect either changes in the implicit valuations or changes in the local characteristics of the property, including the environment in which it is located. This last point becomes particularly important in Chapters 5 and 8, where models of urban location are discussed. Locations within the metropolitan area may, in fact, experience relative price shifts because of urban decay or gentrification for example.

The relationship between house prices in the regions has been a major concern of the UK literature and, indeed, of policy in recent years. The questions raised provide a useful starting point for the other countries as well. In the most comprehensive descriptive analysis of UK house price trends, Holmans (1990, 1995) points to the three central time-series features of UK regional house price data:

- the geographical percentage differences in house prices are much greater than those in incomes,

- the difference in house prices between the north of the country and the south (the North/South divide) widened to record levels in the eighties, but narrowed again in the nineties,
- the South appears to lead the house price cycle and its downswing is greater than elsewhere.

At first sight, these patterns appear to conform to the theoretical expectations for regional housing markets outlined above, i.e. in the short run, prices differ because labour is immobile, but the differences are gradually eroded over time through migration. In fact, life turns out not to be so simple (see Chapter 4) but, for the moment, we merely describe these time-series features, rather than provide behavioural explanations.

Holmans' observations are closely allied to a further major concern of the UK regional house price literature - the so-called "ripple effect". Over successive cycles, house prices have risen first in the South East and gradually spread out over the rest of the country[7]. As a result, regional price differentials exhibit considerable short-term volatility, but longer-term relativities tend to be restored. Alternatively, regional house prices appear to cointegrate in the long term. In the literature to date, there is little evidence of a similar ripple effect in other countries.

However, any tendency for regional house prices to change at different rates must be caused by *either*;

different changes in the economic influences on house prices - for example, regional incomes may grow at different rates and, particularly in the short term, regional income differentials do, indeed, change,

or,

differences in the responsiveness of regional house prices to common changes in economic variables. These, in turn, arise from differences in the structure of regional housing markets. For example, differences in the availability of substitutes to owner-occupation between regions will affect responsiveness. Models that incorporate both of these features are developed in Chapter 4.

Holmans, in fact, criticises the view that a long-run relationship between prices in the North and South exists and it is certainly true that the time-series tests conducted in the best-known studies by MacDonald and Taylor (1993) and Alexander and Barrow (1994) are carried out on data since 1968. Holmans points out that if data are taken back to the thirties, the ratio has *widened* over time, rather than remaining stationary as cointegration tests had suggested. This is shown clearly in his later paper, Holmans (1995, figure II).

[7] At the time of writing, there is considerable speculation whether the ripple effect will again occur, following the boom in prices in the south over the 1997-1999 period.

The differential between prices in South East England and the North reached record levels in the boom years of the late eighties and the divide in house prices became a major policy concern for the first time in those years (see Hamnett 1988). The ratio is graphed in figure 2.3. Fluctuations in *national* prices had been a policy concern since the first boom in 1972/73, but interest in the North/South differential and the policy problems to which this led is a more recent concern. In fact, 1989 turned out to be the peak year and the differential returned closer to the post-1968 average by the mid-nineties. The differential has subsequently widened again. More formally an ADF test on the ratio over the period 1969 quarter 3 to 1999 quarter 3 yields a value of ADF(4)= -2.27. At least on this test, there may be a weak trend. Visually, figure 2.3 also suggests that stationarity is no longer so clear as when Taylor and MacDonald carried out their study.

The record differential in prices at the end of the eighties was eliminated by a fall in nominal house prices concentrated on London and the South East. Using DETR data, between 1990 and 1995, prices in the South East (excluding London) fell by approximately 17.5% whereas prices in the North *rose* by 19%. Nationally, prices fell by 5%.

Much of the empirical literature has concentrated on the North/South divide, e.g. Giussani and Hadjimatheou (1991), because of the policy issues, such as migration, to which it gives rise. But this is only part of the story. Complex interactions take place *within* the southern and northern regions and, indeed, with the Midlands. A feature of the data already suggested by the previous paragraph is that the post-1990 slump was a southern phenomenon. This is particularly clear from figure 2.7, where all the standard regions are considered, but are graphed as blocs - Southern (South East, East Anglia, South West), Midlands (East Midlands, West Midlands, Wales) and Northern (North West, Yorkshire and Humberside, the North).

The figures indicate that the slump became less severe as we move northwards so that, in the North, no slump occurred at all. Furthermore, *within* the broad groupings, house prices appear to have behaved in a similar manner not only in the long run (as cointegration would imply), but also in the short run. In this case, the interrelationships between these regions are likely to be very strong, perhaps through commuting patterns. This very close correlation in price movements in both the short run and the long run has led to the suggestion that prices can, in fact, be modelled as three interrelated blocs, rather than as separate regions since they approximate integrated housing market areas.

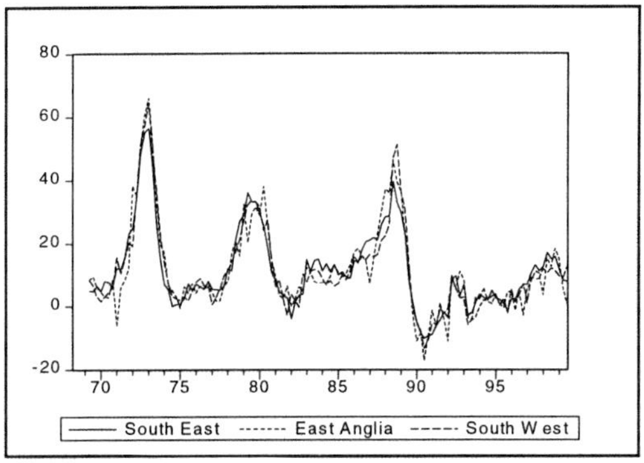

Figure 2.7a. Regional House Prices (annual percentage changes) -Southern England

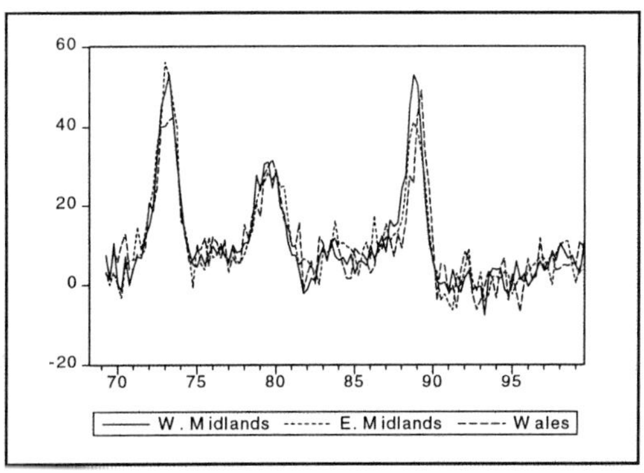

Figure 2.7b. Regional House Prices (annual percentage changes) - Midlands and Wales

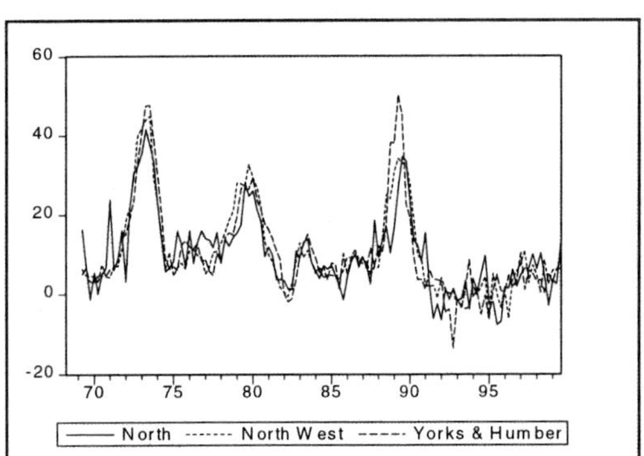

Figure 2.7c. Regional House Prices (annual percentage changes) - Northern England

The distinctive properties of the regional data and the idea of a ripple effect have made this a fertile area for tests of unit root processes and cointegration between prices in the regions. The key papers in the UK literature are those of Alexander and Barrow (1994), MacDonald and Taylor (1993), Rosenthal (1986) and Drake (1995). All the studies use data that begin either in or after 1968 and hence need to be interpreted in the light of Holmans' comments on pre-sixties trends. MacDonald and Taylor examine three questions:

- is there a stable long-run relationship between regional house prices?
- is there a segmentation in house prices between North and South?
- is there a ripple effect?

Bivariate Engle-Granger cointegration tests are conducted for all pairs of regions, followed by Johansen tests on all eleven regions together, finding that there are up to nine cointegrating relationships. The paper tests for the presence of the ripple effect by constructing a moving average representation of the VAR and calculating the effects of shocks beginning in London on the other regions. There is strong support for the view that there is a stable set of long-run relationships among the prices. Also, there is some weak evidence of segmentation between the North and South and the ripple effect, indeed, appears to exist.

Alexander and Barrow's work is closely related but, in contrast to MacDonald and Taylor, a narrower range of pair wise cointegrating regions is found using Johansen tests. They suggest that this may be because Engle-Granger techniques provide weaker tests. A vector error correction model is, then, used to test for causality through weak exogeneity restrictions with some evidence of causality running from the South East to East Anglia and from East Anglia to the South West. Multivariate tests suggest that there are three cointegrating vectors amongst the regions, although the conclusion is dependent on the lag length in the VECM.

Rosenthal (1986) adopts a different approach using cross-spectral methods to examine the long-run and short-run relationships between house prices. Although the study uses monthly data, it has the disadvantage that the sample only covers the period 1975-81, which includes only one major cyclical peak. Rosenthal's analysis suggests that there is a high degree of coherence between the regional series at low frequencies, i.e. regional prices move together in the long run, but at high frequencies (the shorter term) distinct, consistent patterns in the spatial leads and lags are less evident. The South East does not appear convincingly as the driving force for prices in the other regions.

Finally, Drake (1995) tests for convergence between regional house prices using a Kalman filter, based on equation (2.3).

$$(ph_{uk} - ph_i)_t = a_t + b_t(ph_{uk} - ph_{se})_t \qquad (2.3)$$

where:
ph_{uk} = index of UK house prices
ph_{se} = index of house prices for the South East
ph_i = index of house prices for all other regions.
lower case denotes logarithms

The key parameter is b_t which, in contrast to conventional models, is assumed to vary over time. If regional prices converge on the national value (apart from a differential a_t), b_t is expected to take a value of zero. If regional prices converge on the South East value, b_t will tend to unity. The ripple effect would be expected to generate a value cycling around unity.

In fact, the estimated parameters do not strongly support either convergence or the ripple effect and, in particular, prices in the North appear to show evidence of divergence from the South East.[8] Furthermore, with the exception of London and the South West, no evidence of a ripple effect is found.

A further approach to convergence comes from the US literature. If regional house prices appreciate by the same amount over time then, since the initial *level* of prices differs between areas, equal growth implies that the absolute level of prices diverges over time. Gyourko and Voith (1992) do not find this plausible in a study of US prices over the period 1971-89 for 56 metropolitan areas. They suggest tests, adapted from the growth convergence literature, of the hypothesis that the real growth in prices in any area will be negatively related to the initial level of prices, i.e.

$$\Delta \ln(g_{it}) = \alpha_i + B_t + \gamma \ln(g_{it-1}) + \varepsilon_{it} \qquad (2.4)$$

where (α_i) are area specific effects and (B_t) represent national trends. Gyourko and Voith find a value of (γ) of -0.14, similar to a value found for Sweden by Hort (1997). These coefficients imply that prices eventually converge across areas. Nevertheless, the first section of table 2.6, for the nine US census divisions, shows considerable diversity in nominal house price growth over the period 1975-98 with the coastal districts showing the strongest increases over sustained periods. These data do not readily suggest either a ripple effect or convergence over time[9]. The second part of the table, for the Australian state capitals, shows nominal price growth over the period 1987-99 and again indicates considerable diversity, with Sydney showing

[8] But cointegration tests also suggest that there are differences between the North and South.
[9] Further tests are conducted in Chapter 7.

the largest gains. Tu (1999) shows that there is very little evidence of cointegration in prices amongst the state capitals. Each operates as an independent market. At least on a sample of three, therefore, the UK (over the period 1969-98) appears to exhibit the most stable relative growth rates. Some caution is required, however, since census divisions, cities and regions differ in size and are, consequently, not entirely comparable.

Table 2.6. Nominal House Price Growth - US, Australia and UK (annual average percentage changes)

US Census Division	**Growth Rate (%)**	**Australian State Capital**	**Growth Rate %**	**UK Region**	**Growth Rate %**
New England	6.7	Sydney	7.9	South East*	10.8
Middle Atlantic	6.2	Melbourne	6.0	E. Anglia	10.1
South Atlantic	5.2	Brisbane	6.6	South West	10.5
East South Central	5.0	Adelaide	2.9	East Mids.	10.6
West South Central	4.2	Perth	6.0	West Mids.	10.1
West North Central	4.8	Hobart	3.5	Wales	10.2
East North Central	5.5	Darwin	6.1	Yorks.	10.4
Mountain	5.8	Canberra	4.5	North	9.8
Pacific	7.8			North West	10.3
				Scotland	9.8
USA	5.7	Australia	5.5	UK	10.6

Source: Freddie Mac CMHPI , Australian Bureau of Statistics, DETR
* excluding London

2.3.2 New Construction

Far less work has been conducted on regional construction, which is perhaps surprising given that long runs of time-series data exist. As in the last sub-section, our concern at this stage is only with data properties. In particular, does construction exhibit the same correlations between regions as prices, with the South leading the North?

Figure 2.8 is equivalent to figure 2.7 (although omitting the Midlands) but, in this case, looks at new English regional housing starts. Even visually, there appears to be a high degree of correlation (although the absolute level of construction varies considerably by region). But, more formally, we can look at the relationship between construction in the South East and the North of the country. A simple first test is to estimate the relationship between starts in the North and the South East to examine whether a ripple again occurs. We use an error correction model on quarterly data, covering the period 1969 to 1993, to see if *(i)* there is a long-run relationship between the two and (*ii*) to see the timing of any relationship.[10] The error correction term, in fact, takes a significant value of -0.28, suggesting that there is a long-run proportionality between starts in the two regions but, in the dynamics, there is a contemporaneous unit elasticity between starts in the two areas. By contrast, the equivalent contemporaneous elasticity in a house price equation for the two regions is approximately 0.4. This suggests that the timing of cycles in construction is much closer than for prices - the same ripple effect does not exist. Meen (1996) takes this further by constructing a behavioural model of housing starts, again in error correction form, for each of the nine statistical regions of England. Across seven of the regions, remarkably, the restriction that the error correction coefficient is the same cannot be rejected, although Lagrange Multiplier tests indicate that the errors are spatially correlated over the areas. The only exceptions are the South East and London, where the error correction coefficients differ slightly.

Since most of the remaining coefficients in these models also turn out to be similar across space, different movements in the regressors must primarily cause variations in construction cycles.[11] There is no evidence that the industry itself is intrinsically different between the regions. This foreshadows a theme of Chapter 4. Since the regional coefficients are broadly homogeneous, construction can be treated as an integrated national market. This is certainly not true for the demand side of the market, which is characterised by heterogeneity.

[10] More precisely, the equation relates the change in the log of northern starts to a lagged dependent variable, the change in the log of starts in the South East and the log ratio of starts in the two regions.

[11] An exception is that differences in the strength of planning constraints across the country contribute to variations in the price elasticities of supply.

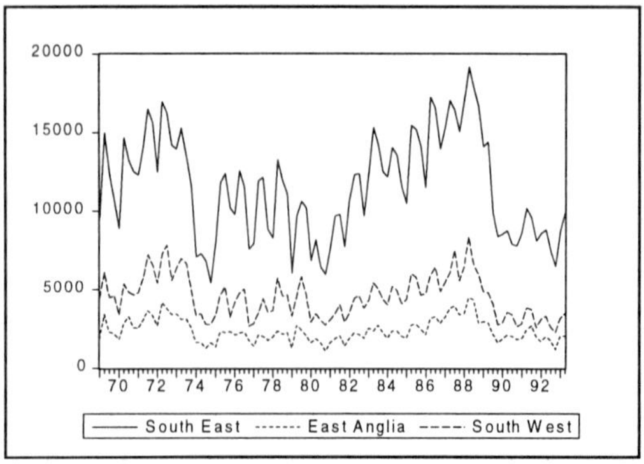

Figure 2.8a. English Regional Housing Starts (Nos) - Southern England

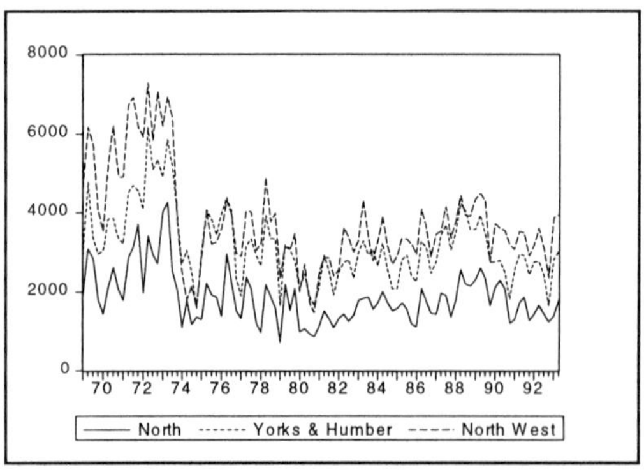

Figure 2.8b. English Regional Housing Starts (Nos) - North

Source: Housing & Construction Statistics (various issues)

2.4 Metropolitan House Prices

As noted earlier, the appropriate definition of housing market areas has proved a difficult problem. With mobile buyers and sellers, it might be argued that arbitrage should ensure that relative property prices move together over time within urban areas, which constitute common labour market areas. In this case, price variations will simply reflect differences in the price of land. If one location has a price higher than others, demand will fall and supply will increase until unit prices are common to the whole labour market area. But implicit in this view is an assumption that all characteristics are reproducible and are, hence, perfectly elastic. The problem becomes more complex if some factors, for example, neighbourhood quality, are not reproducible. In this case, distinct spatial sub-markets emerge.

Regional and urban models based on administrative boundaries are typically estimated because of data constraints rather than because of any belief that they conform to the most appropriate concept of housing market areas. By contrast, the literature on housing sub-markets, e.g. Goodman (1981), Maclennan and Tu (1996), Goodman and Thibodeau (1998), Bourassa *et al* (1999), base their estimates on hedonic equations. Areas, which exhibit similar implicit prices of housing characteristics, may be aggregated into sub-markets and used as a basis for analysis, since similarity of prices indicates a high degree of substitution between properties within the area. Precise methods of construction differ – Goodman and Thibodeau use a hierarchical approach in which housing markets are segmented by the quality of available education in Dallas. Bourassa *et al*, in an analysis of Melbourne and Sydney, use a combination of principal components and cluster analysis to identify local market areas. But, typically, markets constructed by these methods do not match local authority areas.

With inelastic supplies of some characteristics, relative prices may change over time either if valuations of the attributes of properties change or if characteristics of the properties vary. The former might occur if the demographic characteristics of the resident population alter (who may have different tastes) – an increase in the proportion of households with families in an area might increase the implicit valuation of extra bedrooms. The latter could occur if an area experiences a worsening of the neighbourhood - for example, an increase in the local crime rate, a worsening of pollution or a decline in the quality of local schools. More generally, changing relative prices could be a symptom of increasing urban deprivation.

Bearing in mind, therefore, that metropolitan price data are unlikely to correspond to the appropriate theoretical concept in any country, our *a priori* expectations of relative urban price movements are not clear. Furthermore, at least in the UK, data at the urban scale are not usually quality adjusted and may, therefore, be highly misleading. Leishman (2000), for example, shows that in local housing market areas across the West of Scotland, simple averages of prices are heavily biased compared with quality-adjusted measures. Nevertheless, it is still interesting to compare price movements across what might be considered integrated labour market areas. For the UK, Nationwide Building Society data distinguish between London, the Outer Metropolitan area and the Outer South East[12], each of which are within the London commuter belt. However, Nationwide data do *not* suggest that prices have risen by similar amounts over the long term. Between 1973 and 1999,

[12] At this level, data are quality adjusted.

prices rose by 916% in London (approximately 9% per annum) and by 721% (8% per annum) in the Outer South East. Outer Metropolitan prices rose by 827%. Therefore, prices have been increasing faster in the inner areas. This could reflect greater competition for land with the commercial sector in the inner areas. DETR and Halifax data (which distinguish only between London and the Rest of the South East) tell a similar story - London prices have risen more sharply than those in the South East generally. This is despite the fact (as we shall see later) that London has lost households in the middle-aged groups.

Table 2.7a. Housing and Deprivation in Inner London

Borough	Deprivation Rank 1998	Over-crowding	Private Housing 1996	Public Housing 1996
Newham	2	4.06 (2)	0.24	0.15
Hackney	4	4.02 (3)	0.17	0.26
Tower Hamlets	6	4.39 (1)	0.16	0.26
Southwark	8	3.71 (6=)	0.19	0.29
Islington	10	3.41	0.18	0.27
Lambeth	12	3.67 (8)	0.22	0.21
Haringey	13	3.56 (10)	0.30	0.13
Lewisham	14	3.27	0.26	0.18
Camden	17	3.44	0.28	0.20
Hammer-smith	18	3.43	0.31	0.17
Wandsworth	30	3.22	0.33	0.11
Westminster	57	3.71 (6=)	0.40	0.14
Kensington	63	3.47	0.37	0.12

It is useful at this stage to introduce, in tables 2.7a and 2.7b, basic indicators of social deprivation and housing conditions in the London boroughs, disaggregated between Inner and Outer London. These become important in later chapters but, here, the main point to note is the fact that neighbourhood conditions vary considerably within the overall labour market area, suggesting that neighbourhood quality is, indeed, not easily reproducible. The second column shows the rankings (for England) according to the 1998 DETR deprivation index. Although Liverpool is the most deprived authority overall in England, thirteen out of the top 20 most deprived areas are in London, although only three are in Outer London. The third column shows a basic indicator of housing conditions – overcrowding. This is a sub-component of the overall deprivation index and is calculated as a signed Chi-square value. High values indicate the poorest conditions. The figures in brackets show the rankings in terms of the housing indicator of the ten worst authorities. Therefore, Tower Hamlets suffers the worst degree of overcrowding in the country. None of the major northern cities matches London in terms of overcrowding.

Table 2.7b. Housing and Deprivation in Outer London

Borough	Deprivation Rank 1998	Over-crowding	Private Housing 1996	Public Housing 1996
Greenwich	11	2.8	0.24	0.18
Barking	15	3.0	0.25	0.18
Brent	20	3.98 (4)	0.30	0.18
Waltham Forest	22	3.38	0.32	0.10
Ealing	36	3.66 (9)	0.32	0.08
Hounslow	59	3.31	0.30	0.10
Enfield	70	2.61	0.35	0.07
Croydon	88	2.57	0.33	0.07
Redbridge	90	2.35	0.36	0.04
Hillingdon	120	2.71	0.31	0.08
Merton	122	2.43	0.35	0.07
Barnet	130	2.88	0.34	0.06
Havering	143	-	0.34	0.06
Harrow	145	2.65	0.34	0.04
Bexley	148	-	0.36	0.05
Richmond	156	-	0.36	0.06
Bromley	179	-	0.37	0.06
Kingston	220	-	0.36	0.05
Sutton	284	-	0.35	0.07

The fourth and fifth columns provide information on the per capita housing stock in 1996, split between the public and private sectors. The higher levels of public housing in the inner boroughs and higher private housing in the outer boroughs is evident. Although not shown in the table, Outer London has a lower density of housing per head.

2.5 Measurement Errors and Biases

We have already noted that a number of different indices of house prices are available for the UK and USA, producing different results. The problem arises primarily from the heterogeneity of housing – no two houses are identical, particularly when location is taken into account. Therefore, simple indices constructed from transactions data may confound quality changes with true price changes. As Wang and Zorn (1997) point out, whether this matters depends on the intended application. For example, if the aim is to construct national measures of the value of the housing stock, inclusion of quality changes is entirely appropriate. Alternatively, if interest is in measuring the rate of return on housing, the inclusion of quality changes could be misleading. As a result, a large literature exists on the most appropriate way of constructing price indices. Here we summarise the issues and demonstrate the differences between measures that arise in practice, concentrating on the US and UK.

Three sources of time-series data on house prices are available in the UK[13]; the first constructed by the DETR in conjunction with the Council of Mortgage Lenders (CML) is based on a 5% sample survey of mortgage transactions. This is known as the Survey of Mortgage Lenders. Data are available from the second quarter of 1968 and prices are measured at the time of mortgage completion. In addition two lenders, the Halifax and the Nationwide Building Society, construct alternative indices, based on their own mortgage books and are constructed as hedonic indices (see Fleming and Nellis 1984). The indices are based on mortgage approvals data rather than completions so that, in principle, the indices should be more closely related to current market conditions. However, quality-adjusted indices have only been published since the early eighties, although the Nationwide has published unadjusted information since 1952.

In the USA, perhaps the most commonly quoted figures are those of the National Association of Realtors (NAR) from which an index of the median sale price of existing single-family homes is constructed in 119 metropolitan areas (Mason and Quigley 1996). There is no attempt at quality standardisation. Alternatively, an amalgamation of the Fannie Mae and Freddie Mac mortgage transactions databases has created a large database of *repeat sales* for the nine census divisions of the US and numerous metropolitan areas (Pollakowski and Ray 1997). In addition, the US Bureau of the Census publishes a price index for new one-family houses, using *hedonic* methods.

The problem with the measures was illustrated in figure 2.2; for the UK, the graph compares the DETR and Nationwide indices – both of which are adjusted for quality. For the US, the Freddie Mac repeat sales index is compared with the US Bureau of the Census data. Although the former refers to existing houses and the latter to new dwellings, we should still expect the two to move similarly since they are close substitutes. Each graph

[13] Data are also published by the Land Registry. However, despite fuller coverage, the series are only publicly available from the mid-nineties and currently lack sufficient information on dwelling characteristics to construct quality-adjusted indices, although the Bank of England is making attempts to do so.

is expressed as the log difference between the two series[14]. In fact, in each case, the differences are non-stationary; an ADF(4) test for the UK yields a value of 0.13 over the period 1975-1999 and an ADF(1) value for the US of -1.29 (1977-98). As noted above, it is conceivable that the measures may diverge in the short run - prices, for example, are measured at different times. But differences of this form only affect the *dynamics* of any relationship. However if, as the graphs suggest, the differences between the two series are non-stationary, then the same economic theory cannot readily explain both series in the long run.

The differences partly arise from variations in methods of construction. Without defining terms, we have already referred to *mix-adjusted indices*, *repeat sales* and *hedonic* models, all of which are methods of adjusting for quality to obtain constant quality price indices. Each may be subject to different forms of bias in construction.

Hedonic models are regression-based and require information on the price of each dwelling in a sample and the associated set of characteristics, such as the number of rooms, lot size, presence of a garage etc. The coefficients, derived from regressing house prices on the characteristics, yield an estimate of the implicit price of each characteristic. The simplest form of hedonic model is given by equation (2.5)[15].

$$PH_{it} = \sum_{j=1}^{k} \beta_{jt} X_{ijt} + v_{it} \tag{2.5}$$

where, (PH_{it}) is the price of dwelling (i) at time (t); (X_{ijt}) is the associated vector of characteristics, (β_j) are the implicit prices of the (k) characteristics which may vary over time and (v) is an error term. For example, if (X_1) is the number of bedrooms, then (β_1) represents the increase in property value that would occur from adding an extra bedroom. Since these implicit prices may change over time, one approach is to estimate an equation such as (2.5) for each time period as new information becomes available and a quality-adjusted index can be constructed by standardising on a given set of characteristics. Empirical applications of the hedonic method have been enormous worldwide.

[14] Since the series have different base periods (and the Census Bureau figures are expressed in dollars), the values on the vertical axes are not particularly meaningful. DiPasquale and Wheaton (1996, Chapter 8) compare the Freddie Mac and NAR figures over the seventies and eighties; these indicate significant differences particularly in the eighties.

[15] As noted in the last section, areas, which are found to have common coefficients, may be grouped together as housing sub-markets. Here we ignore the spatial dimension.

In principle, repeat sales methods are simpler. The basic idea, first introduced by Bailey *et al* (1963)[16], is that the problem generated by the heterogeneity of the housing stock can be avoided by including in the sample only those houses that have been traded more than once. Apart from improvement work, by definition, the quality of those houses must be constant. Given sufficient information, the sample can exclude those dwellings where changes to the property have been made. Of course, the inclusion only of repeat sales implies that the size of the sample is drastically reduced and there is no necessary reason to assume that repeat sales represent a random sample of the total stock. Sample selection biases are discussed further below. With the exception of Leishman (2000), who looks at twenty-one local housing market areas in the West of Scotland, there have been no attempts to construct repeat sales indices in the UK, although the approach is widely used in the US. The Freddie Mac index is, perhaps, the best known.

The European literature has conducted relatively little research on the problems associated with different measures, although a series of articles on Swedish data sets (see Englund, Quigley and Redfearn 1998, 1999 and Englund, Gordon and Quigley 1999) provides exceptions. Most European studies have been based on hedonic analysis. Therefore, comparative studies have been almost entirely limited to the USA, driven partly by the concern with testing housing market efficiency. An exception for the UK is Rosenthal (1984) who compares the differences between four methods using UK data over the period 1975-81 - simple averages, mix-adjusted, and two hedonic-based methods, concluding that, for this sample, there are few advantages from using the more complex methods. Many working in the field would consider this controversial. By contrast, in the US, there has been no shortage of comparisons. Wang and Zorn (1997) summarise the findings of comparisons by Mark and Goldberg (1984), Case *et al* (1991), Case and Quigley (1991), Crone and Voith (1992), Hosios and Pesando (1991), Clapp and Giacotto (1992), Gatzlaff and Ling (1994) and Meese and Wallace (1997). Peek and Wilcox (1991) provide a further early comparison (including econometric estimates of the determinants of house prices). It would be fair to conclude, however, that no one method consistently turns out to be superior.

The Journal of Real Estate Finance and Economics for January/March 1997 is entirely devoted to the measurement problems that arise under different methodologies. The problems of hedonic models have been known for many years, for example, choice of functional form, collinearity of the

[16] In practice, the use of the method did not become widespread until the studies of efficiency by Case and Shiller (1989, 1990).

included characteristics, biases due to omitted characteristics, the instability of the coefficients over time, large variations in the implicit prices in different studies. Biases due to the omission of spatial or neighbourhood characteristics have received considerable attention and Can (1992), Can and Megbolugbe (1997) propose methods from the spatial econometrics literature to deal with the problems. We return to these in Chapter 4. Yet despite all these drawbacks the method remains highly popular. Wang and Zorn (1999) also set out the problems associated with repeat sales methods. The first set of problems arises from the sampling process. Because the samples are obtained only from observed transactions, biases may be introduced because the samples are non-random. This problem is common to other methods, but is enhanced in repeat sales indices by the exclusion of properties whose sales are observed only once. In addition, Wang and Zorn discuss the possibility of asymptotic inconsistency, i.e. if the price of every house is eventually observed for a second time, will the constructed price index converge on its true value. They speculate that the answer is, no, in the absence of non-random sampling. A further issue that appears in the literature following the work of Case and Shiller concerns potential heteroscedasticity in the errors. Case and Shiller examined the possibility that the errors from repeat sales regressions are related to the number of periods between the two sales of the dwelling, finding a significant effect. Although heteroscedasticity does not lead to biased estimates of the index, it will affect the efficiency of the parameter estimates. The nature of the error term is discussed further below.

But, first, in order to demonstrate some of the more important issues further, consider a more general version of the hedonic equation (2.6), which nests both the hedonic and repeat sales approaches (see, for example, Dombrow *et al* 1997);

$$PH_{it} = \sum_{j=1}^{k} \beta_{jt} X_{ijt} + \alpha_t T_t + v_{it} \tag{2.6}$$

where, again, (PH_{it}) is the price of dwelling (i) at time (t), (v_{it}) is an error term and (X_{ijt}) is the associated vector of characteristics; (T_t) is a set of time dummy variables due to the property being sold in that time period. (T_t) only takes a non-zero value if the property is sold in that period, either for the first or second time. (α_t) is, therefore, the associated value from being sold in that period, standardising for the remaining characteristics and, hence, a price index can be constructed from the coefficients. The coefficients on the characteristics, (β_{jt}), are written as time variant which may or may not turn out to be the case in practice. In long-run equilibrium, we might expect these coefficients to be constant if the supply of the characteristics is perfectly elastic. In the short-run, however, supply may be inelastic and the implicit prices become time-variant. Alternatively, as noted above, changing population characteristics may alter the implicit valuations over time. However, coefficient heterogeneity over time introduces further problems for the repeat sales method.

If (*f*) represents the price at first sale and (*s*) the price at second sale, we may write;

$$PH_{is} - PH_{if} = (\sum_{j=1}^{k} \beta_{js} X_{ijs} - \sum_{j=1}^{k} \beta_{jf} X_{ijf}) + (\alpha_s T^*_s - \alpha_f T^*_f) + \varepsilon_i \quad (2.7)$$

(ε_i) is a further error term whose relationship to (v_{it}) is discussed later. Therefore, the change in the price of the dwelling between its first and second sale consists of three components, (*i*) the effect of changes in the implicit prices, (*ii*) the effect of changes in the characteristics, (*iii*) the effect of the dwelling being sold in a particular period. But the conventional repeat sales method ignores the first two terms, yielding;

$$PH_{is} - PH_{if} = (\alpha_s T^*_s - \alpha_f T^*_f) + \varepsilon_i \quad (2.8)$$

Hence a regression of the change in the sale price between the two dates is conducted on a set of dummy variables[17] and the repeat sales price index can be constructed from the coefficients. Note that if the estimated coefficients are the same in each period then the price has not changed. But the ability to drop the first term in (2.7) relies on (*i*) the characteristics of the property not changing between the two periods and (*ii*) the implicit prices being constant, but we have already seen that there is no necessary reason why this should be the case. Although it may be possible to control for (*i*) by appropriate sample selection, (*ii*) is more difficult. This is an example of the general problem that arises in Chapter 4 in sub-national house price modelling - that of coefficient heterogeneity. Dombrow *et al* (1997) demonstrate the nature of the biases that arise by adding the omitted characteristic variables back into the standard repeat sales model.

Meese and Wallace (1997) conduct related tests by constructing a nested hedonic/repeat sales model. Their aim is to test whether the coefficients derived from repeat sales data are subject to sample selection bias. We have

[17] Here, T^* represents a slightly different set of dummy variables; if a property is sold for the first time, the appropriate dummy takes a value of minus one; if it is sold for the second time it takes a value of one.

already mentioned that there is no reason to assume that houses traded more than once represent a random sample drawn from the housing stock. Since they find that the implicit prices derived from repeat sales data alone are not the same as those derived from the full sample of all traded properties, they conclude that there must be sample selection biases from the repeat sales.

Furthermore, in the US, there is some evidence that sample selection problems vary with the state of the economic cycle. Gatzlaff and Haurin (1997), for example, using repeat sales data for Florida, attempt to correct for sample selection bias by using the Heckman (1974) sample selectivity correction model. The correction involves the estimation of a joint model of the probability that a house will sell and its sale price. The probability that the house will sell is estimated as a probit model related to macroeconomic conditions. From this the inverse Mills ratio acts as a correction term in a standard repeat sales model. Omission of the term would lead to a form of omitted variable bias.

Sample biases may also arise from the fact that repeat transactions, which are likely to be traded more frequently than the stock as a whole, are not necessarily typical in their house price appreciation. Case *et al* (1997), for example, find that appreciation is systematically higher amongst properties transacted more frequently. Search is clearly important in the housing market, but because of the existence of search costs, the prices of houses of the same quality are not necessarily equalised over space. Rather there will be a dispersion of prices. Steele and Goy (1997) suggest that buyers who are particularly well-informed can exploit this dispersion by purchasing houses at the low end of the distribution and re-selling at a higher price at or above the mean. If repeat sales are more likely to be held by such individuals, then an index based on repeat sales will over-estimate true price appreciation.

A further set of problems arises from the nature of the error terms in the hedonic and repeat sales equations, which are, in fact, related. Consider again (2.6) and (2.8). Appropriate estimation of the repeat sales equation depends on the nature of the stochastic processes. Following Englund *et al* (1999)[18], assume that the errors of the hedonic model follow the autoregressive process (2.9),

$$v_{it} = \rho v_{it-1} + \eta_{it} \tag{2.9}$$

[18] Note that the more general model used by Englund *et al* (1999) allows for both age and vintage effects in the hedonic and, hence, repeat sales models, which are ignored here. However in the absence of a panel of observations, such effects cannot be identified.

$$E[\eta_{it}] = 0 \;\; ; \;\; E[\eta_{it}]^2 = \sigma^2{}_{\eta i}$$

If the errors in the hedonic model follow a random walk (ρ=1.0), then the errors in the repeat sales model are,

$$\varepsilon_i = v_{is} - v_{if} = \sum_{j=f}^{s} \eta_{ij} \tag{2.10}$$

$$E[\varepsilon_i] = 0 \;\; ; \;\; E[\varepsilon_i]^2 = (s-f)\sigma^2_{\eta i} \tag{2.11}$$

However if ($-1<\rho<1$), then the error variance becomes,

$$E[\varepsilon_i]^2 = 2\sigma^2_{\eta i}(1-\rho^{s-f})/(1-\rho^2) \tag{2.12}$$

It can be shown that the error variance in a transformed version[19] of the repeat sales model is unrelated to the sales interval only if the random walk hypothesis holds. Applying the model to house sales in Sweden over the period 1981-1993, Englund *et al* (1999) find that the random walk model can be decisively rejected in favour of first order serial correlation, casting doubt on the results from any repeat sales models which ignore serial correlation.

Finally, hybrid methods, introduced by Case and Quigley (1991) should also be mentioned. The method attempts to combine both repeat sales and hedonic methods by estimating a system of two equations. The method falls out naturally from our previous discussion and avoids the loss of information associated with the repeat sales method. Equations (2.6) and (2.8) can be combined into a system of pooled equations which may be estimated jointly, taking advantage of the fact that (α) enters both equations, thus increasing the efficiency of the estimates. Efficiency can be increased further by Generalised Least Squares (GLS) to account for differences in the variances of the error terms in each equation. The model has been extended by Hill *et al* (1997) to account for the potential autocorrelation in the error term in the hedonic equation, discussed above. Maximum likelihood estimation methods are proposed for the extended model. Englund *et al* (1998) provide an application of the hybrid method on Swedish data.

[19] The transformed equation basically divides (2.8) through by (s-f) so that the error variance in (2.11) does not depend on the time interval.

Chapter 3

SELECTED TOPICS IN HOUSING THEORY: A NATIONAL PERSPECTIVE

3.1 Introduction

This chapter considers the micro and macroeconomic foundations underpinning models typically used to analyse national and international housing markets. The biggest difference between this and the two following chapters, which are concerned with regional and urban markets, is the absence of any spatial dimension. By contrast urban analysis, (Chapter 5), is dominated by spatial considerations and regional analysis, (Chapter 4), at least pays lip service to spatial structure; but national models are almost entirely set in a spatial vacuum. As we shall see, however, many modern models are based on life-cycle theory and standard arbitrage conditions can be derived which form the basis of many house price equations.

The chapter is designed to build gradually an integrated model of the housing market, consistent with the life-cycle approach, starting with single equation models and ending with a full general equilibrium model. The chapter, therefore, contains the following sections:

- single equation house price models,
- extensions to include credit constraints and financial liberalisation,
- lags in prices,
- joint models of prices and property transactions,
- stock/flow models of prices and construction activity,
- full general equilibrium models.

3.2 The Determination of House Prices

House prices might almost be described as a national obsession in the UK, both amongst professional economists and the public at large. This arises, at least partly, from the strong cycles that have occurred over the last thirty years, which were described in the last chapter. We saw that both real growth and the amplitude of cycles have been considerably greater than in the US and this may account for the larger number of time-series studies purporting to explain national price movements in the UK than in the US (despite the fact that there are fewer housing economists).[1] The cost to the UK literature has been that some other areas of empirical housing economics, which are at least as important, have been neglected. The US literature shows a broader range of concerns. Nevertheless, chronologically, four classes of price model may be identified in the literature;

- early *ad hoc* models which contained only limited theoretical structure,
- mark-up models which related house prices to construction costs,
- reduced form models, derived from structural housing demand and supply equations,
- life-cycle models.

The first class of ***ad hoc*** studies began to appear in the UK during the early seventies, primarily as a response to the boom in prices in the 1972/73 period. These models attempted to identify the factors responsible for the boom. Two camps were formed. One view was that strong growth in mortgage credit was to blame. Since, at that time, mortgages were generally rationed, at least in principle, a surge in new credit availability could generate an increase in the demand for housing. Since the supply of housing is inelastic, the increase in demand could only lead to a rise in house prices. If true, then the natural policy conclusion was that mortgage controls were necessary to prevent any boom from re-occurring. Naturally such a view did not find favour with the mortgage lenders and the alternative view was that house price fluctuations were caused by strong income growth. Therefore, even at this early stage, the central question became the quantitative response of house prices to income and mortgage credit, a theme that has re-occurred under a variety of guises over the years and is still relevant today. To these variables, the cost of credit as well as its availability might be added. A number of different studies adopted specifications, incorporating these factors - the early work of Duffy (1970), London Business School (1979), and Mayes (1979) are all reviewed in Nellis and Longbottom (1981). The first modelled real house prices as a function of real net mortgage

[1] Whatever the quality, the availability of long time-series data on house prices has also been a factor.

advances, the second as a function of real income, the mortgage interest rate and the number of housing starts and the third as a function of real income, the mortgage rate, private and public completions and gross mortgage advances. There are a number of features of these specifications that are worthy of comment:

- typically early studies made only limited attempts at theoretical specification, compared with modern-day work;
- dynamic lag structures were rudimentary;
- credit market restrictions were modelled by the inclusion of net or gross mortgage advances. This is valid as long as the market is rationed, but is inappropriate if households do not face constraints, since credit becomes an endogenous variable. As we shall see, UK mortgage markets were liberalised in the early eighties so that credit became much more readily available.

Mark-up models of house prices in the UK have never been popular. However, in principle, if the supply of housing is perfectly elastic then, in the long run, house prices should simply be formed as a mark-up on construction costs. However, there appears to be no evidence from cointegrating regressions that any such relationship holds in the UK. Indeed house prices appear unrelated to construction costs at all. But construction costs typically exclude land prices and, as we saw in the last chapter, there is a close relationship between house and land prices. The key issue here, however, is the direction of causality. The relationship between land and house prices reflects land supply constraints. In contrast to the UK literature, even excluding land prices, US work finds construction costs to play an important role. In, for example, Abraham and Hendershott (1996) the short-run elasticity of house price *growth* with respect to construction cost *growth* is approximately 0.35 with a longer-term effect of approximately 0.6.

The ***reduced form*** approach specifies separate housing demand and supply equations and then equates the two to derive a price equation. (3.1)-(3.4) is an example taken from Nellis and Longbottom (1981)[2]. Dynamic adjustment processes augment this static model; Nellis and Longbottom's model was the first published in this field to use the error correction form[3]. Most of the variables appearing in (3.4) are similar to the earlier generation, although demographic factors are also included.

[2] Nellis and Longbottom's final model is slightly more complex and includes housing completions, but no significant effect from population was found.

[3] Although Hendry's house price model using the error correction method was not published until 1984, an unpublished version was available by this time.

$$h_t^d = \alpha_1 + \alpha_2(ph)_t + \alpha_3(ry)_t + \alpha_4(pop)_t + \alpha_5(RBM)_t + \alpha_6(m)_t + \alpha_7(pc)_t \tag{3.1}$$

$$h_t^s = \beta_1 + \beta_2(ph)_t + \beta_3(h)_{t-1} \tag{3.2}$$

$$h_t^d = h_t^s \tag{3.3}$$

$$ph_t = \gamma_1 + \gamma_2(ry)_t + \gamma_3(pop)_t + \gamma_4(RBM)_t + \gamma_5(m)_t + \gamma_6(pc)_t + \gamma_7(h)_{t-1} \tag{3.4}$$

where;
$H^{d,s}$ = housing stock demand and supply
PH = nominal house prices
RY = real incomes
POP = population
RBM =mortgage interest rate
M = mortgage stock
PC = consumers' expenditure deflator
lower case denotes logarithms

In fact, Nellis and Longbottom's model was the subject of a number of criticisms from Buckley and Ermisch (1983) and Barrow and O'Sullivan (1984), but many of the features of the approach remain in models of today.

Perhaps the most widely quoted house price model using the reduced form approach was that of Hendry (1984). Although the underlying model was standard, the paper was seen as an important example of appropriate econometric technique, using the error correction approach in a single equation framework. As a part of the model, Hendry proposed a cubic adjustment process for house prices out of equilibrium, which becomes particularly important when excess demand is large. This requires the inclusion of the lagged, cubed rate of house price inflation as a regressor in the price equation. A related term has proved important in the national house price equation of Muellbauer and Murphy (1997) as a "frenzy" effect.

For reasons outlined below, it has proved difficult to distinguish empirically between reduced form models and ***life-cycle*** models, at least in the UK, because of data deficiencies. Nevertheless the life-cycle model is the starting point for most modern house price models, the first example in a UK context being Buckley and Ermisch (1982). Since then the approach has been used by Meen (1990), Giussani and Hadjimatheou (1990, 1991), Breedon and Joyce (1993), Ashworth and Parker (1997), Brown *et al* (1997), Holly and Jones (1997), Muellbauer and Murphy (1997), Pain and Westaway (1997), Meen and Andrew (1998)[4]. In fact, Brown *et al* (1997) also use a time-varying coefficient approach, through a Kalman filter, to model possible instabilities in the coefficients over time and Hall *et al* (1997) adopt a Markov switching model to capture coefficient change (although not in a life-cycle framework).

In the following intertemporal utility maximising model, there are two goods, housing services and a composite consumption good (C). Assuming that the flow of housing services is directly proportional to the housing stock (H) and, given a real discount rate (β), lifetime utility can be described by equation (3.5).

$$\int_0^\infty e^{-\beta t}\mu(H(t),C(t))dt \tag{3.5}$$

This representation has a long history, see for example Dougherty and Van Order (1982). Equation (3.5) is maximised with respect to the period-to-period budget constraint (3.6) and technical constraints (3.7) and (3.8) which describe the evolution of asset stocks (housing and financial) over time.

$$g(t)X(t)+S(t)+C(t)=(1-\theta)RY(t)+(1-\theta)i(t)A(t) \tag{3.6}$$

$$\dot{H}(t)=X(t)-\delta H(t) \tag{3.7}$$

$$\dot{A}(t)=S(t)-\pi A(t) \tag{3.8}$$

where:

$g(t)$	=	real purchase price of dwellings
$X(t)$	=	new purchases of dwellings
$S(t)$	=	real savings net of real new loans
θ	=	household marginal tax rate
$RY(t)$	=	real household income

[4] Papers where the underlying theory is not explicit include Stern (1992) and Drake (1993).

$i(t)$ = market interest rate
$A(t)$ = real net non-housing assets
δ = depreciation rate on housing
π = general inflation rate
$(.)$ = time derivative
δ, π, θ are assumed to be time invariant

From the first-order conditions, the marginal rate of substitution between housing and the composite consumption good, μ_h / μ_c, is given by (3.9);

$$\mu_h / \mu_c = g(t)[(1-\theta)i(t) - \pi + \delta - \dot{g}^e / g(t)] \tag{3.9}$$

This is the widely-used standard definition of the real housing user cost of capital and represents the real price of housing services, where ($\dot{g}^e / g(t)$) is the expected real capital gain. The definition may be extended to include such elements as property taxes, maintenance expenditures and transactions costs but, at least in time-series models, movements in (3.9) are dominated by changes in the interest rate and in capital gains on housing. More important in practice (and an issue on which we shall spend some time) is to allow for the impact of credit constraints. Dougherty and Van Order (1982) and Meen (1990), for example, show that the addition of credit constraints leads to a revised version of the user cost (3.10), where $\lambda(t)$ represents the shadow price of the rationing constraint.

$$\mu_h / \mu_c = g(t)[(1-\theta)i(t) - \pi + \delta - \dot{g}^e / g(t) + \lambda(t)/\mu_c] \tag{3.10}$$

Equation (3.10) captures the investment (through the capital gains term) as well as the consumption aspect of housing decisions and, in a slightly different form, can be expressed as a market efficiency condition or an arbitrage relationship. If $R(t)$ represents the real imputed rental price of housing services, arbitrage requires;

$$g(t) = R(t)/[(1-\theta)i(t) - \pi + \delta - \dot{g}^e / g(t) + \lambda(t)/\mu_c] \tag{3.11}$$

Equation (3.11) implies that the return on housing, represented by the imputed rental plus any capital gain on housing net of depreciation, equals the post-tax return on alternative assets, allowing for any credit constraints. Two important points should be noted, however. First, (3.11) makes no allowance for housing market risk. However the addition of risk can be handled within the framework, (see Nordvik 1995).

Second, the model lies behind the large, predominantly US, literature on the interactions between inflation and housing markets that arose during the seventies. The literature, which is both theoretical and empirical, concentrates on the interaction of high rates of inflation during the seventies with a tax system that conferred benefits to owner-occupation that other forms of investment did not enjoy. The interaction implies that real house prices and the housing capital stock are non-neutral with respect to the rate of inflation (see Poterba 1984, for an exposition). Although the effects of inflation on real interest rates are not always clear-cut in general equilibrium, in simpler partial models, an increase in the inflation rate, typically, reduces the post-tax real interest rate if $\theta \neq 0$. If the arbitrage condition (3.11) is to hold, this implies an increase in the real house price. Some studies were partial in nature, examining the effect of inflation on the housing market alone, but others were more general concentrating on either rental versus owner-occupancy decisions, (Weiss 1978, Titman 1982, Henderson and Ioannides 1983, Swan 1984) or on the differential return to owner-occupation as opposed to non-residential investment where tax provisions differ (Ebrill and Possen 1982, Hendershott and Hu 1981, 1983, Summers 1981, Kau and Keenan 1983). The implication was that, at times of high inflation, the relative return to housing rises, leading to a reduction in stock market prices and to a misallocation of the capital stock between housing and other uses. This lies at the heart of the view that housing crowds out "productive" investment, an issue considered in more detail later in a general equilibrium context[5]. Since the UK had similar rates of inflation and tax provisions at that time, the conclusions of the US literature, in principle, carry over to the UK (see Buckley and Ermisch 1982). The literature has, however, become less topical with the reduction in general inflation, the cut back in owner-occupation subsidies and, indeed, the fall in US house price inflation in the 1980s[6]. It should be noted, however, that the fall in US house prices for a part of the eighties cannot be explained fully in these terms, (see Poterba 1991). More recently, Berger *et al* (2000) examine the capitalisation of tax subsidies into single-family house prices in Sweden. Using a data set covering 290,000 dwellings, of which approximately 10% received subsidised interest rates, they find strong evidence that subsidies are fully capitalised into prices.

[5] Amongst other factors that need to be considered are price uncertainty and the form of taxation. Rosen *et al* (1984) argue that, if price uncertainty enters the analysis, the effects of the tax system on tenure choice are more limited. Hendershott and Slemrod (1982) consider the appropriate measurement of taxation in the user cost, which is a far from straightforward issue since tax rates vary across household types.

[6] Note, however, that Capozza *et al* (1998) have recently returned to the issue, bringing housing supply responses into the analysis.

Empirically, house price models suggest two departures from the arbitrage conditions. First, rewrite (3.11) as;

$$g(t) = R(t)/[(1-\theta)i(t) + \delta - \gamma(\pi + \dot{g}^e / g(t)) + \lambda(t)/\mu_c] \quad (3.12)$$

$\gamma(\pi + \dot{g}^e / g(t))$ represents the *nominal* capital gain on housing and γ may take a value between zero and unity. Market efficiency requires $\gamma = 1.0$. The implications of this may not be clear. A value of less than unity implies that *nominal* as well as real interest rates are a determinant of prices. This is usually justified in terms of a front-end loading problem, but it is important to remember that front-end loading issues, themselves, arise from a form of capital market imperfection (see Schwab 1983). An implication of this, as shown in Meen (1989), is that if nominal interest rates affect housing demand as well as real rates, then a rise in inflation will typically reduce real house prices, in contrast to the conclusions of the standard model. Second, for given values of *R(t)*, efficiency also requires $\delta \ln(g(t))/\delta \ln[.] = -1.0$, where [.] denotes the denominator in (3.12). This, in practice, is difficult to test in house price models since the term [.] may take negative values and, therefore, cannot be expressed in logs. Instead, most studies impose a semi-logarithmic specification without appreciating that the equation may then violate the efficiency condition.

The role of the user cost in house price studies should be clear; in effect (3.12) is a real house price equation that can be estimated directly, once allowance has been made for dynamic specification (although, arguably, if markets are fully efficient there should be no need for further dynamic specification). In many US studies of housing market efficiency, this provides the basis for measuring the "excess return to housing". Conceptually the excess return measures the total percentage gains from investing in housing (capital gains and imputed rental) minus the costs (in our case mortgage costs and depreciation) relative to the return on an alternative risk free asset. With the exception of Muellbauer and Murphy (1997), most UK studies of house price determination have preferred to work with the user cost of capital rather than the excess return. But as Muellbauer and Murphy show, there is a direct correspondence between the two. In Muellbauer and Murphy's terms, the excess return on net equity from housing, (*ER)*, (using our notation) is given by (3.13);

$$ER(t) = \frac{\{\gamma[\pi + \dot{g}^e / g(t)] + R(t)/g(t) - lvr(t)i_m(t)(1-\theta) - \delta\}}{(1 - lvr(t))} - (1-\theta)i_f(t) \quad (3.13)$$

where:

i_m = mortgage interest rate
i_f = risk free interest rate
lvr = mortgage loan to house value ratio

The term in {.} represents the return to housing net of borrowing costs. In the standard model we expect (γ=1.0) although, for the reasons given above, it may not in practice. The gross return is equal to the capital gain, [.], plus the imputed rental expressed as a percentage of the asset price, *R(t)/g(t)*. The costs incorporate depreciation, (δ), and mortgage costs net of tax, $i_m(t)(1-\theta)$. Since most households borrow less than 100% of the house value, mortgage costs are multiplied by the loan to value ratio. For the outright owner, (*lvr*=0) and the mortgage interest rate disappears from the expression. This net return is compared with the post tax return on alternative investments, $(1\text{-}\theta)i_f$. Muellbauer and Murphy show that the excess return on housing has been positive in the UK for most of the period from the fifties until the early nineties, although the calculations make no allowance for credit restrictions.

In addition to the problems of measuring the real house price, raised in the previous chapter, measurement difficulties also arise with respect to imputed rentals; particularly in the UK there is only a limited private rental market, which can be used as a basis of comparison. In practice, empirical studies of house price determination in the UK generally substitute out for *R(t)* in terms of its expected determinants, for example, real incomes, wealth and demographic variables. However this means that the efficiency condition cannot easily be tested directly as a single equation.

Nevertheless, in principle, equations (3.12) and (3.13) provide direct tests of housing market efficiency; in efficient markets, excess returns should not be autocorrelated. But surveys by Gatzlaff and Tirtiroglu (1995) and Cho (1996) confirm that, over a wide range of US studies, covering different spatial areas, both house price inflation and excess returns are highly autocorrelated and investors can make persistent excess returns[7]. One view is that autocorrelation arises from the existence of transactions costs, both financial (which are higher in the US than in the UK), and in terms of search costs, which limit the spatial range of the search. Therefore, although excess

[7] The autocorrelation properties of house price inflation were also discussed in Chapter 2.

returns exist, exploitable trading rules are not necessarily available. We return to the question of constraints that generate persistence in the following sections. Much less information is available on the efficiency of the UK housing market, although it would be surprising if UK markets were to be found efficient whilst the US market was not. In one of the few comparable UK studies, Barkham and Geltner (1996) find that the market is semi-strong inefficient and housing returns are predictable on the basis of past stock market returns.

Although direct tests in the UK are few, the extent of housing market efficiency can be inferred through the structure of housing models themselves. UK models do not generally assume nor find efficiency to be a sustainable hypothesis. Also, in the US, there have been attempts to estimate the underlying house price equation directly and to infer the degree of market efficiency from the equation. Perhaps, the best-known examples are the studies by Mankiw and Weil (1989) and DiPasquale and Wheaton (1994).

Recent US time-series models of house prices have moved away from an assumption of efficiency in order to explain changes in house prices during the eighties, but views of housing market efficiency are inevitably tied up with the modelling of expectations in equation (3.11). Doubt has been expressed in both the US and UK literatures whether an assumption of rational expectations is appropriate in the case of housing, despite its dominance in other areas of theoretical and empirical economics. The impact of rational expectations in housing models is, however, explored further below. Historically in Britain, where house prices rose almost continuously until the early nineties and the return on housing was greater than on other assets, the potential net gains from forming rational as opposed to backward-looking expectations were probably small. Muellbauer and Murphy (1997) argue strongly that house prices should not be modelled as though expectations were fully rational. Support for this view in the US can be found in Mankiw and Weil (1989), Poterba (1991) and DiPasquale and Wheaton (1994).

3.3 Credit Rationing and Downpayment Constraints

In Section 3.2, we noted that the role of credit markets in generating house price volatility has been a controversial issue in the UK since the early days of modelling in the early seventies. Credit availability also played an important role in the early US literature. In early work, constraints on changes in the interest rates on federally underwritten mortgages were suggested as a cause of the counter-cyclical nature of housing investment.

Such constraints led to a shortage of mortgage funds. However, even then, the view was controversial; because of the close integration of financial markets, alternative funding sources were available, implying that the supply of credit was highly elastic. But since those early days the nature of the argument has moved on, although credit still plays a central role in housing theory and policy.

Although institutional changes in the nature of mortgage markets are not considered in detail, in the UK, the main changes that took place during the eighties and nineties concerned, (*i*) the abolition of the building society cartel, which controlled mortgage interest rates at below market clearing levels (*ii*) the gradual adoption of more commercial objectives by building societies (*iii*) the entry of the banks into the mortgage market (*iv*) large scale consolidation, conversion and take-over in the mortgage industry. At the dawn of the new millennium, mortgage lenders now bear little relationship to those that existed twenty years earlier. The increase in credit availability, resulting from restructuring, has been one of the most important developments in housing over that period.

It was certainly true that rationing was the norm in the sixties and seventies, because mortgage rates were artificially held low by the cartel and this disappeared by the mid-eighties. Consequently, it is sometimes argued that credit is now "freely available", but such statements have to be carefully interpreted. In general, potential mortgagees still face constraints on loan to value and loan to income ratios and, in the UK, the gradual introduction of pricing-to-risk is increasingly likely to generate differential interest rates between classes of borrower.

Similarly, in the US, downpayment requirements on mortgages remain in operation. The needs of the secondary market mean that standardised products are required and downpayments ensure that packaged mortgages meet minimum criteria (DiPasquale and Wheaton 1996 p. 200). Downpayment requirements arise from the potential for adverse selection in a world of asymmetric information (see, for example, Stiglitz and Weiss, 1981)

Equation (3.10) has already shown that the presence of credit market constraints raises the user cost of capital and, therefore, affects the equilibrium asset price of housing. In this section, we take this argument further, considering the following topics:

- the wider effects of downpayment constraints. This has been an important topic in the US literature,
- the implications of mortgage liberalisation for the conduct of monetary policy. This has received considerable attention in the UK since the market boom in the late eighties.

However, in order to consider some of these questions, we require extensions to the basic model.

3.3.1 Downpayment Constraints

This sub-section looks at the implications of constraints for individual households, reserving discussion of aggregate market effects until later. In particular, in this section, we consider differential effects between two potential classes of borrower, broadly the "rich" and the "poor", both of whom would prefer to be owner-occupiers. Surveys in the UK (e.g. Smith 2000) indicate that a much higher percentage of households aspire to owner-occupation than can realistically achieve that status. But tenure issues are deferred until Chapter 5. Because of adverse selection, the lender imposes downpayment requirements on each borrower, but the constraints are more likely to be binding on the "poor" than the "rich". Therefore, each borrower has to pay a percentage of the property value (plus any transactions costs) up front. The idea that the rich are less likely to face binding credit constraints has a long history in consumption analysis and adaptations of the Brueckner (1986), Plaut (1987), Nakagami and Pereira (1991, 1993) and Engelhardt (1994) models provide useful insights on the effects of credit constraints on the housing (and consumption) demands of low-income households.

The starting point is, again, the standard multi-period utility maximising model. Extending equation (3.5), the utility function, (3.14) now allows for potential bequests.

$$\int_0^T e^{-\beta s}\mu(H(s),C(s))ds + e^{-\beta T}V(W) \tag{3.14}$$

where *V(W)* is the value of terminal wealth at time (*T*) and μ is an instantaneous utility function. Equation (3.14) is maximised with respect to slightly extended intertemporal budget constraints (3.15-3.18), and a downpayment constraint, (3.19);

$$\dot{W}(t) = S(t) - \pi W(t) \tag{3.15}$$

$$S(t) = RY(t) + i(t)W(t) - C(t) - RP(t)/PC(t) \tag{3.16}$$

$$RP(t) = MT(t)/\{[(e^{-i(t)})/i(t)][1 - e^{-i(t)N}]\} \tag{3.17}$$

$$MT(t) = [MT(t) - RP(t) + i(t)MT(t)](1 - D(t)) + [(1 - DC(t)) * PH(t) * H(t)](D(t)) \tag{3.18}$$

$$DP(t) = [DC(t) + T(t)] * PH(t) * H(t) - \{PH(t) * H(t) - MT(t) + W(t) * PC(t)\} \tag{3.19}$$

where, (W) is real financial wealth, (S) is real savings, (π) is the general rate of inflation, (RY) is real earned income, (RP) is the nominal mortgage repayment, (PC) is the general price level, (MT) is the nominal mortgage outstanding, (i) is the nominal interest rate on borrowing and lending, (N) is the period of the mortgage loan, (D) is a dummy variable taking a value of one when the household moves and zero otherwise, (DC) is the downpayment percentage, (PH) is the nominal house price, (DP) is the downpayment constraint, (T) are transactions costs expressed as a percentage of the purchase price.

Equation (3.15) defines real financial wealth, which increases with real savings, but falls because inflation depreciates the existing real asset stock. Equation (3.16) defines savings, which increase with earned and unearned income, but fall with consumption and mortgage repayments. Earned income is taken to be exogenous. Mortgage repayments are defined in nominal terms and, therefore, have to be deflated by a general price index. In (3.17), mortgage repayments are defined by a standard annuity formula and hence all mortgages are assumed to be of the repayment form. Equation (3.18) gives the outstanding mortgage and depends on whether the household moves or not in any time period. If no move takes place then, by identity, the outstanding mortgage is the same as last period plus interest due minus repayments, a part of which covers repayment of principal. The model ensures that the mortgage is repaid over (N) years, where (N) below is assumed to be twenty-five. However if the household moves, then a new mortgage is taken out equal to one minus the downpayment percentage multiplied by the value of the new house. Equation (3.19) represents the key change to the model. This constraint compares the required downpayment with available resources represented by the term {.}. Resources are equal to equity in the existing house plus financial wealth. If the expression is positive, then the household cannot move in the current period and has to wait until further assets are accumulated as income rises. However, as Chapter 9 shows, an alternative response (for which some empirical evidence exists) is for households to become discouraged. Rather than saving more to meet the constraint, particularly if the household has a high rate of time preference, the household may give up on owner-occupation altogether, decide on renting instead and spend more on other goods.

Actual housing consumption may, therefore, deviate from the unconstrained optimum and the length of time spent in disequilibrium will be positively related to the downpayment percentage. Furthermore, housing paths will experience discrete jumps and credit unconstrained (rich) households will, typically, have smoother housing profiles than constrained (poor) households. To take an example, if the utility function takes the additive form $U(C,H) = [C^{1-\gamma} + H^{1-\gamma}]/(1-\gamma)$, utility maximisation leads to housing (3.20), and consumption (3.21) demand functions (here written in discrete time for convenience):

$$H_t = (1-D_t) * H_{t-1} + D_t * [e(\ln(C_t) - (1/\gamma)\ln(1+UCC_t))] \qquad (3.20)$$

$$\ln(C) = \ln(C^e_{t+1}) - (1/\gamma)\ln[(1+r)/(1+\beta)] \qquad (3.21)$$

where: $UCC = (i - \dot{P}H) * (PH / PC)$ and is a simplified version of the housing user cost of capital; (r) is the real interest rate $(i - \dot{P}C)$. Equation (3.20) captures the downpayment constraint so that if the constraint is binding then the household cannot move and housing consumption is the same as in the previous period. The second part of the equation is the standard housing consumption rule. The ratio of housing to composite consumption depends on the housing user cost, which represents the relative price of housing. If the relative price is unchanging, then the consumption ratio will also be constant over time. But the ratio will change with downpayment constraints. Equation (3.21) is the standard Hall (1978) consumption rule under rational expectations where C^e_{t+1} is expected consumption in the next time period and $(1/\gamma)$ is the elasticity of substitution. If the market interest rate is equal to the discount rate, then consumption will be constant over time. Rationing constraints could also be added to the consumption function since liquidity constraints are an important part of the aggregate consumption literature (see, for example, Muellbauer 1983).

We are particularly interested in the effect of the introduction of a downpayment constraint.[8] Related issues are considered by Artle and Varaiya (1978), Miles (1992) and Patterson (1993). We examine, first, housing patterns when there is no constraint. These provide a baseline for

[8] Note that transactions costs can also be analysed using the same framework. Note also that strictly the following diagrams compare the position of the *same* household before and after the introduction of the constraint, rather than the relative positions of two households on different incomes. However the same principle applies.

comparison. If the user cost of capital is constant over time and the discount rate equals the real interest rate, the unbroken lines in figure 3.1 show the desired positions for housing demand, the mortgage outstanding and mortgage repayments as a proportion of income. Time is shown along the horizontal axis; the vertical scale in figure 3.1a denotes units of housing consumption (but does not correspond to any directly observed market variable); in figure 3.1b, the outstanding mortgage is defined in pounds sterling, whereas figure 3.1c is expressed as a percentage. Since the household is unconstrained, the household can maintain its desired position in each period. But in the absence of unexpected shocks, for example to income, both the housing and composite consumption paths will be constant over time. Under perfect foresight, having reached the desired position in the first time period, the household has no need to move even if (expected) income rises over the household's lifetime[9]. As shown in the third segment mortgage repayments as a proportion of income will fall over time.

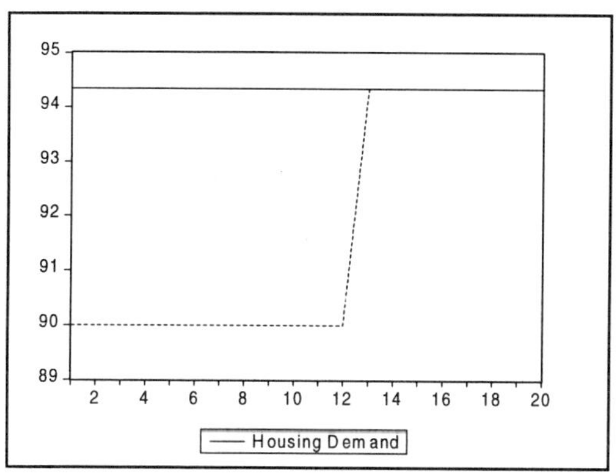

Figure 3.1a. Housing Demand: Constrained & Unconstrained Households

But the broken lines in figure 3.1 reflect the position for constrained households, facing a downpayment requirement[10]. If the constraint is binding, then the household, initially, has to under-consume owner-occupied housing[11]. This is shown in the first segment of figure 3.1. For the first part of the period housing consumption is sub-optimal. However over time, as the

[9] The graph, in fact, assumes real income growth of 3% p.a. Note that models of this form take no account of changing demographic circumstances, e.g. ageing, which would affect the profile. Such issues are delayed until Chapter 5.

[10] Taken to be 20% of the purchase price.

[11] Or rent or remain in the parental home.

household accumulates assets, the constraint is no longer binding so that housing consumption jumps to the optimal path. Note, however, that although the mortgage outstanding jumps at the time of the move, the requirement for a deposit means that both the size of the mortgage and repayments are *permanently* lower than in the unconstrained case.

Figure 3.1b. Mortgage Outstanding: Constrained & Unconstrained Households

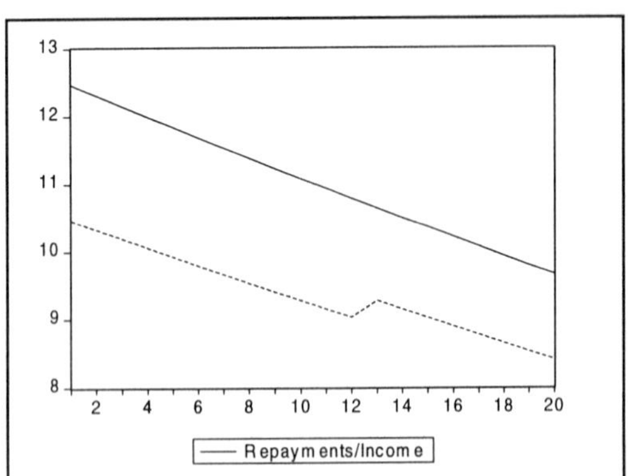

Figure 3.1c. Repayment to Income Ratio: Constrained & Unconstrained Households

Amongst the most important results, the model implies;

- for a given state of the economy, housing (and consumption) streams are typically bumpier for low-income households, who are more likely to face credit constraints, and, who are reliant on current rather than permanent incomes.

- But, given changes in the economy, low-income households are likely to adapt more slowly because of downpayment constraints. Therefore, they will deviate for longer periods of time from their optimal consumption and housing profiles. To anticipate later results, if certain locations experience either negative or positive shocks, high-income groups will be in a better position to move to alternative locations quickly to take advantage of those shocks. Furthermore, low-income households are more likely to become locked into declining areas, not only because of lower incomes, but also because of declining relative house prices. In later chapters, we model the mobility of different household types and show that low-income groups are relatively immobile. This is consistent with the presence of credit constraints.
- Although not yet demonstrated, shocks generate *persistence* in price movements. One explanation is that not all groups are able to move at the same time, because of credit constraints.[12] This is consistent with the observed autocorrelation in house price inflation. The presence of transactions costs generates a similar result.
- Low-income households are more likely to be affected by variations in national policy, such as interest rate changes, than high-income groups. This again arises from the front-end loading problem. The rich can borrow against purely nominal interest rate changes, leaving lifetime wealth unchanged. The poor cannot.
- Recently, Ortalo-Magné and Rady (1999) demonstrate that the effects of credit market constraints vary by age cohort. In particular, the rise in owner-occupancy amongst the young in the UK in the eighties is consistent with a relaxation of credit constraints at that time. Furthermore, they suggest that the bust in the market and the fall in owner-occupancy rates in the early nineties is consistent with a transitory income fall for the young.

3.3.2 Credit Constraints and the Conduct of Monetary Policy

The potential for adverse selection means that downpayment constraints exist in the UK[13] in a similar manner to the USA. However, prior to the eighties, constraints on loan to income and loan to value ratios existed not only for precautionary reasons, but also because of market rationing. Liberalisation of mortgage markets, which eliminated rationing, was one of

[12] Credit constraints and transactions costs are, by no means, the only reasons for persistence. Later we explore alternative explanations.

[13] In fact, during the late eighties, loan to value ratios sometimes exceeded 100% in the frenzy of the time. However lenders and households now appear to have become a little more cautious again.

the most important events in UK housing markets during the eighties. As noted above, liberalisation was closely related to the abolition of the building society cartel and the entry of the commercial banks into the market. For the government, the primary motivation for encouraging change was microeconomic and fitted in with the general climate of freeing markets from controls. However, in practice, arguably the main effects were macroeconomic. The work of Muellbauer and Murphy (1990) proved particularly influential (and controversial), arguing that financial liberalisation and rapidly increasing house prices were major factors in explaining the boom in consumers' expenditure that occurred in the second half of the eighties. This controversy is discussed further in Chapter 9; here we concentrate on some of the theoretical macroeconomic effects of the removal of rationing and the implications for monetary policy, showing that monetary policy becomes more powerful as liberalisation takes place.

Consider equation (3.10) again; the two key elements of the user cost are the interest rate ($i(t)$) and the rationing constraint ($\lambda(t)$)[14]. Deregulation reduces the implicit price of owner-occupier housing services. In the UK, it was widely argued that this reduction in cost was responsible for the boom in house prices that occurred in the second half of the eighties. But, in fact, the explanation is slightly more complex. Liberalisation initially took place in the *early* eighties, but prices did not boom until much later. How can this occur? The explanation lies in terms of the conduct of monetary policy. In the first half of the eighties, the government maintained relatively tight policy, despite deregulation. Between 1980 and 1985, pre-tax mortgage interest rates averaged 13%. Therefore, the elimination of rationing was offset by a rise in mortgage interest rates towards market clearing levels. Meen (1996a) shows that, over the period, the user cost of capital remained fairly invariant to deregulation.

But from 1986 through to the middle of 1988, monetary policy was relaxed, with mortgage rates falling to a minimum of 9.8% in the second quarter of 1988. Prior to the eighties, equation (3.11) would have predicted that the effect on housing demand and prices would have been muted, because the length of the mortgage queue would have acted as a buffer i.e. any increase in housing demand as a result of the lower interest rates would not come to fruition because of the unavailability of credit. But after deregulation, mortgage queues no longer acted as a buffer and, therefore, monetary policy became more powerful.

Table 3.1 simulates the effects on aggregate demand of a two percentage point reduction in interest rates before and after liberalisation. These results

[14] Meen (1996a) combines the two terms into a virtual price (see Rothbarth (1941)).

are taken from Meen (1996a) and use the estimated model developed in Chapter 6.

Table 3.1. Impact of Interest Rate Changes on GDP - Before and After Liberalisation (percentage changes in GDP relative to base)

Year	Rationed	Unrationed
1	0.2	0.5
2	0.2	1.4
3	0.3	2.2
4	0.4	2.6

Source: Meen (1996a)

The table looks at the impact on demand in both the short run (year 1) and in the longer term. The table suggests that the economy is *inelastic* with respect to interest rate changes under rationing (GDP is only 0.4% higher even after four years), but clearly much more elastic under liberalised markets. Monetary policy becomes much more effective after liberalisation.

3.4 Lags in Prices

The price equation derived from the arbitrage relationship (3.11) requires no lags; demand shocks, therefore, should be immediately reflected in price changes in an efficient market. But empirical models, without exception, suggest that lagged adjustment is a feature of price behaviour. Without appealing to inefficiencies, can lags be explained in terms of theory? In fact, downpayment constraints, housing market search, expectations formation and construction delays can all introduce lags into price adjustment and become important topics later in this and in subsequent chapters. But, first, there are other issues to resolve.

Note that conventional autocorrelation tests are, as shown in Chapter 2, conducted in terms of house price *inflation* rather than the *level* of prices. The problem is that, as specified, temporary random shocks have permanent effects on the level of prices i.e. the level of prices is undetermined. By contrast, the theoretical models of prices considered so far, determine the level of prices.

In fact, both elements can be combined into a joint model, determining processes of dynamic adjustment and a long-run equilibrium solution in terms of levels. In the empirical literature on price formation, by far the most important approach has been to use error correction models, which can be derived as a form of dynamic optimisation model. But before deriving the dynamic model, it is useful to return to the static model and deal with a problem noted above that the imputed rental (*R(t)*) is generally not directly observable. Although the UK national accounts include estimates of imputed rentals as a part of household income, there are considerable doubts about the quality of the estimates because the private rental sector, which in some countries is used as a basis for comparison, is only approximately 10% of the UK housing market and has, historically, been subject to rent controls. As a result all UK studies, and those in most other countries, substitute out in terms of the factors believed to determine the imputed rental.

One of the features of the life-cycle approach is that it considers the consumption of housing services and the investment role of housing simultaneously. The former is summarised by the imputed rental. The market in housing services is assumed to clear in each time period so that, in a reduced form, the rental reflects all the factors determining housing demand and supply. The most important factors are taken to be incomes, wealth, demography and (since the supply of housing services is assumed to be proportional to the stock), the housing stock. This is summarised in equation (3.22);

$$R(t) = h(RY(t), W(t), HH(t), H(t)) \tag{3.22}$$

Substituting equation (3.22) into equation (3.11), and suppressing the time notation, yields a general equation (3.23);

$$\ln(g) = f(\ln(RY), \ln(W), \ln(HH), \ln(H), \ln(M), \ln[(1-\theta)i + \delta - \pi - \dot{g}^e / g]) \tag{3.23}$$

where:

RY = real personal disposable income
W = real wealth
HH = number of households
H = housing stock
M = measure of mortgage rationing

However, note that the explicit relationship given by (3.11) has already been lost in (3.23), since we do not know the precise relationship determining *R(t)*; in (3.23) we have assumed a logarithmic specification, but testing the arbitrage equation or efficiency condition directly is no longer straightforward.

In fact, there are further difficulties, which we have already noted. First, in (3.23) the final term, the real interest rate, is defined in logs as the theory would predict, but since the series may take negative values (and did so for long spells in the sixties and seventies), this implies that housing demand is infinite. Measurement errors and the presence of credit constraints suggest that the real rate is, in fact, never negative (see Meen 1996a) but, nevertheless, the usual approach in the literature has been not to take logarithms of the term, which again may violate the efficiency condition. Second, *nominal* interest rates may affect housing demand as well as real rates. Taking all these factors into account, the basic equation (in logs) used by many researchers is given by equation (3.24)[15]. Clearly much of the theoretical structure of (3.11) has disappeared. Indeed, if the equation is compared with the reduced form demand/supply model given by equations (3.1)-(3.4), their structures are similar. Distinguishing empirically, therefore, between the two hypotheses is difficult.

$$\ln(g) = a_1 \ln(RY) + a_2 \ln(W) + a_3 \ln(HH) + a_4 \ln(H) + a_5 \ln(M)$$
$$+ a_6(i) + a_7(\dot{ph}^e) + \varepsilon$$

$$a_1, a_2, a_3, a_5, a_7 \geq 0 \qquad a_4, a_6 \leq 0 \tag{3.24}$$

$\dot{ph}^e = \pi + \dot{g}^e / g$ = the expected nominal capital gain on housing. Adding dynamics, the generic form of the error correction model is given by (3.25) where γ_3 is the error correction coefficient determining the speed of adjustment to the long-run equilibrium;

$$\Delta \ln(g) = \gamma_1 \Delta \ln(g)_{-1} + \gamma_2 \Delta \ln(X) + \gamma_3 [\ln(g) - \gamma_4 \ln(X)]_{-1} + \mu$$
$$X' = [RY, W, HH, H, M, i, \dot{ph}^e] \tag{3.25}$$

In the UK literature, equation (3.25) has been estimated directly, e.g. Nellis and Longbottom (1981), Hendry (1984), Meen (1990), through the Engle-Granger methodology, Munro and Tu (1996) or through the Johansen approach, Drake (1993), Ashworth and Parker (1997). Error correction models of house prices have also been estimated widely in other countries, for example, Kosonen (1997) for Finland, Hort (1998) for Sweden and Bar-Nathan *et al* (1998) for Israel. In the USA, the error correction approach is,

[15] In fact, few studies incorporate all the variables, which might be considered as a nested equation.

perhaps, less common, although Malpezzi (1999) provides an exception and Abraham and Hendershott (1996) might be interpreted in the light of error correction models.

We might also mention three US studies that partly fit into this framework. First, Mankiw and Weil's (1989) study employs the life-cycle framework, and attracted considerable publicity both within the academic world and outside, because of its prediction that real house prices would fall by 47% in real terms by 2007. Clearly, if true, (and house prices rose in the nineties) then the asset bases of both individual households and financial institutions would be severely undermined.

Econometrically, their approach to modelling real house prices is very different from that employed in the UK. Mankiw and Weil's work consists of two models; the first is primarily a data-determined approach and is the model that attracted most publicity. The model is constructed in two stages. Initially, a cross section model is estimated, regressing housing demand by age on a set of age dummies. From this regression it is possible to construct a time-series of housing demand, based purely on demographic factors assuming that housing demand for each age group is constant over time. Therefore movements in the variable reflect only demographic changes, in particular both the baby boom and the baby bust. Related, demographic measures, have been constructed in the US by DiPasquale and Wheaton (1994) and by Buckley and Ermisch (1982) and Meen (1990) for the UK. This demographic variable then becomes a regressor in a further empirical equation, where the (log of the) real price of housing (measured by the investment deflator and hence excluding land costs) is regressed on the (log of the) demographic variable, a time trend, real GNP and an after-tax interest rate. The equation includes no lags and, therefore unsurprisingly, an autocorrelation coefficient is highly significant, reflecting dynamic misspecification. The demographic variable has an elasticity of approximately five and, hence, demographics have a very strong effect on house prices. The estimated equation is used to predict the future, using the fact that demographic changes are known well in advance with a high degree of precision. From the equation, the authors reach their well-known and controversial conclusion.

Their second model is not estimated, but uses a dynamic model similar to the two-equation rational expectations model of house prices and construction of Poterba (1984), discussed in Section 3.6, to test whether housing markets are efficient, given that population movements are predictable. They find that observed house price movements are not consistent with an efficient market.

Mankiw and Weil's work received a great deal of academic criticism. A 1991 edition of Regional Science and Urban Economics was almost entirely devoted to the issue. Perhaps the criticisms of Hamilton (1991) are most telling, who points out that the negative time trend in the equation reduced real prices by 8% per annum on its own and is responsible for most of Mankiw and Weil's predictions. Holland (1991) finds an absence of cointegration between the real house price and the demographic variables. Further criticisms came from Woodward (1991) who suggested the results were sensitive to specification and violated theoretical priors, Engelhardt and Poterba (1991) who pointed to similar demographic trends in Canada, but very different house price patterns and Hendershott (1991) who showed that although the model fitted the fifties and sixties reasonably well, the fit in the seventies was poor and, therefore, provided a weak basis for predicting the future. In a detailed study using 1980 census data, Green and Hendershott (1996) examine the effect of education and income as well as age structure and show that, in contrast to Mankiw and Weil, the ageing of the population has only a limited effect on price, having controlled for these other variables.

The second model by DiPasquale and Wheaton (1994) estimates a stock/flow model of house prices and construction activity on US national data. Again the model adopts a very different econometric approach from UK work, but there are some similarities in terms of model structures. The model relates house prices to the ratio of the dwelling stock to the number of households, market rents, the home-ownership rate, permanent income (measured by consumption) and the user cost of ownership. A simple partial adjustment process is included to capture gradual price adjustment. Here, demographics are still important, but a wider set of regressors is included and demographics do not dominate the results in the same way as in the Mankiw and Weil study. Furthermore there is no time trend. In contrast to UK studies, market rents are included, reflecting substitution between tenures. In the UK, almost no time-series house price study includes private rents. This partly reflects poor UK rents data, but also the fact that, until recently, there was a lower degree of substitution between private renting and owner-occupation than in the US. This issue is examined further in Chapter 5. DiPasquale and Wheaton reject housing market efficiency and argue that the correlation in house price movements over time is due to incomplete market adjustment in which prices respond only slowly to demand and supply changes, pointing to the role of market search in preventing faster adjustment. They also argue that expectations are better modelled as backward-looking processes, which introduce lags into the model.

The third study, by Abraham and Hendershott (1996), has attracted attention as a test for the existence of speculative bubbles. The authors estimate a model of house price inflation covering thirty US cities over fourteen years. The model has some similarity to an error correction specification, although not estimated in the conventional manner. The lagged dependent variable in the equation is interpreted as a bubble-builder - house price inflation is self-reinforcing in the short term - and the equivalent of the error correction term, measuring market disequilibrium, is a bubble-burster, ensuring that in the longer term, prices are determined by fundamentals. Disaggregating the data between the coastal and inland areas, the authors find that the disequilibrium terms are only significant in the former; in other words bubbles are stronger on the coast (where planning controls are stronger).

3.5 Joint Models of House Prices and Property Transactions

Chapter 2 estimated a very simple bivariate model of prices and transactions, which suggested that both price inflation and transactions exhibit positive autocorrelation in the short run and some evidence of longer-term mean reversion. Although there appears to be a strong correlation between movements in the two series, as yet, we have no convincing explanation as to why the correlation might occur.

The literature poses a conundrum. The basic arbitrage equation, (3.11), predicts that shocks to the market will result in an instantaneous adjustment to prices in an efficient market in the absence of trading frictions and given an inelastic supply of housing. Perfect price adjustment implies that the level of transactions should remain unaffected. But, in contrast to the basic theory, US studies, in particular, have pointed to the presence of a short-run correlation between movements in prices and transactions. Berkovec and Goodman (1996), for example, find that changes in real house prices and changes in turnover are positively correlated and note, in addition, that transactions respond more quickly than house prices to shocks. Most theoretical explanations of the correlation have been couched in terms of trading frictions which arise from search costs, transactions costs, or, once again, liquidity constraints. Other US studies also support an empirical relationship; Stein (1995) finds a positive correlation between the level of sales and the percentage change in real house prices for existing single-family homes between 1968 and 1992. On the other hand, Follain and Velz (1995) observe a negative correlation between the level of house prices and the level of sales between 1986 and 1993 for twenty-two metropolitan markets. Outside the USA, the only studies are by Hort (2000) for Sweden and Meen (2000) for the UK, who also find correlations. However each of the studies differs in terms of whether the variables are specified in levels, first differences or a combination. This, clearly, affects the orders of integration.

Search models are discussed in a little more detail in Chapter 4. Wheaton (1990), for example, constructs a theoretical model of search to analyse the relationship between vacancies, turnover, and pricing. In Berkovec and Goodman's (1996) model, search is driven by mismatches in the valuations of properties by buyers and sellers. In particular, if sellers adjust their reservation prices only slowly in response to negative demand shocks (and there is considerable anecdotal evidence that this is the case), then the volume of transactions will be affected before prices. Since the inverse of transactions is time on the market, sales time then acts as an indicator to sellers to lower reservation prices. Therefore, in the short run, prices and transactions will be positively correlated. In the longer term, prices will fall to a new permanently lower level, whereas transactions return to their original level.

As we have already seen, both **transactions costs** and **liquidity constraints** generate lock-in costs, reducing the propensity of households to move. Stein (1995), for example, demonstrates that a short-run correlation between prices and transactions can result from the nature of credit markets. As shown in (3.19), meeting any downpayment constraint, and hence the ability to move, depends on the price fetched for the existing house. Falling prices mean that liquidity constrained households are less likely to be able to repay their mortgage debt and, at the same time, to be able to transfer sufficient equity to meet the deposit on a new home. Therefore, the probability of moving declines, again, generating the observed positive correlation. Linneman and Wachter (1989), Zorn (1989) and Engelhardt (1994) amongst many others provide empirical support for the view that credit constraints affect owner-occupation and mobility rates. Stein also shows that "equity transfer" problems can generate self-reinforcing multipliers and multiple equilibria in the housing market. Relative to perfect capital market models, downpayment constraints magnify the effects of housing demand changes. Furthermore, such models can generate booms and slumps in housing markets, independently of the existence of speculative bubbles. With multiple equilibria solutions, a small change in economic fundamentals can result in dramatic changes in prices. The housing market experiences a "catastrophe" – a discrete jump in prices from one candidate equilibrium to another. Lamont and Stein (1999) also find that house prices are more sensitive to shocks in cities where a high percentage of borrowers is heavily leveraged. In the UK, Ortalo-Magné and Rady (2000) use a related approach to explain the boom in residential transactions in the late eighties and the subsequent slump in the nineties. They argue that the boom was caused by a one-off adjustment to mortgage liberalisation in the eighties, which reduced the constraints that households faced.

The relationship between prices and transactions can also be expressed in terms of vacancies. In contrast to the US literature, UK theoretical and empirical housing work almost entirely ignores the role of vacancies. This is partly because of a paucity of regular time-series data. Nevertheless Wheaton (1990) and DiPasquale and Wheaton (1996) identify vacancies as a key variable in explaining prices, rents, sales and construction. As noted above, increasing sales times indicate that seller reservation prices are above the equilibrium and need to be reduced[16]. DiPasquale and Wheaton (1996, p.228, figure 9.2), indeed, show that there is a strong negative relationship between real price inflation and expected sales time. But average sale time is determined by equation (3.26);

$$(vacancies\,/\,transactions) = average\ sale\ time \tag{3.26}$$

Therefore, we expect a negative relationship between house price changes and the vacancy rate. However vacancies (in excess of some "normal" level) are an indicator of overall housing market disequilibrium. Therefore the vacancy rate (*VR*) may be explained by (3.27);

$$VR_t = f(H_t - H_t^*) \tag{3.27}$$

where (H^*) defines the desired housing stock. Precisely how the desired stock is to be defined is postponed until Chapter 6, where we demonstrate that an estimate can be derived from (3.24). However this suggests that the bivariate model of prices and transactions from Chapter 2 may now be extended, allowing us to derive long-run levels solutions for both prices and transactions, set in an error correction framework. This is given, in general terms, by equation (3.28). Both transactions and prices, in principle, respond to the vacancy rate or market disequilibrium. We, therefore, have a joint model for prices and transactions, conditional on the excess demand for housing.

$$\begin{bmatrix} \gamma_{11}(L)\ \gamma_{12}(L) \\ \gamma_{21}(L)\ \gamma_{22}(L) \end{bmatrix} \begin{bmatrix} \Delta \ln(g) \\ \ln(TR) \end{bmatrix} = \begin{bmatrix} \alpha_1 \\ \alpha_2 \end{bmatrix} [VR_{t-1}] + \begin{bmatrix} \varepsilon_1 \\ \varepsilon_2 \end{bmatrix} \tag{3.28}$$

[16] As shown in Chapter 4, the optimal pricing rule for sellers suggests that prices are negatively related to time on the market.

In this general form, both prices and transactions respond to housing market disequilibrium induced by shocks. However, different speeds of adjustment are captured through different values of the α terms. Models of perfect price adjustment are encompassed within the general model, and imply that transactions are unaffected by market disequilibrium.

3.6 Joint Models of Prices and Construction (Stock/Flow Models)

Stock/flow models, determining the level of house prices and the volume of housing construction, remain one of the main workhorses of theoretical and empirical housing economics. Early British examples include Whitehead (1971, 1974, 1975). For the USA, the model of DiPasquale and Wheaton (1994), already discussed, provides a more recent example. But perhaps the most influential version has been that put forward by Poterba (1984), which sets out a two equation model, (3.29) and (3.30). Equation (3.29) is, again, an arbitrage relationship for the housing market and is consistent with (3.11) – note that the equation includes no lags; the return on housing made up of the (imputed) rental, *R(.)* plus any capital gain is equal to the return on alternative assets, represented by $(a_1 g)$. In terms of (3.11), $a_1 = (1-\theta)i - \pi + \delta + \lambda / \mu_c$ which, here, is assumed to be constant. (a_2) summarises the coefficients in (3.22). The imputed rental is, again, determined by conditions in the market for housing services and, hence, is expected to be related to the size of the housing stock, the number of households, income and wealth.[17] Equation (3.30), however, represents *flow* housing supply and is positively related to the real house price (as a proxy for profitability) and negatively to the size of the existing stock through depreciation.

$$\dot{g} = a_1 g - a_2 R(H, HH, RY, W) \qquad (3.29)$$

$$\dot{H} = b_1 g - \delta H \qquad (3.30)$$

Equations (3.29) and (3.30) are shown in the phase diagram, figure 3.2. Both stock and flow markets are initially in equilibrium at (*A*) at the intersection of the two loci, $\dot{g}_0 = 0$, $\dot{H} = 0$, i.e. where neither prices nor the housing

[17] In fact, here, the negative relationship to the size of the housing stock is the only important variable.

stock are changing. The former is derived from the solution to (3.29) and the latter from (3.30). Since the model contains one predetermined variable – the housing stock – and one stable characteristic root, there will be unique convergence following any shock. If $b_1 \neq 0$, then the locus $\dot{H} = 0$ will be upward sloping. But if supply is perfectly inelastic, then the locus will be vertical, passing through the points, (*H*AD*). Now consider a positive demand shock – for example a rise in income. The locus $\dot{g}_0 = 0$ shifts to the right and prices jump to the saddle path at the point (*D*). Over time, supply adjusts through new construction to a new long-run equilibrium at (*B*). If supply is perfectly elastic, real prices will return to the original equilibrium, but if supply is perfectly inelastic, the long-run equilibrium remains at (*D*) with permanently higher prices. But even with relatively large elasticities, the restoration of full stock-flow equilibrium may take decades.

The size of the supply elasticity is, therefore, a key coefficient. The general consensus is that short-run supply elasticities are lower than long-run elasticities because of the required time-to-build e.g. Topel and Rosen (1988) for the US and Tsoukis and Westaway (1994) for the UK, but empirical evidence strongly suggests that long-run price elasticities are considerably lower in the UK than the US. This is a commonly quoted reason for the stronger trends in UK house prices than in US prices, as found in Chapter 2. Malpezzi (1996), for example, suggests that the long-run UK supply elasticity on post-war data is between 0.9 and 2.1, but pre-war the elasticity was between 4 and 7. For the US, the comparable figures are between 9 and 16 and 11 and 18 respectively. Therefore, the elasticity is close to infinite for the US but not for the UK

A further important feature is that the model will exhibit overshooting. As we have seen, in response to any shock, prices "jump" to a saddle path and gradually fall back over time. Note, however, that prices will typically exhibit autocorrelation and mean reversion, because of lagged quantity adjustment, even in an efficient market. We cannot, therefore, necessarily conclude that autocorrelation implies inefficiencies. Furthermore, it is not necessary to conclude that housing necessarily exhibits speculative bubbles. As noted above, Abraham and Hendershott (1996), for example, argue that the short-run positive autocorrelation in prices reflects a "bubble builder", whereas a form of error correction reflects a "bubble-burster". This is not to deny that bubbles may occur, but observed behaviour is consistent with other explanations as well.

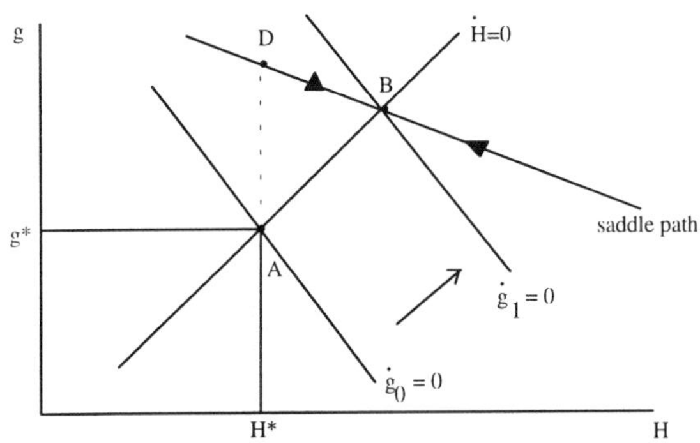

Figure 3.2. Dynamic Adjustment in Stock-Flow Models

Finally, note that figure 3.2 does not exhibit cycles, which, as shown in Chapter 2, are a key feature of the market. It follows, therefore, that cycles must arise either from cyclical behaviour in the independent variables (e.g. income or interest rates) – and it would be hard to deny that this has occurred – or from absent features of the model. One feature concerns the modelling of expectations. This is demonstrated by DiPasquale and Wheaton (1996), who use their stock/flow model to demonstrate the importance of different assumptions concerning expectations formation. They show that, depending on assumed parameter values, neither exogenously formed nor rational expectations will typically generate housing cycles in the two-equation model, but cycles are consistent with backward-looking expectations.

There is an additional effect from prices not covered in the Poterba framework. DiPasquale and Wheaton (1996), supported by Topel and Rosen (1988), argue that new construction is heavily dependent on the expected sales time for a given *level* of house prices. But, in their view, the expected sales time is related to the *change* in prices so that either the change in prices or the sales time could be an additional determinant in (3.30); even if b_1 is very low, prices could still be important in determining housing cycles and, indeed, this is precisely the finding in Meen (1996). Across all the English standard regions, the rate of change of prices has a strong positive effect on construction, even though the level of prices only has a weak influence. We shall see the influence of this result later in Chapter 6. To anticipate, because the rate of change of real prices is highly volatile, so is construction activity.

A related issue is raised by Stein (1995), who argues that new construction requires builders to put money up front to finance construction (a form of downpayment constraint). The builder's ability to do so will depend on the prices obtained from properties just completed. If sale times are short (prices rising rapidly), liquidity constraints that the firm faces are less binding. Once again, current levels of prices may not be a good indicator of the state of liquidity, which may be better captured by the rate of change of prices.

These amendments to the basic model suggest that the nature of both the long-run equilibrium and the dynamic adjustment in stock/flow models are difficult to derive from theory alone. Empirically based vector autoregressive (VAR) models provide an alternative approach. Baffoe-Bonnie (1998), for example, estimates a VAR model of US house prices and sales designed to look at the effects of macroeconomic variables on housing market activity. VAR models in this area are not unusual but, as Baffoe-Bonnie indicates, such models are not structural and the coefficients are not generally interpretable in terms of behavioural parameters. However, recent models of general business cycles suggest an improvement on the standard VAR, e.g. Evans and Reichlin (1994), Blanchard and Quah (1989, 1993). Meen (2000) adapts the approach to construct a four variable VAR, covering prices, housing starts, construction costs and interest rates. Structural models with readily interpretable coefficients in terms of (3.29) and (3.30) can, then, be obtained by the imposition of identification and weak exogeneity restrictions, which determine the model's long-run properties. However, the lags are data-determined and generate short-term movements consistent with both overshooting and cycles. The empirical results are explored further in Chapter 6.

3.7 General Equilibrium Models

So far, we have examined in some detail models of prices, construction and transactions all within a similar theoretical framework. However, the model is still essentially partial since all other elements of the economy – in particular incomes - are taken as exogenous factors. In fact, some of the most interesting work in recent years has relaxed these restrictions and considered housing in a general equilibrium context. In particular, the interrelationships between housing and labour markets and housing and business investment have proved particularly important. The former is considered primarily in Chapters 4 and 5, since issues of migration and commuting are central. Here we deal with the latter, concentrating on the question of whether housing investment crowds-out business investment. This was a live issue particularly in the seventies and eighties when the view held that subsidies led to over-investment in housing at the expense of manufacturing investment, reducing the economy's long-run growth rate. However, more recent research suggests that this view was over-simplistic and in some instances the effects are neutral. Indeed in Chapter 8, when a spatial dimension is added, housing may actually crowd-in business investment.

Excluding the spatial dimension, a simplified version of the two-sector growth model of Turnovsky and Okuyama (1994)[18] provides a suitable vehicle for demonstrating the central issues. The two sectors are housing and the rest of the economy, treated as an aggregate good. The model can be used to demonstrate that, in the long run, the effects of housing subsidies depend on constraints on the mobility of labour between the two sectors. Constraints in other markets have similar effects. Meen (1989), for example, shows that housing credit market constraints limit any crowding-out effects from subsidies. Constraints operate as a form of second-best solution in the presence of tax distortions. At least in the UK, for these reasons, the negative effects of subsidies in the seventies and early eighties were probably overstated.

More formally, now consider an *aggregate economy* model where, once again, households consume two goods, housing services (H) and a composite good (c), whose price is used as a numeraire and is normalised to unity. The per capita utility function remains as in (3.14), but the per capita budget constraint is revised as in (3.31);

$$\dot{k} + n(k) + (g.\dot{h}) + n(g.h) + c + R.H = w + r(k) + (r_h + \dot{g}/g)g.h(1-\tau_h) \tag{3.31}$$

where:

n	=	population growth rate
k	=	per capita capital stock
g	=	real asset price of the housing
h	=	per capita housing stock
c	=	per capita consumption of the non-housing good
R	=	real imputed price of housing services
H	=	per capita flow of housing services
w	=	real wage rate
r	=	real return on non-housing capital
r_h	=	real imputed rental rate on housing
τ_h	=	tax rate on housing

In this version of the model, output of the two goods is endogenised by the inclusion of the capital stock, allowing us to consider crowding out.

[18] This, in turn, builds on the Ramsey (1928) growth model.

Since savings are used for the accumulation of physical capital, (k) appears directly in the budget constraint rather than savings.

The left hand side of (3.31) expresses per capita expenditure; households may spend their income on consumption goods and housing (the imputed rent) or save through accumulating non-housing or housing assets[19]. Capital markets are assumed to be perfect and all borrowing and lending takes place at the market interest rate (r). The terms in n(.) arise because of possible population growth. For a given level of output, a growing population implies that per capita consumption is falling. The right hand side of (3.31) represents total per capita income as the sum of the real wage and interest receipts on non-housing capital and the return on housing made up of imputed rents and a capital gain. In order to look at the effects of taxes and subsidies, we assume that the return on housing is taxed (or subsidised if τ_h is negative).

The economy is assumed to produce the two goods, housing (Y_H) and non-housing (Y_N), according to technologies (3.32);

$$\begin{aligned} Y_H &= Z(K_H, L_H) \\ Y_N &= F(K_N, L_N) \end{aligned} \tag{3.32}$$

where (K_i) = total capital employed in sector (i) and (L_i) is labour employed in sector (i). The subscript (N) refers to the non-housing sector and (H) to the housing sector. Under diminishing marginal productivity and constant returns to scale, the production functions can be expressed alternatively in per capita terms as (3.33);

$$\begin{aligned} y_H &= z(k_H) \\ y_N &= f(k_N) \end{aligned} \tag{3.33}$$

$$f'>0, \quad f''<0, \quad z'>0, \quad z''<0$$

$$\begin{aligned} L_N + L_H &= L \\ K_N + K_H &= K \end{aligned} \tag{3.34}$$

From the first-order conditions for utility and profit maximisation we obtain;

[19] The original Turnovsky and Okuyama model also includes government bonds, taxation and a government budget constraint, which we ignore here.

$$f'(k_N) = gz'(k_H) = r \tag{3.35}$$

$$f(k_N) - k_N f'(k_N) = w = [z(k_H) - k_H z'(k_H)]g \tag{3.36}$$

$$\rho(k_N) + (1-\rho)k_H = k \tag{3.37}$$

$$\mu_c = \lambda \tag{3.38}$$

$$\dot{g} / g = r/(1-\tau_H) - \mu_H / g\mu_c \tag{3.39}$$

$$\dot{\lambda} / \lambda = \beta + n - r \tag{3.40}$$

$$\dot{k} = \rho f(k_N) - c - n(k) \tag{3.41}$$

$$\dot{h} = (1-\rho)z(k_H) - n(h) \tag{3.42}$$

where $\rho = L_N / L$

The first two equations are standard, equating marginal productivities across the two sectors (3.35 for capital and 3.36 for labour), allowing for the relative price of housing, whereas (3.37) is an identity defining the economy-wide factor intensity. (λ)[20] is the costate variable associated with the household budget constraint and (3.38) is the standard condition which equates the marginal utility of consumption with wealth; (3.39) relates the ratio of the marginal utilities to the real price of housing services. Both (3.39) and (3.40) are arbitrage relationships equating the returns on the different assets. The equations imply two familiar results. First, intertemporal consumption of the non-housing good is determined by (3.43);

[20] Note that this is not the same constraint as in (3.11).

$$\mu_c(c) = (1+n)^{-1}(1+\beta)^{-1}(1+r)\mu_c(c_{+1}) \tag{3.43}$$

which is the Hall (1978) consumption function, allowing for a growing population and is consistent with (3.21) above.

$$\mu_H / \mu_c = g(r/(1-\tau_h) - \dot{g}/g) \tag{3.44}$$

Second, rewriting (3.39), the ratio of the marginal utility of housing to consumption is determined by (3.44), which is a simplification of the housing user cost of capital. Equations (3.43) and (3.44) together again represent the standard life-cycle housing and consumption model, but embedded in a two-sector model of production. Notice that, from (3.43), the time path of consumption is independent of the tax, although the absolute level will change. (3.41) and (3.42) are capital accumulation equations. Since we are primarily interested in the *long-run* relationships between the capital stocks, the long-run solutions, setting $\dot{k} = \dot{h} = \dot{g} = \dot{\lambda} = 0$, give;

$$r = f'(k_N) = \beta + n \qquad (3.45)^{21}$$

$$\mu_H / \mu_c = (\beta + n)(g/(1-\tau_h)) \tag{3.46}$$

$$\rho(f(k_N) = c + n(k) \tag{3.47}$$

$$(1-\rho)z(k_H) = n(h) \tag{3.48}$$

$$R = (\beta + n)g/(1-\tau_h) \tag{3.49}$$

and for all periods, equations (3.35)-(3.38) remain relevant. As noted above, the long-run effects of taxes and subsidies vary according to whether labour is mobile or not between the two sectors; we initially assume mobility.
First, since neither (β) nor (n) are affected by the tax then, from (3.45), neither (r) nor $f'(k_N)$ will change. Second, if labour is perfectly elastic between the two sectors, as we saw in the Poterba model, then the real house

[21] Note that this is the Modified Golden Rule. See, for example, Blanchard and Fischer (1989 Chapter 2).

price (g) also cannot change. Consequently, from (3.35), $z'(k_H)$ is unaffected. In other words, the capital-labour ratios are unchanged in *both* sectors by the imposition of the tax. But from (3.46), the tax must raise the ratio of the marginal utilities (μ_H/μ_c), which, under diminishing marginal utility, can only be achieved by a reduction in the demand for housing. From (3.49), this requires an increase in real imputed rental (R). The reduction in housing demand generates a flow of labour into the non-housing sector (a rise in ρ), so that, from (3.47) and (3.48), production of the non-housing good rises and production of housing falls. Again from (3.47), equilibrium implies that consumption of the non-housing good, (c) must increase. The reduction in housing demand is compensated by an increase in non-housing consumption in equilibrium. But since (L_N) has risen and (L_H) has fallen and the capital-labour ratios are unchanged, in equilibrium, (K_N) will increase and (K_H) will fall. Subsidies to housing will lead to more of the capital stock being devoted to housing and less to the production of other goods. However as the factor intensities *within* each sector are unchanged, the change in the capital-labour ratio for the economy as a whole will depend on the relative capital intensities of each sector. Only if housing is relatively labour-intensive will a subsidy reduce the overall capital stock.

Now consider the alternative case in which labour is perfectly immobile between the two sectors. The results are intuitively clear. Since labour is immobile, (ρ) is fixed by definition. It remains the case that $f'(k_N)$ is unchanged by the tax, but since labour is also now fixed, the capital stock (K_N) must be unchanged. However any subsidy lowers the tax-adjusted relative price of housing and, hence for equilibrium, (g) now has to rise. But the marginal productivity condition (3.35) can only be maintained by a fall in the marginal productivity of housing capital or, in other words, by a rise in the capital-labour ratio in the housing sector. Therefore, in equilibrium, the housing capital stock rises. But with (k_N) and the output of the non-housing good unchanged, this can only occur by crowding-out private consumption.

Evidence from full econometric models on the extent of crowding-out from housing suggests that, although crowding-out is a reasonable representation (in the absence of labour and credit market constraints) in the long run, in the short-run crowding-out is less than complete. This implies that a role remains for fiscal policy. The depths of housing cycles might be mitigated, for example, through demand management policies without generating negative effects on the economy as a whole (see Meen 1995). These conclusions arise from inertia. As we have seen, house prices typically do not immediately adjust to demand shocks so that quantity adjustments occur in the short run. These conclusions are reinforced if inertia exists in the non-housing sector as well, for example, in wages. There is ample empirical evidence to indicate that inertia exists in wage formation because of the existence of contracts.

3.8 Concluding Remarks

Compared with many markets, one of the key issues that arises in housing economics concerns the importance of constraints. The previous sections have concentrated, in particular, on credit and labour market constraints and we have demonstrated how standard conclusions radically alter in their presence. Later we shall also see how credit markets contribute to housing market volatility.

An equally important constraint arises from land markets and the nature of the land use planning system. The general equilibrium model in the last section completely ignored this issue. Sectoral shortages arose in the labour market but, implicitly, there is no shortage of non-reproducible production factors such as land. We shall have more to say on this issue particularly in Chapters 6 and 9, but planning constraints have been put forward as one of the most important explanations for the weak price elasticity of supply found in the UK and, consequently, for the non-stationarity of real house prices. In the US, Malpezzi (1999) has demonstrated the importance of the regulatory environment for house price to income ratios. Areas with strong controls are associated with high ratios.

Chapter 4

HOUSING THEORY: REGIONAL ISSUES

4.1 Introduction

The majority of theoretical analysis in housing deals either with the national or the urban dimension but, as we saw in Chapter 2, the fact that labour markets are typically not integrated at the regional level, i.e. commuting is not widespread between regions, gives rise to a further set of issues. Space enters the analysis for the first time and the main issue with which we are concerned is *convergence* in spatial markets over the course of time. In Chapter 2 we saw that we could describe statistically the time-series properties of regional price differentials using cointegration analysis, for example, but theoretical explanations for the relative movements were deferred until this chapter. Furthermore we saw that degrees of regional convergence appeared to differ internationally. Table 2.6 showed that whereas prices in the UK regions have grown at similar rates, this was not true in either the USA or Australia. This might, of course, simply be a function of size and, indeed, results by Hort (1997) suggest that Swedish experience has been more akin to that in the UK.

Broadly, there are at least six potential theoretical explanations for the observed spatial price patterns (and the so-called ripple effect to which we referred in Chapter 2):

- migration,
- transactions and search costs,
- equity transfer,
- spatial arbitrage,
- leads/lags and convergence in the determinants of housing activity,
- spatial coefficient heterogeneity.

However before considering these issues, it is convenient, first, to examine briefly past studies of regional house prices and, then, to introduce empirical issues that are helpful in explaining the patterns; these are concepts from the spatial econometrics literature, notably spatial lags and errors and coefficient heterogeneity. Also, the idea of common stochastic trends and related issues in aggregation bias are covered.

4.2 Regional House Price Models

We begin by looking at previous approaches, particularly in the UK, to modelling regional prices[1]. As mentioned in Chapter 2, the main stimulus to research since the late eighties has been the strong short-run variation in price growth between the North and the South and the implications of this divide for labour market adjustment. Although regional studies have expanded considerably in recent years, compared with *national* time-series studies, the number of regional models remains more limited. However the number is still considerably greater than in most other countries and these give rise to important modelling issues concerning the nature of spatial interactions. Other countries have constructed models at the sub-national level, but these are often treated as panels, where the coefficients are implicitly assumed to be the same in each area. As we shall see, this causes estimation problems. Furthermore all studies, both in the UK and elsewhere, are essentially based on theory derived at the national level; in other words the theory is very similar to that discussed in Chapter 3. Spatial features are rather crude add-ons to the basic structure, rather than being fundamental to the model. This is why, in the next section, we introduce concepts from the spatial econometrics literature.

The main UK studies are those by McAvinchey and Maclennan (1982), Giussani and Hadjimatheou (1991, 1991a), Reilly and Witt (1994)[2], Muellbauer and Murphy (1994), Ashworth and Parker (1997), Munro and Tu (1996, 1996a) and Meen (1999). The time gap between the first study in (1982) and subsequent work reflects the policy concerns noted above. Regional price differentials were not considered a major concern until the late eighties. Consequently, the objectives of the McAvinchey and Maclennan study were different from all later work and, in fact, reflect more

[1] There has been only one attempt to model regional construction in the UK, Meen (1996) and no attempts to model regional transactions.

[2] This study uses regional data, but is not primarily interested in regional modelling *per se*. Rather they examine the effects of housing possessions and use panel data to increase the number of observations.

closely our own concerns. The authors highlighted the fact that micro and macro analyses of housing markets have, typically, been conducted independently and they considered the modelling of house prices as an example of the dichotomy. They saw their work as a step towards the development of a micro-based approach to modelling house price change. Few of the other studies rigorously discuss the effect that local market differences and interactions have on the structure of the systems, in the manner expressed by McAvinchey and Maclennan and later by Maclennan and Tu (1996)[3].

The study by McAvinchey and Maclennan is, in fact, more detailed than many of the later studies in terms of the included regressors. However the paper was written before the advent of cointegration and, therefore, did not model the long-run relationships between regional house prices. Consequently the dependent variables are specified as the rate of house price *inflation*, rather than the *level* of house prices. The range of regressors included is comprehensive, although a number are collinear, for example housing starts and completions, minimum lending rate and the mortgage rate. The effects of credit market constraints are captured by the inclusion of building society asset and mortgage advances variables. Demographic factors are included through the marriage rate. The study is one of the few to include building costs. The study finds a high degree of variation in the coefficients across the regions.

The two papers by Giussani and Hadjimatheou (1991, 1991a) are based on the life-cycle model, but address slightly different questions and employ different estimation techniques. The first study begins by looking for evidence of a ripple effect in terms of cross-correlations between the growth in house prices in London and in the other regions and then carries out Granger causality tests to examine the direction of causality. This part of their work has more in common with Alexander and Barrow (1994) and MacDonald and Taylor (1993) discussed in Chapter 2. But the main part of their paper estimates regional price equations, using the Engle-Granger cointegration technique. Its main novelty was to include spatial interactions in the model through adding the rate of growth of London prices in the dynamic equations for each of the other regions. As we shall see in the next section, this is a simple example of what is known as a "spatial lag". However its inclusion raises further issues. First, the spatial lag only enters into the dynamics. By itself, this technique does not ensure that the observed long-run relationships in regional house prices hold. Second, the inclusion of

[3] But see the discussion of housing sub-markets in Chapter 2.

the spatial lag may improve the model's fit, but does not necessarily tell us more about the nature of the transmission mechanism[4].

In their second paper, Giussani and Hadjimatheou are explicitly concerned with the North/South divide in house prices and estimate an equation for the ratio of house prices in South East England relative to North West England. They relate relative house prices to relative incomes, banks' base interest rate, changes in unemployment in the two regions, and housing wealth relative to the number of households. The authors point particularly to the impact of income differentials in explaining variations and also to the different regional responses to financial conditions through the interest rate - a theme we pick up later.

Muellbauer and Murphy's regional study is closely related to the structure of their national model (Muellbauer and Murphy 1997). The equations are all expressed in terms of deviations from the national average price. The model emphasises both the excess return to housing and the importance of financial liberalisation. In terms of a behavioural analysis of the workings of regional housing markets, this provides the most detailed discussion of interrelationships between the regions. However, estimation is over a short sample period and the number of regressors is limited. To overcome the data shortages, in some cases, the authors impose common elasticities across the regions. This procedure, we suggest below, has problems.

One of the interesting features of the Muellbauer and Murphy approach is its treatment of spatial interactions. As we shall see, the literature emphasises two forms of spatial interdependency - spatial errors and spatial lags. In this particular case, spatial errors are captured through estimation by Seemingly Unrelated Regression (SUR). Spatial lags are included by assuming that house prices in any region are not just related to, say, own region income but also to incomes in bordering regions. In Muellbauer and Murphy's model, the spatial lag variables generate the ripple effect.

Ashworth and Parker's study is simpler and relates regional prices to per capita incomes, a real interest rate and the number of private sector starts. Their study is the first to use the Johansen cointegration methodology in a regional house price modelling context and the study attempts to capture spatial interactions in terms of both lags and errors. Rather surprisingly, the coefficients show only limited spatial variation, again, an important issue to be studied further below.

Munro and Tu (1996, 1996a) also adopt relatively simple specifications. In their first paper, Munro and Tu adopt the Engle-Granger approach. In the long run, prices in each region are related to real household income, a real

[4] This paper was heavily criticised by Muellbauer and Murphy (1994).

interest rate and either national average or South Eastern prices. In contrast to the Giussani and Hadjimatheou (1991) paper, the links occur in the long run as well as in the dynamics. Munro and Tu group together regions into larger aggregates, although Meen (1996) suggests that grouping is only valid if standard aggregation conditions hold - again to be discussed below.

4.3 Econometric Issues

As we have seen, existing studies of regional prices adopt very different approaches. However, it would be useful if general principles could be established concerning, first, the modelling of spatial interactions and, second, tests of parameter variation. These are, perhaps, the areas where the current housing literature is at its weakest. In fact, using ideas taken from spatial econometrics and recent work on dynamic heterogeneous panels, a more general perspective can be established. Perhaps the two most commonly discussed features of spatial data are (*i*) the existence of spatial dependence and (*ii*) spatial coefficient heterogeneity. Here, spatial dependence arises because housing typically consists of a set of interlinked local markets. Heterogeneity measures the extent to which local markets exhibit structural differences, perhaps, because of different household characteristics in each location.

We shall find that, in many circumstances, aggregate national models of the type discussed in the last chapter may be invalid as a result of different forms of aggregation bias. But aggregation biases can arise in two different dimensions - over space and over individuals. In fact, in Chapter 6, when empirical results for national house price models are considered, we shall argue that structural changes in the UK national housing market in the nineties arose from precisely these two factors. In particular, increasing dispersion in economic conditions across the population and different regional growth patterns from the norm reduce the value of aggregate national models.

We show in the following sub-sections that the validity of national analysis relies on two aggregation conditions. Either all households (and spatial areas) must behave in an identical manner, i.e. coefficient homogeneity must hold, or the factors affecting housing demand, e.g. incomes, must grow at the same rate (or exhibit common stochastic trends), again, across both individuals and space. But if these conditions hold, then there is only a limited role for regional analysis, since there is no regional "problem". There would be no trend in regional unemployment differences, for example, and house prices would be expected to grow at the same rate in each area. Neither of these events, of course, occurs.

In summary, then, the digression into econometric theory in the following sub-sections is motivated by four arguments; first, housing markets are not independent, even at the regional level; second, the economic theory underlying our housing models suggests that coefficients will vary over both space and individuals. Third, in this case, the aggregation conditions that allow us to treat housing as a single national market do not hold and, fourth, any spatial model must explicitly allow for this heterogeneity. Heterogeneity and aggregation become key issues. Therefore, this section develops the appropriate econometric techniques. In Section 4.4 and in Chapter 7, these techniques are employed to explain the pattern in British regional house prices.

4.3.1 Modelling Spatial Dependence

Consider the general spatial *cross-section* model taken from Anselin (1988).

$$y = \rho W_1 y + X\beta + \varepsilon \tag{4.1}$$

$$\varepsilon = \lambda W_2 \varepsilon + \mu \tag{4.2}$$

$$\mu \sim N(0,\Omega) \tag{4.3}$$

$$\Omega_{ii} = h_i(z\alpha) \;\; h_i > 0 \tag{4.4}$$

Regional housing models can also be expressed in these terms. Equation (4.1) defines the basic relationship where (y) - perhaps house prices - is related to a set of regressors (X) and a spatial lag ($W_1 y$) i.e. to (y) in other locations, where the form of the spatial lag is determined by the matrix W_1. This weights matrix attempts to quantify the strength of the relationship between the variables in different locations. The weights are usually based on spatial contiguity or distance decay. In a housing context, the weights matrices might specify the relationship between house prices in different locations. However the error term (ε) is not necessarily white noise and may exhibit an autoregressive relationship in space, determined by (4.2). The nature of the spatial autocorrelation is determined by a second weights matrix, W_2. The error term (μ) has a general covariance Ω allowing for possible heteroscedasticity in terms of a set of exogenous variables (z).

Equations (4.1)-(4.4) model the two usual forms of spatial correlation in the literature, i.e. in terms of lags or errors. In the housing literature, the use of regional data sets that do not correspond to local housing market areas will often introduce a form of spatially correlated errors. Many forms of neighbourhood effect, e.g. Can (1992), Can and Megbolugbe (1997), will introduce spatial lags.

Note, however, that in cross-sectional models, the weights matrices, which are used both in estimation and in spatial autocorrelation tests, have to be specified on an *a priori* basis rather than estimated directly. This means that all specification tests are conditional on the validity of the weights matrices and, indeed, the form of the matrices can make a considerable difference to the results.

We can see that several of the studies discussed in the previous section include spatial lags, although not expressed in these terms. The models of Giussani and Hadjimatheou (1991) and Munro and Tu (1996) relate prices in each region to those in London and the South East as a way of capturing the ripple effect. In these cases, the only non-zero value in the weights matrix is that for London and the South East. Clearly this is an exceptionally simple form for the weights matrix and the interactions considered by Muellbauer and Murphy, where relationships between a wider set of variables are taken into account, provide a more general application of the weights matrix.

4.3.2 Spatial Coefficient Heterogeneity in Static Models

The second issue is spatial coefficient heterogeneity i.e. the extent to which the coefficients vary over space in either a random or non-random manner. Surprisingly, in all the studies considered, none discusses this fundamental issue. McAvinchey and Maclennan find a very wide range of coefficient values between the regions, whereas Ashworth and Parker find fairly similar values across space. But no study considers whether there is any formal spatial structure in the coefficients - for example, are values systematically higher or lower in the South than in the North? But this is a central issue in spatial econometrics.

In equation (4.1), it is assumed that the β coefficients are constant over space. In *cross sectional models*, if any coefficient variation is purely random, then assuming all coefficients to be equal leads to heteroscedastic errors and inefficient estimates. Alternatively, the β coefficients may not vary randomly, but may be systematically related over space. If this is the case, then failure to take account of the spatial differences will lead to parameter biases as a form of omitted variable bias. One solution to this problem in the regional science literature has been to use the spatial expansion method. The expansion method is a form of variable parameter model in which the underlying approach has been set out in a series of papers, the most recent of which is Casetti (1997). The expansion method allows the parameters themselves to be defined as functions of a set of spatial variables, for example, locational co-ordinates. Alternatively, in the house price model used by Can (1992), for example, the expansion is based on neighbourhood quality, so that the implicit prices of housing characteristics vary according to neighbourhood.

The parameter expansions may be defined in either a stochastic or non-stochastic framework. If the expansion is non-stochastic, this is known as a fixed part expansion. But the coefficients may also have a random component. In a static model, failure to allow for this will, again, generate heteroscedastic errors in the estimated equation. Jones and Bullen (1994) provide a comparison of the relative merits of fixed versus random coefficient expansion methods, using house prices in the London boroughs as an example. Since, with random effects, estimation is not efficient under OLS a form of GLS estimator for cross-sectional models is required. Jones and Bullen show that, in many cases, the fixed and random effects results are very different, but the extent of any difference depends on the sample sizes in each district. As the number of dwellings sampled in each district rises, the fixed and the random effects models tend towards the same value[5].

4.3.3 Econometric Issues in Dynamic Heterogeneous Panels

The use of static models estimated on cross-section data imposes methodological limitations. However an increasing amount of regional analysis now uses *dynamic*, panel data. In fact, regional house price studies have panel data of the appropriate form available - this is an important difference from urban analysis, where cross-section data still often have to be used.

This eases some of the problems imposed by cross-section estimation, but adds new problems. If the number of time-series observations is large relative to the number of spatial observations - as in regional house price models, (*i*) it is no longer necessary to pre-specify the form of the spatial weights matrices either for lags or errors, (*ii*) estimation methods become straightforward and (*iii*) the use of the expansion method in either the fixed or random effects versions becomes unnecessary. The data can tell us the most appropriate spatial forms and the validity of contiguity or distance decay functions, for example, can be formally tested. In the case of spatial

[5] There is a direct analogy to panel data estimation where, as the number of time-series observations increases, fixed and random effects estimation tend to the same values; see Meen and Andrew (1998a).

errors, the model may be efficiently estimated using SUR to capture the form of the cross equation error covariance matrix. Diagonality of the covariance matrix may, then, be tested by using Lagrange Multiplier tests, for example. White and Hewings (1982) recommend the use of SUR in a model of employment in the US states in order to avoid some of the problems of pre-assigned spatial weights matrices. SUR provides a general framework for testing for spatially correlated errors where data permit.

Even though panel data ease some problems, Pesaran and Smith (1995) show that, in contrast to static models, in *dynamic* models even random coefficient variation over space introduces inconsistencies into the estimated coefficients of panel models. Unless all coefficients are identical in each spatial unit (an extremely strong condition and one that will not exist when coefficients exhibit spatial patterns), then separate equations need to be estimated for each spatial unit in order to avoid bias. Price models that are simply estimated as panels (perhaps allowing for fixed effects) across metropolitan areas are likely to experience significant biases. But if the number of spatial units is fairly small, such as regions, then the option of estimating separate equations is technically feasible. Furthermore, Pesaran and Smith show that, in heterogeneous panels, even if cointegrating relationships exist at the individual (regional) level, aggregate (national) relationships typically will not cointegrate, because of coefficient heterogeneity. However, Hall *et al* (1999) introduce a caveat. Suppose, for example, that regional house prices are a function of regional incomes, but the coefficients vary between the locations. Hall *et al* demonstrate that, if incomes in each region are driven by a common stochastic trend (constant regional income shares are a special case), then the estimation of a dynamic panel, assuming homogeneous parameters, still provides consistent estimates. In fact, this result is a generalisation of the aggregation conditions originally set out by Theil (1954) to a stochastic framework.

This point is worth stressing since it has wide implications. In cases where common stochastic trends exist across the regions, then the estimation of dynamic panel models does not lead to inconsistent estimates, even if models exhibit spatial coefficient heterogeneity. Therefore, the identification of changes in stochastic trends or regional departures from the stochastic trend is critical.

More formally we can illustrate these points, using the following time-series/spatial model, adapted from Anselin (1988):

$$y_{it} = x_{it}\beta_{it} + \eta_i + \varepsilon_{it} \quad t = 1 \ldots T,\ i = 1 \ldots N \tag{4.5}$$

$$E(\varepsilon_{it}) = 0 \tag{4.6}$$

$$E(\varepsilon_{it}\varepsilon_{js}) \neq 0 \tag{4.7}$$

To make the example more concrete y_{it} is a stacked vector where the first T observations represent, say, house prices in region (1) from time periods (1) to (T), then the next T observations represent the next region and so on to region N. The x_{it} represent the independent variables, e.g. income, demography for each spatial unit.

(β_{it}) represent the parameters attached to each x_{it}. In this general form, each spatial unit and time period has a different coefficient. Since this means that the number of parameters exceeds the number of observations, for estimation, some structure needs to be imposed on the coefficients. (η_i) are fixed effects. Here they are variables, which do not vary over time, but vary across space. Typically these are incorporated as spatial dummy variables in fixed effects panel models. (ε_{it}) represents the error term. Equation (4.6) sets the expected value of the error term across both time and space equal to zero. (4.7) expresses a general form of error covariance matrix.

The number of classes of model covered by (4.5) to (4.7) is very large, but given that our interest is primarily in variation over space, we abstract from any time variation in parameters or errors. Hence the model becomes;

$$y_{it} = x_{it}\beta_i + \eta_i + \varepsilon_{it} \tag{4.8}$$

$$E(\varepsilon_{it}) = 0 \tag{4.9}$$

$$E(\varepsilon_{it}\varepsilon_{it}) = \sigma_i \qquad \mathrm{i} = \mathrm{j} \tag{4.10}$$

$$E(\varepsilon_{it}\varepsilon_{jt}) = \sigma_{ij} \qquad \mathrm{i} \neq \mathrm{j} \tag{4.11}$$

Hence the coefficients (β_i) vary over space but not time and our main interest concerns the effects of these variations. Consider the following example from Pesaran and Smith (1995). The basic dynamic model is described by (4.12);

$$y_{it} = \alpha_i + \beta_{i1}x_{it} + \beta_{i2}x_{it-1} + \varepsilon_{it} \tag{4.12}$$

$$\beta_{i1} = \beta_1 + \xi_{i1} \;; \qquad \beta_{i2} = \beta_2 + \xi_{i2}$$

$$x_{it} = \rho x_{it-1} + \mu_{it} \;; \quad |\rho| < 1 \tag{4.13}$$

$$E(\xi_{i1}) = E(\xi_{i2}) = 0$$

$$Var(\xi_{i1}) = \omega_{11} \; Var(\xi_{i2}) = \omega_{22} \; Cov(\xi_{i1}\xi_{i2}) = \omega_{12}$$

In the true model (4.12), y_{it} is determined by current and lagged values of an exogenous (scalar) variable x_{it} and the parameters vary randomly across regions (i); x_{it} is, itself, determined by a first-order stationary autoregressive process, (4.13). But suppose, instead of the true model, (4.14) is estimated;

$$y_{it} = \alpha_i + \gamma_1 x_{it} + \gamma_2 x_{it-1} + \lambda y_{it-1} + v_{it} \tag{4.14}$$

This assumes that the parameters are homogeneous across the regions (apart from a fixed effect) and adds a lagged dependent variable. Such a specification is commonly estimated on either aggregate or panel data and may be reparameterised into error correction form under appropriate restrictions, in the manner used in the last chapter. We are interested in whether the estimates of γ_1, γ_2 and λ are consistent. The following results hold for fixed effects estimation of (4.14);

$$\text{plim}\,(\hat{\gamma}_1) = \beta_1 \tag{4.15}$$

$$\text{plim}\,(\hat{\gamma}_2) = \beta_2 - \lambda^*(\beta_1 + \rho\beta_2) \tag{4.16}$$

$$\text{plim}(\hat{\lambda}) = [\rho(\omega_{11} + \omega_{22}) + (1+\rho^2)\omega_{12}] / [\omega_{11} + \omega_{22} + 2\rho\omega_{12} + (1-\rho^2)(\beta_2^2 + \sigma^2/\tau^2)] \quad (4.17)$$

where; σ^2 is the mean of the variances of ε_{it} ; τ^2 is the mean of the variances of μ_{it} and $\lambda^* = \text{plim}(\hat{\lambda})$.Therefore (*i*) the short-run effect, β_1, is estimated consistently by the aggregate/panel model (ii) the inconsistency in β_2 depends on λ^* (which is zero in the true model) and ρ. Now as $\rho \to 1$, then $\text{plim}(\hat{\lambda}_2) \to (1-\lambda^*)\beta_2 - \lambda^*\beta_1$. If we make the additional assumption that λ^* is close to unity then the estimated value of γ_2 will approximate the negative of β_1. The conditions under which λ^* is likely to be close to unity are, therefore, important. But from the third condition as $\rho \to 1$, so will λ^*. Finally it is clear from the third condition again, that the parameter inconsistencies disappear when the spatial parameters are homogeneous ie $\omega_{ij} = 0 \;\; \forall\; i,j$. They do not disappear, however, when $\rho=0$.

There is, however, a special case. Consider the model used by Hall *et al* (1999). Let there be, by assumption, a set of cointegrating relationships across the spatial units, but the coefficients in each relationship vary randomly;

$$y_{it} = \beta_i x_{it} + \varepsilon_{it} \quad (4.18)$$

$$\beta_i \neq \beta_j ; i \neq j \quad (4.19)$$

We assume that y_{it}, x_{it} are non-stationary. Now suppose we aggregate over the spatial units to obtain the variables;

$$\bar{y} = \sum y_i ; \bar{x} = \sum x_i \quad (4.20)$$

These might represent the national aggregates of the regional variables. But Pesaran and Smith argue that the aggregate relationship will not cointegrate, since exact aggregation over the *N* areas yields;

$$\bar{y} = \beta_1 \bar{x} + \sum_{i=2}^{N} (\beta_1 - \beta_i) x_{it} + \sum_{i=1}^{N} \varepsilon_{it} \tag{4.21}$$

If we carry out a standard aggregate regression of $\bar{y}$ on $\bar{x}$, then the error term will be;

$$v = \sum_{i=2}^{N} (\beta_1 - \beta_i) x_{it} + \sum_{i=1}^{N} \varepsilon_{it} \tag{4.22}$$

which will be non-stationary and, hence, we will not find cointegrating relationships at the aggregate level. But take the following special case. Suppose that the regressors follow the following common stochastic trend;

$$x_{it} = \alpha_i x_t + \mu_{it} \tag{4.23}$$

(x_{it}), for example, might represent regional income and (x_t) the corresponding national total. μ_{it} are assumed to be stationary processes. Then, by substitution, the aggregate relationship becomes;

$$\bar{y} = (\sum \beta_i \alpha_i / \sum \alpha_i) \bar{x} + \sum (\varepsilon_{it} + \beta_i \mu_{it}) \tag{4.24}$$

Since the error term now only consists of a linear combination of I(0) variables, a cointegrating relationship between the aggregate variables can exist in contrast to the Pesaran and Smith result. However the result arises directly from the assumption of a common stochastic trend (4.23). If the nature of the relationship between the sub-national and national variables changes, then cointegration in the national relationship (and any panel relationship which assumes common coefficients) breaks down.

In summary, the Pesaran and Smith results suggest strongly that simply incorporating fixed effects in dynamic spatial models will be inadequate and will lead to inconsistent estimates. Some method is required that allows slope coefficients to vary systematically across space except in the case of common stochastic trends. Below, we attempt to show how spatial structure can be added parsimoniously without imposing *a priori* parameter constraints or without relying on spatial expansion methods, by exploiting the extra dimension of the panel data set.

4.3.4 Aggregation Across Households

Finally, aggregation problems may also arise across individuals as well as across space (see Meen and Andrew 1998). Although strictly the concern of Chapter 5, it is convenient to discuss the issues here, since they are closely related to the previous sub-section. Consider the linear micro housing demand function (4.25);

$$h_{it} = \alpha_i + \beta_i y_{it} + \delta_i g_{it} + \mu_{it} \tag{4.25}$$

where;
$h_i =$ housing demand by individual (i) at time (t); $i=1...N$
$y_i =$ individual income
$g_i =$ real house prices which may or may not vary between individuals

$$H_t = \sum_{i=1}^{N} h_{it}; Y_t = \sum_{i=1}^{N} y_{it}; G_t = \sum_{i=1}^{N} w_i g_{it} \tag{4.26}$$

$w_i =$ aggregate house price index weights

In (4.25), each of the individuals potentially has a different response to income and price changes. But if we are interested in aggregate, national housing demand, a natural question to ask is whether there are restrictions on the parameters of the individual equations or particular values for y_i and g_i that will ensure an aggregate equation (4.27) is consistent with the underlying micro equations.

$$H_t = \alpha + \beta(Y)_t + \delta(G)_t + \mu_t \tag{4.27}$$

As before, exact linear aggregation is possible if (*i*) there are no changes in the income distribution - or incomes follow common stochastic trends, (*ii*) all the coefficients are the same across households so that a change in income from the rich to the poor does not affect aggregate housing demand. In the linear model, changes in the income distribution generate an aggregate equation (4.28);

$$H_t = \alpha + \sum \bar{\lambda}_i \beta_i Y_t + \sum (\lambda_{i_t} - \bar{\lambda}_i)\beta_i Y_t + \delta(G)_t + \mu_t \tag{4.28}$$

where, $\lambda_{i_t} = y_{i_t} / \sum y_{i_t}$ and represents the share of each household's income in the total, and $\bar{\lambda}_i = 1/T(\sum_{t=1}^{T} \lambda_{it})$ is the time mean of each household's income share over the sample.

Therefore, in general, some measure of income dispersion is required. Alternatively, consider the effect of different propensities to consume housing out of income from different sources i.e. wage income (W) as opposed to investment income (V). The true aggregate model is assumed to be given by (4.29), but we estimate instead a model that sums income from the different sources (4.30), where $Y_t=W_t+V_t$. For simplicity, we assume that the coefficients do not vary over households.

$$H_t = \beta_1 W_t + \beta_2 V_t + \delta(G) + \varepsilon_{1_t} \tag{4.29}$$

$$H_t = \beta Y_t + \delta(G) + \varepsilon_{2_t} \tag{4.30}$$

The relationship between the two is given by (4.31), where $\bar{\beta} = 1/T \sum_{t=1}^{T} [(W_t / Y_t)\beta_1 + (V_t / Y_t)\beta_2]$, is the time mean of the true "aggregate" coefficient, (which is the weighted average of the two income coefficients).

$$H_t = \bar{\beta} Y_t + (\beta_1 - \bar{\beta})W_t + (\beta_2 - \bar{\beta})V_t + \delta(G) + \varepsilon_{it} \tag{4.31}$$

(4.31) implies that if either the two income sources grow at the same rate or $\beta_1 = \beta_2 = \beta$, then aggregation over income sources does not matter and (4.30) may be estimated validly. But if wage income and investment income have not grown at the same rate over time (and they have not in the UK) then the omission of the disaggregated terms becomes important. Given the observed income movements in the UK in recent years, typically (4.30) will overestimate the growth in housing demand.

4.4 Convergence and Divergence in Regional Housing Markets

In Chapter 2 we saw that, statistically, it is not too difficult to model regional house price patterns through a combination of cointegration and, through what turns out to be spatial lag techniques. However it is less straightforward to provide convincing theoretical explanations of these patterns, particularly in the UK. Section 4.1 suggested six possibilities, which are discussed in turn.[6] The final possibility relies on the heterogeneity issues raised in the previous section.

4.4.1 Migration

At first sight, the idea that households take advantage of differences in regional house prices to move between locations, is appealing. In the UK, the existence of short-term changes in price differentials, followed by the maintenance of relativities in the longer term appears to be consistent with the view that the regions constitute differentiated labour markets and adjustment, therefore, takes time. The longer-term differentials simply reflect the valuations of the characteristics of each location. Alexander and Barrow (1994) discuss (but do not demonstrate) this as an explanation for their empirical findings. If prices are high in the South relative to the North, then households should migrate to the North, leading to an equalisation in house prices over time as the ripple effect would suggest. Such a view is compatible with the standard human capital framework underlying much of the work on migration theory. Furthermore, the view that the differential in house prices between the South East and the North prevents migration from high to low unemployment areas is an important part of the story told by Bover *et al* (1989) in their explanation of labour market segmentation.

The literature suggests that three classes of variable influence migration patterns, personal characteristics, environmental factors and aggregate market variables (see, for example, Groenewold 1997 or Champion *et al* 1998). In a time-series context, the latter are the most important and are generally captured by a combination of labour market and housing market variables. The former include such factors as wage, unemployment and employment growth differences, whereas the latter concentrate primarily on

[6] A further possibility arises if house prices are related to construction costs. Since construction costs do not show a high degree of regional variation (labour costs are similar and materials are partly imported), we might expect regional prices to be similar. However, we have already argued that, in the UK, there is little relationship between house prices and construction costs and, in any case, the simple relationship breaks down in the presence of land scarcity.

relative house prices, but also take into account the effect of tenure structure. The series of articles by Hughes and McCormick (1981, 1985, 1987, 1990) which suggested that local authority tenants have a lower propensity to migrate have proved particularly influential, although still disputed by McGregor *et al* (1992) who argued that the tenure structure is proxying more general socio-economic considerations[7]. For example, moving firms tend to bring with them their more highly skilled workforce, but recruit the less skilled workforce locally.

There is little doubt that housing market factors are a major determinant of short distance (intra-regional) moves and there is also empirical evidence that interregional migration is negatively related to house price differentials[8], but a debate still exists over the relative *quantitative* importance of labour and housing market influences. There is also no reason why the same ranking should apply in all parts of the country. *A priori*, those areas favoured by retiring households, for example, might be more influenced by housing than by labour market factors. Attempts have been made to distinguish between households moving for housing as opposed to labour market reasons and these studies do find significant effects from relative house price differences. Thomas (1993), for example, finds strong deterrent effects from high relative house prices for non-job related moves. However, the relationship between migration and house prices is not straightforward and requires the modelling of house price expectations. But the consensus from the literature would probably be that labour market factors have a stronger overall role than the housing market in influencing migration decisions, Gordon (1990).

A large number of empirical studies concerning regional or state adjustment processes have been published. In the UK, examples include Pissarides and McMaster (1990), Hyclak and Johnes (1992), and Blackaby and Manning (1992). In Australia, Groenewold (1997) provides a similar analysis. In each of these studies, the emphasis is on labour market adjustment, where equations are generally estimated for wages, migration, employment and unemployment. UK and Australian studies suggest that migration plays only a limited role in the elimination of regional unemployment differences, whereas Blanchard and Katz (1992) indicate that migration is the central adjustment mechanism between US states. Evidence from these time-series models is also supported by cross-section and panel

[7] In fact, moving patterns by tenure have changed significantly in recent years.

[8] We should note, however, that one line of argument in the literature suggests migration and house prices are positively correlated. However as Evans (1990, 1993) shows, the correlation probably reflects disequilibrium. For example, a positive demand shock in any area in the short term will induce both a migration inflow and a rise in house prices, although in the longer term we expect a negative relationship between the two.

studies, which examine migration patterns in considerable detail, e.g. Pissarides and Wadsworth (1989), Jackman and Savouri (1992).

In the UK, net migration flows are, in any case, small relative to the US, particularly amongst manual workers. Despite US findings, it is unlikely that migration plays the same stabilising role in the UK. But if migration flows are weak and house price differences are not the major factor in influencing flows, then it appears unlikely that migration could be entirely responsible for the observed pattern of relative house prices in Britain and the generation of a ripple effect. Illustrative calculations by Holmans (1990) also support the view that migration flows are not quantitatively large enough to bring about the observed price movements.

Table 4.1 shows regional migration trends in the UK. Although shown only for 1997, the North-South population drift is typical of the trends that have taken place for many years. The net gainers have been the East, South East and the South West. As we shall see in the next chapter, continuing movement away from urban areas, towards the suburbs, has accompanied these flows. These are most obvious in the table for London, which loses population through migration on a significant scale to the surrounding areas. Again these short-distance moves need to be explained in Chapter 5. Note, however, that the population of London has not declined. London gains both from international migration and from a higher birth rate (since it has a relatively young population).

Table 4.1 Net Internal Migration: UK 1997 (000s)[9]

Region	**Net Gain**
North East	-5.9
North West	-5.1
Merseyside	-6.2
Yorks. & Humberside	-7.2
East Midlands	10.1
West Midlands	-10.8
East	20.2
London	-54.5
South East	23.9
South West	31.5
Wales	4.1
Scotland	2.1
Northern Ireland	-2.2

Source: Office For National Statistics

[9] Note that the regions differ slightly from those used in Chapter 2. This results from a recent re-classification of the UK regional accounts.

4.4.2 Transactions and Search Costs

We have already briefly discussed the importance of transactions costs in the previous chapter. Their existence typically leads to forms of inertia in behaviour. Therefore, given transactions costs, a finding that prices do not change at the same rate in all areas simultaneously should, perhaps, come as no surprise. But, particularly in a spatial setting, further trading frictions need to be taken into account, notably the possibility of search costs. Here, however, we have to be more speculative in our conclusions.

The prime objection to migration as the main explanation of regional price patterns concerned the volume of activity. We suggested that the number of interregional moves was insufficient, at least in the UK, to drive price convergence. By contrast, migration in the USA is greater but, in fact, there is less evidence of convergence in prices. However market search, which is related to migration, is not subject to the same criticism. Even if we cannot easily directly observe search behaviour, in general, we expect that, for every housing market trade, the number of property visits will be higher and it is *search* rather than *moves* that drives price changes. The idea of spatial price patterns based on search behaviour is intuitively appealing. In search models, agents do not have to physically move to exert an influence on the price.

Search models applied to housing markets are reviewed in Clark and Flowerdew (1982). Here we simply highlight one or two points, which are particularly relevant to our interests. Since the earliest work of Stigler (1961), the number of searches undertaken by potential buyers depends on the dispersion of prices relative to search costs. If house prices in a market follow a uniform distribution between an upper value P^U and a lower value P^L and the cost of each visit to view a new house is constant, then Stigler shows that a wide dispersion of prices will be associated with a greater number of searches (since the gains from doing so are increased), but searches will decrease with the cost per search. However the relationship is non-linear since search yields diminishing returns in terms of the expected reduction in the minimum asking price. Although the number of property visits is not directly observable from published data, we expect the number of searches to be greater than one[10]. Furthermore, since the costs of search are clearly increasing in distance, we would not expect many households currently living in the south of the country to be searching in northern markets (although, of course, the price dispersion between the two areas is also large). Therefore sets of equilibrium prices can emerge rather than a single spatial equilibrium. On this view of the world, we would expect more

[10] Although anecdotal evidence suggests that the number of searches is typically not large.

dispersion in price movements in large countries such as the USA and Australia than in the UK - which is the case as shown in table 2.6.

Furthermore, Salant (1991) and Berkovec and Goodman (1996), again using a search framework, derive an optimal pricing rule for rational sellers attempting to maximise the discounted expected value of the selling price. This is derived from a value function (4.32);

$$V_{t,j} = \underset{P}{Max}\, \beta(1 - F_t(P))V_{t+1,j+1} + F_t(P)P_t \qquad (4.32)$$

$V_{t,j}$ is the expected value at t of selling a house that has been on the market for j periods. This equals the probability of sale, $F_t(P)$, multiplied by the price, P_t, plus the discounted value function in $t+1$ multiplied by one minus the probability of sale in the current period. The optimal pricing rule for the seller can be solved by standard dynamic optimisation methods, generating (4.33);

$$P_{t,j} = (P^U{}_t + \beta V_{t+1,j+1})/2 \qquad (4.33)$$

In a two period model, the offer price will simply be the average of the upper and lower price (if the seller is forced to sell at the lower price in the second period). In a multi-period model, the offer price will decline with time on the market. Therefore, the offer price of a house of vintage j (i.e. that has been on the market for j periods) will be greater than that of vintage $j+1$. But $F_t(P)$, the probability of sale, is made up of two elements – the probability of being visited by a prospective buyer, (γ_t), which depends on the number of buyers (B_t) relative to sellers, (S_t), and the probability a visitor will purchase an inspected property, which depends on the offer price. Clearly the higher the price set by sellers, the greater the chance that this will be above the reservation price of the buyer.

$$F_t(P_t) = \gamma_t[(P_t^U - P_t)/(P_t^U - P_t^L)] \qquad (4.34)$$

$$\gamma_t = B_t / S_t \qquad (4.35)$$

Although the model does not have an explicit spatial dimension, search models of this form hint at why prices may not change at the same rate in each location. Changes to offer prices depend, again, on the price dispersion - which may not be the same between regions - and also on housing search activity in terms of relative numbers of buyers and sellers.

Little empirical work has been carried out in the UK However, exceptions can be found in Tu and Goldfinch (1996), and Maclennan and Tu (1996). These studies construct empirical models, identifying local housing market sub-systems for Scotland, using multinomial logit methods, in which search plays a role. There have been, however, no attempts to apply these search models to regional quantitative models in the UK.

4.4.3 Equity Transfer

Downpayment constraints may also generate spatial patterns. As we have seen, Stein (1995) suggests that the observed positive correlation between sales and prices arises from the credit market. If, on moving, existing owner-occupiers have to make a downpayment rather than taking out a 100% loan, then sales depend on the value of the existing house. Building on this work, Muellbauer and Murphy (1994) argue that lagged house prices affect current house prices because these are an indicator of the equity available to repeat buyers moving up the housing ladder. Therefore, the finding that prices in other regions are related to prices in the South East may indicate that purchasers moving from the South East have greater buying power as prices rise, forcing up prices in the other regions. Again the explanation is related to migration movements and search behaviour, although Stein also suggests that cities, which have high debt levels (high loan to value ratios), are more likely to experience a crash in prices than cities where there is a wide dispersion of debt ratios. This could occur if home-owners took out high levels of debt at a time of high trading activity and rapidly increasing prices. This makes the market fragile to subsequent negative shocks and is precisely what occurred in London and South East England in the early nineties. Some cities or regions are more susceptible to shocks than others depending on gearing. We return to this important point in Chapters 7 and 9 where we show that, indeed, the patterns of regional house price movements in the UK are consistent with the debt gearing ratios, although a distinction needs to be drawn between gearing in terms of loan to value ratios and loan to income ratios. High levels of one do not necessarily imply high levels of the other. The South East of England has high gearing in terms of the latter, but not the former.

4.4.4 Spatial Arbitrage

The efficiency literature discussed in the last chapter suggests that arbitrage should take place over space to eliminate differences in returns. Financial rather than physical household flows generate the result although, again, the presence of frictions implies that excess returns will not necessarily be eliminated. If markets are spatially efficient, then the returns in one spatial market should not be useable to predict the returns in another. The US literature suggests that this is not the case. Tirtiroglu (1992) and Clapp and Tirtiroglu (1994) find evidence that house price changes in a given sub-market are related to changes in contiguous markets. This might be considered as evidence of a "positive feedback effect", whereby recent strength in one local sub-market feeds into other sub-markets. For example, if new information becomes available in one area, this information is transmitted first to contiguous areas. More recently Pollakowski and Ray (1997) examine spatial interactions in house prices in both the nine US census divisions and more locally around the New York metropolitan area using a VAR approach. This is one of the few studies comparable to UK work on the ripple effect, but the results are not consistent with UK findings. The authors conclude that house prices in the census divisions have some relationship to prices in other divisions, but the diffusion process is not one whereby prices are related only, or even primarily, to contiguous regions. The New York metropolitan area results provide, however, stronger support for the spatial diffusion, positive feedback hypothesis. We extend the Pollakowski and Ray work in Chapter 7.

4.4.5 Leads/Lags and Convergence in the Determinants of House Prices

This view is, perhaps, the simplest. The observed pattern of house prices can occur even if there are no spatial links between housing markets, if the regressors follow similar patterns. Since income is quantitatively one of the most important determinants of house prices, the spatial pattern of income change over time is central. This is the explanation favoured by Holmans (1990); the tendency of house price differentials to widen over time in the UK reflects relative income growth, coupled with an inelastic supply of housing, particularly in the South East (a factor stressed by Evans 1989). Since growth in the economy has often begun in the South with other regions catching up later, then the pattern appears consistent. Similarly the slump of the nineties was primarily concentrated in the South. Clearly different regional growth patterns must be an important part of the story, although there is little evidence that regional income trends are consistent with those in house prices. Indeed, Giussani and Hadjimatheou (1991) argue that there is no evidence of a ripple effect in incomes consistent with that in house prices.

4.4.6 Coefficient Heterogeneity

The final explanation, taken from Meen (1999), adopts a rather different approach, although some of the issues raised by Stein (1995) concerning the dispersion of debt gearing are relevant. In Section 4.3, the econometric issues concerning coefficient heterogeneity were discussed and we argued that structural differences between regional housing markets could lead to parameter differences and subsequent biases in aggregate models. We also noted in Section 4.2 that no study had examined whether systematic patterns in the coefficients across space existed. In fact, coefficient differences turn out to be useful in, at least partially, explaining the ripple effect and spatial price patterns in general, taking account of the Pesaran and Smith criticisms. Although this becomes clearer when empirical results are presented in Chapter 7, the basic idea is that coefficients in the South are consistently larger than those in the North – the patterns are non-random. Therefore, the response to *national* shocks, such as changes in interest rates, will be systematically different between the two regions. Here we set out the appropriate theoretical principles.

First, take the following (long run i.e. static) equation at the national level (denoted by subscript N) and its regional equivalent (denoted i). These might be considered as cointegrating relationships;

$$Y_N = \gamma_{0,N} + \gamma_{1,N}(X_N) + \gamma_{2,N}(Z) + \varepsilon_N \tag{4.36}$$

$$Y_i = \gamma_{0,i} + \gamma_{1,i}(X_i) + \gamma_{2,i}(Z) + \varepsilon_i \tag{4.37}$$

In (4.36) and (4.37), (Z) has no subscript and represents the set of regressors that do not vary regionally. An obvious example is the nominal interest rate; (X_N, X_i) are the vectors of regressors that do vary regionally, for example, incomes, subject to the constraint;

$$X_N = \sum_{i=1}^{n} X_i \tag{4.38}$$

If all the coefficients across the regions are identical, we could model regional deviations from the national average, (4.39);

$$(Y_i - Y_N) = \gamma_{1,i}(X_i - X_N) + (\varepsilon_i - \varepsilon_N) \tag{4.39}$$

But if the coefficients are not identical across space and if we assume that the $(X_i)s$ follow the stochastic process given by (4.40)

$$X_i = \beta_i X_N + \mu_i \quad ; \quad \sum_{i=1}^{n} \beta_i = 1 \tag{4.40}$$

The equation then becomes;

$$\begin{aligned}(Y_i - Y_N) &= (\gamma_{0,i} - \gamma_{0,N}) + (\gamma_{1,i}\beta_i - \gamma_{1,N})X_N + (\gamma_{2,i} - \gamma_{2,N})Z \\ &+ (\varepsilon_i - \varepsilon_N + \gamma_{1,i}\mu_i)\end{aligned} \tag{4.41}$$

Furthermore, if the dependent variable is an I(0) process[11], this imposes constraints on the regional coefficient values. Since (X_N, Z) will typically be non-stationary then, *in the long-run*, the regional coefficients cannot be significantly different from the national average coefficients (appropriately weighted).[12]

Now consider the dynamic processes, again in a cointegration framework. Similar calculations lead to the following equation in deviation form;

$$\begin{aligned}\Delta(Y_i - Y_N) &= (\alpha_{0,i} - \alpha_{0,N}) + (\alpha_{1,i} - \alpha_{1,N})\Delta Z + \alpha_{2,i}(\Delta X_i - \Delta X_N) \\ &+ (\alpha_{2,i} - \alpha_{2,N})\Delta X_N + \alpha_{3,i}(\varepsilon_i - \varepsilon_N + \gamma_{1,i}\mu_i)_{-1} + (v_i - v_N)\end{aligned} \tag{4.42}$$

[11] If, for example, all regional house prices cointegrate, then deviations from the national average will be I(0).

[12] Remember we suggested in Chapter 2 that trends in regional deviations appeared to be weak in the UK, even if stationarity was not fully supported. Stationarity of the deviations would not appear to be valid in the USA and Australia. However, this does not affect the approach, merely the expected values of the coefficients.

Here the (α) coefficients refer to the dynamic terms and the last term is the error term. The equation also includes the errors from (4.41) to capture the cointegrating relationship. Since all the difference terms are stationary (on the assumption that they are I(1) in levels), there is no *necessary* reason why the $(\alpha_{1i}-\alpha_{1N}),(\alpha_{2i}-\alpha_{2N})$ coefficients should be insignificantly different from zero. Hence, if there are differences in coefficients between the regions, cointegration does not rule out the inclusion of national variables such as interest rates in the regional equation in first differences. Studies that exclude national variables are implicitly assuming regional coefficient equality. However, it is perfectly possible that house prices in the South East, for example, might be more sensitive to interest rate changes than the other regions in the short run because of differences in debt gearing. Furthermore, in countries where cointegration of regional prices does not occur, the long-run coefficients in (4.41) may also differ between areas.

Expressed in error correction form, equation (4.42) can be rewritten as (4.43).

$$\begin{aligned}\Delta(Y_i-Y_N) &= (\alpha_{0,i}-\alpha_{0,N})+(\alpha_{1,i}-\alpha_{1,N})\Delta Z+\alpha_{2,i}(\Delta X_i-\Delta X_N)\\ &+(\alpha_{2,i}-\alpha_{2,N})\Delta X_N-\alpha_{3,i}[(Y_i-Y_N)_{-1}-(\gamma_{0,i}-\gamma_{0,N})-(\gamma_{1,i}-\gamma_{1,N})X_{N,-1}\\ &-(\gamma_{2,i}-\gamma_{2,N})Z_{-1}-\gamma_{1,i}(X_i-X_N)_{-1}]+(v_i-v_N)\end{aligned} \tag{4.43}$$

[.] is the error correction relationship representing the equation's long-run structure. Equation (4.43) turns out to be our basic model, although we reserve the results of estimation until Chapter 7. But the key result is that coefficient patterns turn out to be spatially non-random, As a result, national shocks, such as a change in interest rates, generate a distinct spatial pattern in house price movements in the short run, whereas the common stochastic trend, implied by expressing variables relative to the national average, ensures that the results are consistent with observed long-run house price movements. The existence of regionally varying debt gearing ratios, which are reflected in the coefficients are shown to, at least partly, explain why prices in London and the South East typically rise before those in the rest of the country.

4.5 So Why Do Regional Price Patterns Differ?

There is no definitive answer to this question and there is no reason why the same factors should be equally important in different counties. However, to speculate, there are, probably, three key factors.

First, and most obviously, regional economic conditions differ. In Australia, for example, price trends between the state capitals, broadly, reflect relative economic growth rates; New South Wales has consistently proved the strongest growing state both in terms of GDP and property values.

Second, differences in the structures of housing markets, population make-up and credit conditions will all be reflected in the parameters of formal models. But, critically, the distributions are non-random and, as we show in Chapter 7, these lead to spatial patterns in the responses of house prices to national shocks.

Third, and there is no empirical evidence to support this, we suspect that search patterns are more important in explaining spatial price distributions than migration *per se* which is the more commonly quoted view.

Chapter 5

HOUSING CAREERS AND URBAN STRUCTURE

5.1 Introduction

By identity, changes in the number of households in any locality are determined by either natural rates of population increase (along with any associated changes in headship rates) or by moves between different locations. The former involves the creation of *new* households, whereas the latter involves a redistribution of *existing* households. Although this is true whatever the spatial dimension - nation, region or metropolitan area - the relative importance differs with each. Typically, the smaller the spatial scale, the more important is moving or migration relative to "domestically induced" change. At the national level, migration only occurs internationally, usually in response to differences in economic and political conditions. But such flows are often dominated by domestic rates of population increase, although this depends on the size of the country and its degree of openness[1]. Increases in the number of households in recent years have frequently occurred as a result of rises in headship rates rather than population *per se* as average household sizes have fallen. Falling average household sizes and the growth of single person households has been a distinctive trend in many industrialised countries.

At the regional level, we noted in Chapter 4 that inter-regional migration flows are typically important in most countries and take place in response both to differences in employment and housing market conditions, although we suggested that, in terms of *long-distance migration*, employment is probably the most important factor. Nevertheless, natural rates of increase

[1] Australia, for example, has traditionally relied on high levels of immigration.

remain substantial. However, at the metropolitan level, moving is the dominant manner by which areas expand or contract in terms of population. This is because most moves by households are short distance. According to the Survey of English Housing (SEH), for example, for owner-occupiers, 55% of moves were for less than five miles in 1996/97 and 80% less than twenty miles. Although the proportions are slightly less for private renters, the differences are minor. Furthermore, similar patterns emerge in other countries. Clark and Dieleman (1996) or Dieleman *et al* (2000), for example, reach similar conclusions for both the USA and the Netherlands. In contrast to regional flows, typically, short-distance moves are not primarily generated by labour market conditions. Rather moves take place either to improve housing and environmental conditions or because of changes in family circumstances e.g. marriage or family break-up. According to the SEH, only 9% of moves by owner-occupiers in 1996/97 were for job-related reasons. Although the proportion rose to 17% in the private rented sector, almost no-one in the public sector moved for job reasons.

Therefore this chapter, which concentrates on the urban dimension, is much more heavily concerned with location choice and its determinants than either of the last two chapters. The central concern is to identify the factors that determine emerging patterns of spatial structure. Although we have something to say on the important question of new household formation, here, it is a secondary issue. The chapter has both a microeconomic and a macroeconomic dimension. In the former, household housing careers are traced. This provides linkages to the models in Chapter 3 and considers life-cycle behaviour from new household formation, through moving decisions, to retirement. In contrast to standard location theory, urban structure falls out naturally from the housing decisions that different types of households undertake at different stages of their housing careers. Young, single person households have different housing and location requirements from middle-aged couples with children. In Sydney and Melbourne, for example, much of the recent resurgence in central area housing has taken place in high-rise building associated with increasing demand from the former (for whom travel to work times are crucial), whereas counter-urbanisation trends continue amongst the latter e.g. Stimson (1999). This suggests a segmentation of housing markets between different household types. For example, once households have left central areas, it becomes difficult to entice them back again.

As Dieleman *et al* (2000) point out, the dominant factors determining moving decisions are age of the household head and current tenure. The 20-35 age group is the most mobile in most developed economies, triggered by leaving home, changing jobs, marriage and the addition of children. After the age of 35, these triggers become less frequent so that the requirement to move home becomes less at least up to retirement age. Private renters are also more likely to move house than home-owners (although the mobile also have a higher probability of renting) - again this appears to be common across developed economies - since transactions costs are much greater for home-owners. However the propensity to move for public tenants is, as we shall see, slightly less clear-cut. At least in the UK, the traditional wisdom was that public sector tenants had very low mobility rates; but this has not been the case in urban areas in recent years. The concentration on demographic factors as determinants of household formation and moving decisions is not misplaced but economic factors, of course, also have a role, particularly incomes and relative housing costs, and these have to be incorporated into the analysis.

In summary, the areas to be covered are:

- location theory and its extensions,
- urban/suburban drift,
- new household formation and tenure choice,
- moving and location decisions

5.2 Some Aspects of Location Theory and Its Extensions

Some, but by no means all, of the results that follow would be predicted by standard residential location theory. Therefore it is helpful to begin by highlighting the common features and differences from standard theory. Most theoretical models of housing location start from the monocentric model associated with Alonso (1964) and Muth (1969). The basic model assumes that households work in a single location in the city, but choose between living in the city centre and out-of-town (access versus space). Since commuting to the city centre involves both time and transport costs, the price of housing and land must fall with distance from the city centre. Equilibrium requires the household to locate where the marginal increase in commuting costs is exactly equal to the marginal reduction in land prices. Utility maximisation leads to a bid-rent function showing how prices change with distance from the city centre; the bid rent function depends on the (negative of the) marginal valuation of travel time. The rent gradient falls with distance from the city centre, but becomes flatter as commuting costs fall. If commuting costs are low, the required compensation in terms of lower house prices from living further out is correspondingly reduced. In the extreme, if commuting costs are zero, then the bid rent function becomes horizontal.

From Muth and Goodman (1989), one of the key results is given by equation (5.1).

$$du / dy = (\eta_{hy} - \eta_{\psi y})(\psi / y) / (\delta^2 p / \delta u^2) \tag{5.1}$$

u = time spent commuting
y = income
$(\eta_{hy} - \eta_{\psi y})$ = the difference between the income elasticity of housing demand and the income elasticity of the marginal valuation of commuting time.
ψ = the marginal valuation of commuting time
p = price of housing services

The equation states that the effect of a change in income on the time spent commuting depends on the difference between two elasticities, the ratio of the marginal valuation of commuting time to income (which is positive) and a second order derivative, which has to be positive for stability. Therefore, whether a rise in income leads to households congregating in the city centre or moving to the suburbs depends primarily on two elasticities. If the income elasticity of housing demand is high, then households are more likely to reside in the suburbs. In this case, the simple theoretical model provides a useful explanation of the observed population drift to the suburbs by relatively high-income households in some countries. In fact, the model can be pushed slightly further. Muth and Goodman show that, if travel time is valued at the wage rate, then $\eta_{\psi y} = 1$, so the crucial empirical issue is whether the income elasticity of housing demand η_{hy} is greater or less than one. However, although early evidence tended to support the conclusion that the elasticity exceeds one, later evidence has been less supportive (but see the discussion in Chapter 6). Note also that there is no reason why cities should exhibit the same locational structure. In cities where commuting costs are low, concentration of the wealthy in suburban locations might be expected. But if commuting costs are high, the reverse holds. This might, perhaps, be the case in developing cities with an absence of infrastructure. Furthermore, if young single households value travel time particularly highly, they are more likely to be concentrated at the core.

An important strand of the literature attempts to integrate neighbourhood quality as an additional explanatory factor in location choice. But neighbourhood quality does not play a role in the Alonso-Muth model, although it is consistent with the Wheaton (1977) critique. Wheaton argues that the two elasticities in equation (5.1) are similar in size and, therefore, cannot explain observed residential patterns. He suggests that this provides credence to the view that the suburbanisation of wealthier American households is primarily a response to externalities and fiscal incentives. Recent extensions to the monocentric model by Brueckner *et al* (1999) support the importance of amenities in explaining differences in the distribution of wealthy households around the world. This work is discussed further in Chapter 10. Bourassa *et al* (1999) also suggest that the inner areas of Sydney and Melbourne have been successful in retaining wealthy households because of the attractiveness of inner area neighbourhoods. Neighbourhood quality is a key feature of the models developed below.

Although elegant, the simple monocentric model has received further criticisms over its real world relevance. For example, the model assumes that all employment is exogenously determined in the city centre. This is to prove a particularly important drawback in Chapter 8, where housing and labour markets are treated simultaneously in order to explain multi-centred employment patterns. In addition, the model assumes that are no geographical features preventing households travelling in any direction.

The view that the price of housing or land can be characterised only by two characteristics, size and accessibility is not appealing, although both are likely to be important factors. But neighbourhood quality can be introduced into an extended version of the hedonic model discussed in Chapter 2.

$$PH = f(S, N) \tag{5.2}$$

where:
PH = dwelling price
S = structural attributes
N = neighbourhood characteristics

In equation (5.2), S, represents the attributes or characteristics of the dwelling, e.g. the number of rooms, whereas (N) represents the geographical location and includes such factors as nearness to factories, pollution levels and general neighbourhood quality. This could also include distance to the city centre although, as we shall see, specific rent gradients are added into some models. Furthermore although, in principle, neighbourhood spillover effects could be incorporated in (N), some models add spatial spillovers through the use of the spatial lag techniques discussed in Chapter 4. In one sense, the hedonic approach could be seen as a generalisation of the space-access model to incorporate a broader range of economic variables. The cost is the loss of theoretical elegance and explicit predictions.

In the UK, hedonic models that attempt to include neighbourhood or location specific effects are fairly rare, although they are more common in the US. But, in the US literature, neighbourhood effects are often found to be insignificant, implying that neighbourhoods have little influence. More likely explanations of this result lie in variable collinearity and specification problems. Amongst British work, Garrod and Willis (1992) look at the amenity value of forestry and woodland, whereas Pennington *et al* (1990) examine the effects of aircraft noise on property values. But particularly interesting, are the studies of Cheshire and Sheppard (1995, 1998), who use micro data on two towns, Reading and Darlington, allowing the authors to derive implicit prices for amenity values and to estimate the land rent function for each town. Perhaps surprisingly, given the criticisms of the monocentric model, in an extended framework, they find that the monocentric model performs well. The Cheshire/Sheppard model is defined as a Box-Cox transform (5.3);

$$(p^{\psi}-1)/\psi = K + \sum_{i\in D}\beta_i x_i + \sum_{j\in C}\beta_j (x_j^{\lambda}-1)/\lambda + r(d,\theta)(L^{\xi}-1)/\xi \tag{5.3}$$

where;
p = rentalised price of the structure
x_i , x_j = set of location or structure specific characteristics
$K, \beta_i, \beta_j, \lambda, \psi, \xi$ = set of parameters to be estimated (the last three are the parameters of the Box-Cox transformation
L = quantity of land involved in the structure
D = set of dichotomous characteristics
C = set of continuously variable characteristics
$r\,(d,\ \theta)$ = land rent function

Therefore, the house price (transformed into a rental stream) is related to a set of structural and locational attributes in the same way as (5.2) and the quantity of land multiplied by its price, defined by the land rent function. The land function, in turn, depends on distance from the centre *(d)*, a parameter (θ) measuring the angle of deflection of the property from the East and (n) an integer determining the number of radial asymmetries. Therefore, the price of any property will depend on its location. More precisely the rent function is defined by (5.4);

$$r(d,\theta) = \beta_1 \exp\{d[\beta_2 + \beta_3 \sin(n\theta - \beta_4)]\} \tag{5.4}$$

where, $\beta_1 \ldots \beta_4$ are parameters to be estimated.

In the model, rents decrease monotonically (for given locational characteristics) along any linear path from the centre, but the function is sufficiently general to allow asymmetries in different directions.

The model can be used to show why *relative* house prices may not remain constant even within a common labour market area. As DiPasquale and Wheaton (1996, Chapter 13) show, varying levels of crime, education, local services and amenities all imply that the standard bid rent function is not necessarily monotonically decreasing in distance. These factors can dominate the effects of commuting distances. Prices can vary dramatically within very closely related areas. This is certainly true within London, where the relative growth rates of prices in neighbouring boroughs can vary considerably.

It is this recognition of the importance of amenities that leads to the Cheshire and Sheppard model. In their model, the monotonic rent function still holds, but only by standardising on the level of amenities in different locations. The existence of different amenities leads to a complex spatial pricing structure. However, the inclusion of amenities does not necessarily imply that *relative* prices change over time. This depends on variations in the patterns of demand and supply. For example, an increase in families with children in an area would raise the demand for high quality schools. However any impact on the implicit valuation of schools depends on whether supply is inelastic. This, in turn, raises questions of land use planning and zoning, which are discussed in more detail in Chapter 10. But, in general, land use planning, which limits the supply of certain characteristics, changes relative prices even within urban areas.

In the literature there are further approaches to introducing spatial interactions in hedonic-based models, particularly concentrating on neighbourhood and spillover effects. This work is directly related to the spatial econometrics literature, introduced in Chapter 4[2]. The addition of a spatial lag to (5.2) yields an extended version (5.5);

$$PH = f(S, N, W.PH) \tag{5.5}$$

where (W) is an appropriate spatial weights matrix, so that the equation now states that house prices in any location are determined by a set of structural and neighbourhood characteristics and also by house prices in other locations. This is specified as a spatial lag model, although the extension to add a spatial error process is straightforward. This is, in fact, the approach to capturing spillover effects used by Can (1992) and Can and Megbolugbe

[2] See Dubin (1998) for a primer on the use of spatial techniques in housing analysis.

(1997) in a study of property values in the Columbus (Ohio) metropolitan area.

Now consider some of the features of these models, which become important in later chapters. First, standard residential location models imply an absence of social mix. Under certain parameter values, such models suggest that high incomes lead households to move away from city centres in the search for greater space at the expense of longer commuting times. But, under other parameter values, they congregate in cities. Either way households tend to be concentrated in common areas or rings, defined by income. Furthermore, these tendencies will be reinforced if household utilities are interdependent and are increased by living in areas dominated by other households of similar status (Evans 1976). Second, these models are typically static. Without extensions, they are not immediately suitable for explaining dynamic processes of change over time. Third, the location model adopts a partial equilibrium framework - it has nothing to say about firm location and employment opportunities for example.

Fourth, the model has little to say about the market imperfections that low-income households, in particular, may face. For example, in Chapter 3, we looked at the impact of credit market constraints on mobility. The standard model implies that, since any location goes to the highest bidder, the "rich" will have first choice, but there are no housing shortages or excess supply. Homelessness does not exist (see Early 1999 for a recent model of homelessness). All households have incomes and are implicitly employed. All locations are identical except in terms of distance from the city, i.e. there are no deprived areas. An exception is the vast US literature on neighbourhood structure induced by racial discrimination. However, efforts to explain racial concentrations in terms of socio-economic variables alone have largely proved unsuccessful (see, for example, Harsman and Quigley 1995, for a comparative analysis of San Francisco and Stockholm). In summary, it would be difficult to disagree with the conclusion of Brueckner *et al* (1999) that "Despite substantial progress in urban economic theory since the 1960s, the absence of a convincing and robust explanation of location by income represents a significant failure of the standard model" (p. 105).

5.3 Unemployment in London

From the previous section, two of the key issues to be considered further are, (*i*) interactions between housing and labour markets, (*ii*) environmental quality. Both of these affect housing market choices of new and existing households and contribute to urban structure. Since the empirical work in

Chapter 8 is based on London and the South East, it is useful to highlight some of the characteristics of the areas. The South of England is often considered as the most prosperous part of the country with slower growth and higher unemployment in the North, but a North-South divide is a simplification and, as shown in Chapter 2, some of the most deprived areas of England can be found amongst the London boroughs

Until the early eighties, unemployment rates in London and the rest of the South East were similar as shown in figure 5.1. However the gap has increased over the course of time. Clearly a critical issue is why this has occurred when London and the South East together might be considered as a single labour market area, since transport links are generally good compared with many other parts of the country. Other UK metropolitan areas have experienced similar trends – unemployment in the urban core has risen relative to the suburbs; nor are the patterns confined to the UK.

One view that has received a great deal of publicity is that the differential has arisen from a "Jobs Gap". Inner city areas are suffering from a shortage of labour demand. Although this is an old debate, the issue has recently resurfaced with the work of Turok and Edge (1999) who describe the long-term large-scale loss of, particularly, male manufacturing unskilled jobs from London and the major metropolitan conurbations. This has continued into the nineties despite the fact that manufacturing now accounts for less than 10% of jobs in London.

Although the trends in manufacturing are clear[3], the policy prescription that new jobs need to be guided towards cities does not necessarily hold. An alternative view is that urban labour markets are "seamless"; this implies that if governments or the private sector create jobs in deprived areas, there is little effect on local unemployment because labour will commute in from other areas. This view implies that unemployment is due to the characteristics of the resident population (Metcalfe and Richardson 1976, Evans and Richardson 1981, Fieldhouse 1999) and the areas of highest unemployment are simply those with the highest concentrations of low skilled workers. In this case urban unemployment patterns depend on the residential location decisions and constraints that different types of worker face. The view is, however, partial because it takes residential location to be exogenous. A fuller analysis requires the interrelationships between housing and labour markets to be taken into account.

[3] Note that a large part of the loss is due to the nationally declining share of manufacturing output in GDP. However, it remains true that large cities have fared comparatively poorly.

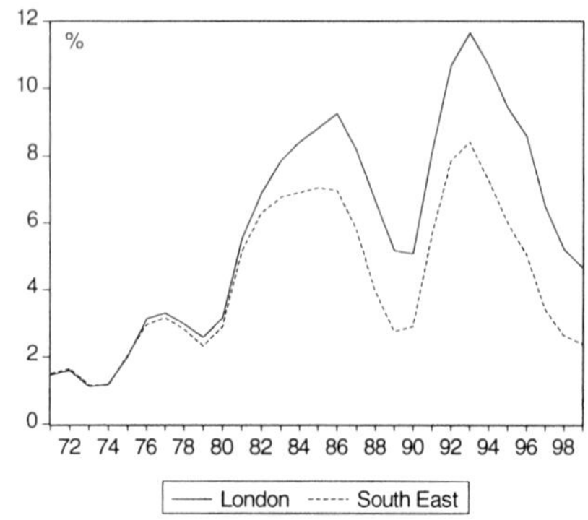

Figure 5.1. Unemployment in London and South East England

5.4 Urban/ Suburban Drift

In contrast to the major northern metropolitan conurbations, London is not now generally losing population. After decades of population loss, London's population in 1996 stood at over 7 million, a 4.6% increase from 1983 (ONS 1998). But from a peak in 1939, London's population fell for 44 years, with a particularly rapid decline in the sixties and seventies. Even the population of Inner London has increased slightly since 1983, now standing at 2.71 million, but the population is similar to that in the 1850s. By contrast population loss in Outer London was relatively slow and, again, has been reversed in recent years.

The gains in recent years in London have occurred partly as a result of natural population increases. London has both a high birth rate and low death rate as a result of its relatively young population compared with the country as a whole. Furthermore London has gained significantly from international in-migration. In terms of internal migration, London continues to gain population from the Northern regions, but loses population to the neighbouring South East and Eastern regions. In terms of the age structure of migration, London benefits from the mobile 16-24 age group, but contracts in the other age groups. These trends have established distinct patterns of urban-rural drift. To caricature the movements, at early stages of an individual's life-cycle, he/she tends to be drawn towards London (as a result of better labour market opportunities) but, as the individual becomes older and household characteristics change, the individual migrates short distances to Outer London or the South East and, in many cases, commutes back to London to work. Under Fielding's (1992) Escalator Hypothesis, the individual may leave the South East altogether later in his/her career. These patterns give rise to the population distributions shown in table 5.1.

Table 5.1. Population Age Structure in London and South East England (% shares)

	0-15	16-24	25-39	40-59	60+
Inner London	19.2	14.0	28.5	20.6	17.8
Outer London	19.7	13.0	24.2	23.3	19.8
Rest of South East	19.9	12.5	21.9	24.7	21.1

Source: 1991 Census of Population

Inner London clearly has a younger population structure than the Rest of the South East, particularly in the 16-24 and 25-39 age bands. The table also demonstrates that individuals tend to move away from the centre as they become older.

The question, however, is why households move away from London as they age. It seems unlikely that age *per se* is the critical factor. Section 5.2 also suggests that explanations in terms of elasticities alone are unlikely to be sufficient. To answer the question, we need to look at the housing careers of households and to ask (*i*) what are the factors that cause households to move and (*ii*) what are the factors that influence the choice of location. These are, of course, interlinked.

5.5 Individual Housing Careers

The objective of this section is to trace the lifetime housing careers of individual households from the point of new household formation.[4] As a part of this, the location choice of each household naturally falls out of the model as one of a set of interdependent decisions concerning the quantity of housing services required, tenure and location, all of which will vary over the life-cycle.

The literature - particularly the most comprehensive study by Clark and Dieleman (1996) - suggests that housing careers have similarities internationally, despite differences in institutional arrangements. As noted above, the factors that affect both new household formation and the moving decisions of existing households can be separated into demographic and economic. However, time-series econometric models cannot readily capture demographic variables, for example, the effect on moving of an additional child in the family. Instead we require individual choice models, which look at the probability of being in a particular state, conditional on a set of economic and demographic characteristics. Qualitative Response models have been widely used in the quantitative housing literature, (see for

[4] In fact, we shall ignore the increasingly important issue of housing in retirement.

example Quigley 1985, Borsch-Supan and Pitkin 1988). The next sub-section looks at *new* household formation whereas the following two sub-sections consider moving and location decisions by *existing* households.

5.5.1 New Household Formation

If, as appears to be the case, young households are more likely to be attracted to the urban centre, changes in new household formation rates and tenure choices have important consequences for cities. But, during the nineties in the UK, there has been a marked decline in the rate of new household formation and, in particular, a rise in the proportion of new households choosing not to go directly into owner-occupation as first tenure. Neither has the UK been alone. Yates and Wulff (1999, 2000) show stronger growth in private renting than in owner-occupation in Australia. Between 1974 and 1994 in Australia, the home purchase rate for the 25-34 age group fell particularly sharply. They point to three factors; (*i*) later marriage and childbirth, (*ii*) increasing costs of house purchase, (*iii*) labour market restructuring and poor job security. Income growth has become polarised with disproportionate increases at the top and bottom of the income distribution. In Australia, between 1984 and 1994 real household disposable income fell by 1.4%. But real incomes of the lowest quintile fell by 9%, whereas income rose by 2.5% in the top quintile. Widening income distributions have not been uncommon internationally, most noticeably in the USA. Gyourko and Linneman (1996, 1997), for example, point to the increasing importance of educational attainment relative to demographic factors in explaining owner-occupation rates in the US; education is, of course, crucial in explaining relative incomes.

Although for young cohorts in the UK, moving into owner-occupation remains the most common tenure after leaving the parental home, the proportion has fallen noticeably and typically depends on the number of employed household members. In addition, we expect rental rates to reflect the structure of financial institutions, credit markets and taxation. Burrows (1998) shows that, in 1988, new households in the UK made up 62% of all entrants to owner-occupation, but this had fallen to 40% by 1996/97. Surveys, (Ford and Seavers 2000), suggest that the aspirations of young households towards owner-occupation have changed, although it still seems probable that most will enter owner-occupation at some stage. Greater reliance on the private rented sector by households at an early stage in their housing careers would not cause great surprise in the US but, in Britain, it has attracted considerable comment, because (*i*) the private rental market is much smaller than in many other countries (around 10% of the housing stock) and households have typically entered directly into owner-occupancy at an earlier age than elsewhere, by-passing the rental sector, (*ii*) the reduction in homeownership amongst the youngest adult age cohort has been partly responsible for lower levels of property transactions in the nineties - approximately 50% of new mortgage loans are to first-time buyers. Unsurprisingly, mortgage lenders have been particularly interested in this phenomenon[5].

Holmans (1996) discusses the extent of this fall. He suggests that, if 1991 ownership rates had been maintained, around 250,000 extra owner-occupier households would have been in existence by 1994/95[6]. Holmans also indicates that, of this number, approximately a half was due to the reduction in the owner-occupancy rate for this group, approximately a third was due to lower household formation and around a sixth was due to lower population in the 20-24 age group. Table 5.2 sheds further light on the changing tenure patterns of the younger elements of the population; these are, again, taken from Holmans (1996) and use data from the Survey of English Housing and the Labour Force Survey. It compares the changes in tenure patterns for two age groups and three household types – married and cohabiting couples and single women. Three key results emerge; first, the owner-occupancy rate for the under 25s fell considerably over the nineties for each of the three household types. This was compensated by a rise in private renting. The changes are much less evident for the 25-29 group. Second, owner-occupancy rates are considerably lower for cohabiting households than for married households. Third, particularly in 1991, even for the under 25s, the owner-occupancy rate for the married is high. The early age at which British married couples enter into owner-occupation is evident.

Although the figures in table 5.2 indicate that the demographic characteristics are an important element in explaining tenure patterns, by themselves, they cannot explain the tenure *changes* over time. An obvious explanation, however, is in terms of the recession. But, although real wages grew only very slowly in the economy as a whole over the 1991-95 period, the more telling statistic is in terms of *relative* income growth of the different age groups. Broadly, the older age groups gained at the expense of the young during the first half of the nineties. Ortalo-Magné and Rady (1999) report data, which suggest that the young fared well relative to the older age groups in the eighties, but the position was reversed in the early nineties. Data taken from the British Household Panel Survey and shown in table 5.3 support this view. The table indicates real income growth for five age bands between 1991 and 1996 and shows that, in total over the period, the younger age groups have done far worse than the over thirties. Incomes

[5] The relationship between house prices and transactions was discussed in Chapter 3.

[6] For comparison, there are around seventeen million owner-occupied dwellings in the UK.

of the 20-24 age group fell by nearly 6%, whereas incomes of the over 35s rose by approximately 13%. The figures, again, demonstrate the potential aggregation problems raised in Chapter 4. Furthermore, since the effect of any downpayment constraint is negatively related to the level of income, from Chapter 3, the young are more likely to be squeezed out of owner-occupation.

Table 5.2. Tenure Status By Household Type (percentages)

	1991		1994/95	
	Under 25	**25-29**	**Under 25**	**25-29**
Married Couples				
Owners	63	75	53	75
Public tenant	22	16	24	15
Private tenant	15	9	23	9
Cohabiting Couples				
Owners	50	66	40	63
Public tenant	22	16	26	19
Private tenant	28	17	35	17
Single Women Living Alone				
Owners	25	52	18	54
Public tenant	25	17	25	23
Private tenant	49	30	56	22

Source: Holmans (1996)

Table 5.3. Real Income Growth By Age Group. 1991-1996 (%)

16-19	**20-24**	**25-29**	**30-35**	**35+**
-15.0	-5.9	-2.0	11.3	12.7

Source: BHPS

It is also true in the UK that low-income groups are more likely to be renters[7]. According to the SEH, the average gross weekly income in 1996/97 of households with a mortgage was approximately 70% higher than those in the private rental sector and 230% higher than public sector tenants. This is, partly, a result of the normal housing life-cycle. Other things equal, the young are more likely to be on low incomes as a part of their standard career progression. But this is not the whole story. Again using SEH data, only 18% of private renters were in the 16-24 age group and a further 20% in the

[7] See Yates and Wulff (2000) for a discussion of the incomes of renters in Australia.

25-29 age group. Furthermore, Burbidge (2000) shows that, for the two largest Australian cities, the owner-occupation rate for households with incomes less than the poverty line stood at 45.5%, but for those with incomes twice the poverty line, the proportion rose to more than 90%. Clark and Dieleman demonstrate similar patterns for both the USA and the Netherlands. Furthermore, on moving, high income renting households are more likely to move to owner-occupation than low-income households.

In contrast to the US, empirical studies of new household formation in the UK have been limited, although the works of Ermisch (1999) and Ermisch and Di Salvo (1997) provide important exceptions. But, in an international survey, Bramley *et al* (1997) draw a number of conclusions;

- in general, demographic factors are quantitatively more important than economic factors in explaining new household formation. Even if incomes grow slowly, such factors as marital status change and the addition of children will have strong effects on household formation rates.
- There is considerable variation in the literature in estimates of the income elasticity of household formation at the aggregate level, which are generally found to be in the range 0.05 to 0.4 with a central estimate of approximately 0.15.
- Young single-person households are more responsive to income changes with a range of elasticities of 0.7 to 1.8. However there is no clear consensus and lower rates of around 0.3 have been found.
- The distribution of income as well as its level is important. Higher incomes of women relative to men increase household formation, partly through effects on marriage and divorce rates.
- Household formation is also affected by changes in housing costs, although methods of measuring housing costs vary considerably. Overall elasticities lie in the range -0.01 to -0.23 with a central value of -0.08. Therefore price elasticities tend to be lower than income elasticities.

Tenure choice models have traditionally not been popular in the UK literature simply because the private rented market has been so small and has not been seen as a substitute to owner-occupation for most households. The work by Holmans (1996) to which we referred earlier and related work by Burrows (1998) are primarily descriptive, pointing to the important changes in tenure flows that have occurred in recent years. The work of Ermisch and Di Salvo (1996) is an important exception. By contrast recent work in North America has been extensive, highlighting the effects of downpayment constraints on both young and recently moving households, for example, Zorn (1989), Engelhardt (1994), and Haurin *et al* (1997). A joint model of household formation and tenure choice for young adults has recently been estimated for Sweden by Åsberg (1999). To speculate, this issue is likely to become increasingly important in the UK.

5.5.2 Moving Propensities

This and the next sub-section are concerned with the moving decisions of households already in existence – the next step along the housing life-cycle. In many ways this fits naturally into some of the models introduced in Chapters 3 and 4. However the issues raised in this section are slightly different. First, the search model of Chapter 4 appears, at first sight, an appropriate framework. But, in the search model, households continue looking for different properties because of the price distribution of houses of common quality, i.e. there is a probability that a buyer will find a lower price by inspecting a further property. In this section, the search process is not explicit and moving takes place because of the changing characteristics of the household and different neighbourhood characteristics. Second, note that in the simplest model of Chapter 3, under perfect foresight and in the absence of credit market constraints, the need for households to move after the initial setting up of the family home might be rather limited. But it is worth stressing the implicit assumptions of that model. First, the model was aspatial – it did not consider the fact that households have to commute or move to different locations as the spatial structure of labour demand changes over the course of time. Second, demographics played no role; implicitly each household was made up of a single individual and the model did not consider that the household might have to move to adapt to changing household size. Third, there were no shocks to income or employment. Unexpected income changes or "surprises" (see Ermisch and Di Salvo 1996) mean that the smooth housing profiles of the basic model no longer occur. Fourth, each location is implicitly identical in terms of housing and environmental quality, which are unchanging over time. Therefore, although the models of Chapter 3 are useful for analysing some aspects of macroeconomic behaviour, these additional considerations suggest that the moving patterns of a typical household over its housing career are far more complex than the simple models might suggest.

In principle, both moving and location decisions are joint and, indeed, we can specify models in which the probabilities of moving and choosing a particular location are jointly determined. Alternatively, we could specify a set of conditional and marginal probabilities for each decision. For example, the probability of choosing location (x) could be modelled conditional on deciding to move at all – which is a marginal probability. Models of this form can be constructed as nested logit models (see Quigley 1985 or Borsch-

Supan and Pitkin 1988)[8]. An example for London and South East England is estimated in Chapter 8 and can be shown as the decision tree figure 5.2.

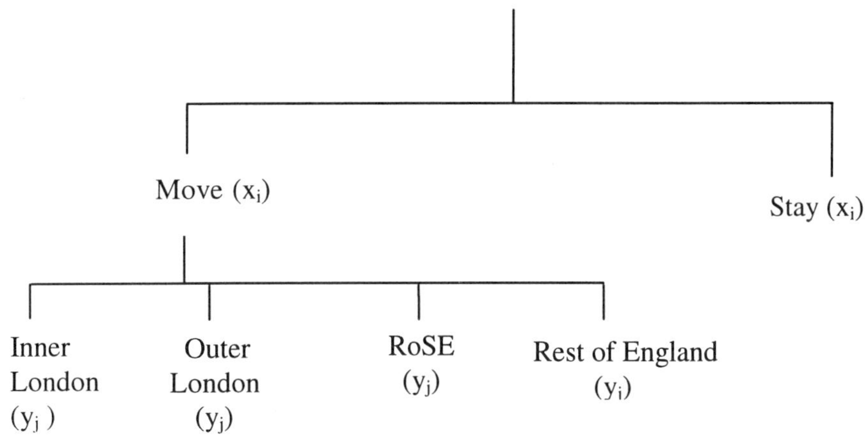

Figure 5.2. Decision Tree for Moving and Location

In this case, the model adopts a two-stage hierarchical structure in which the first stage determines the probability of moving for each household located in London and the South East, whereas the second stage determines the location choice, conditional on the decision to move. More precisely, households are assumed to be able to choose between four locations; Inner London, Outer London, Rest of the South East and the rest of Britain.

The (x_i) and (y_j) reflect the variables influencing the decisions. Note that (i) refers to the characteristics of the individual whereas (j) refers to the attributes of the location. Although both (x) and (y) could influence both decisions, as a simplification, the two are separated, which implies that each household has the same location preferences, independently of individual attributes, including income. But, as we shall see, this may still lead to the establishment of differentiated communities. Put crudely, just because lower income groups prefer good quality locations in the same manner as the rich, it does not necessarily mean that they can achieve this goal.

[8] The housing literature contains a wide range of discrete choice models. Here we are concerned only with joint models of moving and location. Other models consider location and dwelling type or dwelling type and tenure. Extending figure 5.2, it is easy to see the number of choices involved in a full model of moving, dwelling type, location and tenure. Ours is a sub-set of the full model.

The most important factors affecting moving decisions will be a combination of demographic and economic variables. The following are likely to be amongst the most significant;

- change in marital status,
- age of household head,
- retirement,
- number of pre-school children,
- number of children of school age,
- previous tenure,
- income and credit constraints,
- housing costs,
- job change,
- employment status of any spouse.

There is strong evidence that changes in marital status increase the number of households, both in terms of marriage and family break-up. We have already noted that mobility is strongly related to age and that, by the age of 35-40, mobility declines considerably until retirement, when mobility rises again. Dieleman *et al* (2000) show that, for 27 US cities, mobility rates for the under 35s average around 40%, but only 11% for the over 35s. Not only the number of children, but also their ages are important to mobility. Broadly, an increase in the number of children under school age tends to increase moving as space requirements rise, but the presence of older children appears to reduce mobility, so as not to disrupt their education.

One of the critical factors determining moving is previous tenure. According to the SEH, in 1996/97, 40% of private tenants had lived in their current dwelling for less than one year and 75% for less than three years. For the owner-occupier sector, the corresponding proportions were 6% and 18% respectively. Dieleman *et al* (2000) show a similar picture in US cities. The average turnover rate for private renting between 1985 and 1995 was approximately 38% per annum, but less than 8% in owner-occupation. There may be, however, an element of self-selection here; the most mobile members of the population are more likely to choose renting.

Residential mobility varies over the economic cycle. Amongst owner-occupiers, Burrows (1998) shows that, at the height of the UK housing market boom in 1988, 9% moved home, but in the slump of 1993/94, the proportion fell to 5%. Tenure choice also varies over the cycle; using the same source, in 1988, 80% of moves by households with a mortgage were to other mortgaged properties, but the proportion fell to 63% in 1995/96. (Permanent) income and housing costs are probably the key factors.

In addition, although less well documented, we argue that low-income households, have a lower probability of moving than high-income households. This is partly because the former are less able to make the transition from renting (either in the public or private sectors) to owner-occupation but, even amongst existing owner-occupiers, there are constraints on moving for low-income households. The effect of income on tenure transition is well known. The proportional hazards model of Clark and Dieleman (1996, p. 109), for example, shows how the probability of moving into owner-occupation for couples increases with the level of income and the number of earners in the household. According to their study for the US over the period 1970-1987 using the Panel Study of Income Dynamics, the presence of a second earner increases the "risk" of a move to owner-occupation by approximately 60%. The effectiveness of downpayment constraints is also inversely related to income and, as shown in the last section, these constraints have been influential on tenure choice.

But although low incomes and credit constraints affect tenure choice, it does not *necessarily* follow that they affect the number of moves. Low-income households may simply move between rented properties (although there is evidence that some will decide not to move at all). However, given the dominance of the owner-occupier sector in the UK, an important question quantitatively is whether relatively low-income households within the owner-occupier sector are less likely to move. According to Burrows and Wilcox (2000) a half of households in the lowest income quintile are owner-occupiers. The relationship between mobility and income has been subjected to few empirical tests in the UK, although Burrows and Wilcox also show from SEH data that the lower income quintiles have noticeably lower moving propensities. There are good reasons why this might occur. First, again, low income households are more likely to be faced by binding credit market constraints and this affects moving owner-occupiers just as much as households changing tenures. Note that, for these households, *current* income rather than *permanent* income will be the relevant measure. As a result, low-income households are less likely to be able to move in response to changing labour market conditions in particular areas, since expanding areas are likely to be locations of high house price growth. Low- income households can, therefore, become "trapped" in declining areas. This is a theme to which we return later. Second, there is evidence that low income/low skilled groups have smaller local labour market areas than the skilled. Speculatively, we might suggest that, by analogy, low-income households may have smaller housing market areas and, hence, have lower moving propensities. It is certainly true that, in contrast to the USA, migration rates of manual workers are low in the UK.

At least in the UK, relatively small numbers of household heads change job and location at the same time. As noted above, for those with a mortgage, only 9% of households move for job related reasons. Although individuals may well change jobs at a later date to be closer to work, the two are not typically simultaneous. From an econometric viewpoint, this has the advantage that moving decisions can be modelled conditional on the level of income, rather than requiring the joint modelling of labour market and housing decisions. The situation is rather different for newly forming households where location, job choice and tenure are all jointly endogenous processes (see, for example Haurin *et al* 1994).

Finally from the factors identified above, the presence of a spouse in the household may have two effects. First, dual income households are more likely to move due to the higher income levels. But if both partners are earning, the probability of finding a new dwelling, which satisfies the job locations of both is reduced.

5.5.3 Location Choice

The discussion in Section 5.2 stresses neighbourhood quality as a determinant of location choice. The importance of the overall environment is strongly confirmed by survey evidence. According to the SEH, for owners, the most important reason for moving is the desire for a larger dwelling (25%) but, at 16%, the wish to move to a better area is the second most important reason[9]. Furthermore, Burrows (1998) reports that, increasingly, the characteristics of the neighbourhood are as important as dwelling size. Quality of life is also stressed in Champion *et al* (1998).

In Australia, Burbidge (2000) shows that, amongst owner-occupier families in Melbourne and Sydney, low-income households are more likely to be in the outer suburbs. The high quality of many neighbourhoods close to the centre is an attraction for wealthier households and low-income households are forced outwards to lower priced areas. Furthermore, Cheshire (1995) demonstrates that many northern European cities have regained population in recent years but, typically, the cities that are increasing are those of higher environmental quality, such as cathedral and university towns. Older industrial cities have continued to lose population (see Champion and Ford, 1998 for the UK). The following list captures many of the more important environmental (and other) characteristics that have been suggested as important in influencing locational choice and are, at least in principle, measurable:

- crime rate,
- local school quality,
- unemployment rate,
- pollution,
- availability of parkland,

[9] Equally with the desire to change tenure.

- household overcrowding,
- housing lacking basic amenities,
- derelict properties,
- housing availability,
- housing costs in each location,
- current location.

The first five factors are direct indicators of environmental quality. The fear of crime is frequently quoted as one of the most important factors discouraging residence in inner city areas. Similarly the quality of local schools is seen as a key factor, at least amongst parents. In London, educational performance and crime rates are notably poorer in the inner city locations (table 5.4). The proportion of children obtaining more than five GCSEs (the standard school examination, usually taken at age 16) is a commonly used measure of school performance. The crime rate is measured by notifiable offences per resident population. The unemployment rate (which is a characteristic not only of individuals, but of the locality as a whole), pollution and green space are all additional potential indicators of environmental quality. Note, as shown in table 5.5, many of these indicators are highly correlated – although this does not imply causality.

The next three indicators, overcrowding, dwellings lacking basic amenities, and derelict properties are examples of variables that reflect underlying local housing conditions. In terms of the spatial spillovers model, demand for housing in any locality depends on the quality of other dwellings in the neighbourhood. This generates spatial price linkages as in the Can (1992) spatial lag model. By contrast, housing availability indicates new housing supply. Although there are clearly issues of simultaneity, an important policy issue is the extent to which the construction of new homes creates extra demand by attracting households to those localities. This has been used as an argument against the relaxation of planning constraints in South East England. Even if supply has no direct effect on demand, it is still likely to have an indirect effect through housing costs. Any expansion of supply drives down price and attracts population to those locations.

Finally, we have already noted that average moving distances are small. Long (1992) – reproduced in Clark and Dieleman (1996, p.40) - shows that this is true across the developed world. Therefore current location is likely to be an important influence. The desire to maintain the ties of family and friends can be considered as a form of transactions cost, which is probably much more important than direct moving costs in terms of solicitors fees, taxation etc.

Table 5.4a. Housing and Deprivation in Inner London

Borough	**Deprivation Rank 1998**	**% with 5+GCSEs Grade A-C Av. 1992-98**	**Crime Rate Av. 1992-96**
Newham	2	27.3	0.124
Hackney	4	25.5	0.154
Tower Hamlets	6	22.8	0.145
Southwark	8	23.3	0.171
Islington	10	21.7	0.159
Lambeth	12	24.8	0.154
Haringey	13	27.1	0.117
Lewisham	14	29.0	0.121
Camden	17	25.5	0.205
Hammersmith	18	35.1	0.125
Wandsworth	30	31.6	0.117
Westminster	57	30.4	0.333
Kensington	63	39.6	0.108

Table 5.4b. Housing and Deprivation in Outer London

Borough	**Deprivation Rank 1998**	**% with 5+GCSEs Grade A-C Av. 1992-98**	**Crime Rate Av. 1992-96**
Greenwich	11	29.1	0.145
Barking	15	27.3	0.100
Brent	20	36.8	0.107
Waltham Forest	22	33.3	0.076
Ealing	36	35.1	0.101
Hounslow	59	41.3	0.113
Enfield	70	40.3	0.087
Croydon	88	38.4	0.099
Redbridge	90	48.4	0.084
Hillingdon	120	40.0	0.091
Merton	122	36.5	0.091
Barnet	130	51.9	0.081
Havering	143	44.7	0.075
Harrow	145	50.9	0.071
Bexley	148	43.6	0.079
Richmond	156	48.7	0.080
Bromley	179	50.0	0.089
Kingston	220	55.9	0.186
Sutton	284	54.2	0.075

Table 5.5. Correlations Between Social Indicators

	Houses without basic amenities	**Crime Rate**	**GCSE score**	**Overcrowding**
Basic Amenities	1.0			
Crime	0.471	1.0		
GCSEs	-0.472	-0.463	1.0	
Overcrowding	0.549	0.350	-0.752	1.0

Chapter 6

EMPIRICAL FINDINGS FROM NATIONAL HOUSING MODELS

6.1 Introduction

This and the following two chapters present empirical results corresponding to Chapters 3-5; therefore this chapter considers a selection of national and international findings, Chapter 7 looks at regional issues and Chapter 8 deals with the urban dimension.

We begin by returning to single equation house price models, having already set up the appropriate theoretical framework in Chapter 3. However we saw in Chapter 2 that the long-run trends in real house prices differ across counties. It is important to explore why these differences occur. Is there something fundamentally different in the nature of housing markets between countries, which means that the same theories cannot be used internationally or are there merely relatively minor differences in the model coefficients? We investigate quantitative results from different house price models. Furthermore since, under some circumstances, house price equations can be seen as inverted housing demand functions, there should be a correspondence between the parameters of house price equations and direct estimates of price and income elasticities of demand. We compare the results of these different approaches. In previous chapters, we stressed the importance of aggregation biases. Therefore, in the single equation context, we examine evidence for structural price changes arising from the labour market.

The following section considers joint models of prices and housing construction. These can be considered as a generalisation of the two-equation Poterba (1984) model. In Chapter 3 we noted that, typically, such models did not generate housing cycles. Cycles in housing can, however, be investigated by using more general techniques taken from the business cycle literature. By constructing a vector error correction model (VECM) of prices, building activity, construction costs and interest rates, consistent with the stock/flow framework, cyclical behaviour may be modelled. The section also discusses the importance of supply elasticities in the construction equation stressing, as in DiPasquale and Wheaton (1996) and Stein (1995), that although supply may be inelastic with respect to the *level* of prices, the *rate of change* of prices may still have a major influence.

Section 6.4 constructs a joint model of prices and property transactions. This is in the tradition of recent US work but, as in Chapter 3, stresses how prices and transactions respond differently to housing market disequilibrium induced by either demand or supply shocks. The model preserves the property that permanent shocks have permanent effects on prices, but only temporary effects on transactions, although both are positively correlated in the short run. We also discuss the reasons why transactions have been exceptionally low in the UK in the nineties and the relationship to low rates of new household formation.

Finally, Section 6.5 discusses housing as an element of full macroeconometric models of the economy. This allows us to quantify the circular linkages between housing and the economy and the size of any multipliers in both the short run and the long run.

6.2 House Price Models

The starting point is equation (3.12) - which defines the basic life-cycle or arbitrage equation. For convenience this is repeated as equation (6.1). In Chapter 3, in discussing the Poterba stock/flow model, we rewrote the condition slightly, simplifying as in (6.2).

$$g(t) = R(t)/[(1-\theta)i(t) + \delta - \gamma(\pi + \dot{g}^e / g(t)) + \lambda(t)/\mu_c] \tag{6.1}$$

$$\dot{g} = a_1(g) - a_2 R(\overset{-}{H}, \overset{+}{HH}, \overset{+}{RY}, \overset{+}{W}) \qquad (6.2)^1$$

[1] Note that (6.2) ignores the rationing term. Since rationing has been absent since the early eighties in the UK, we ignore this complication for the moment, although this will re-enter the picture later.

where:

g = real house price
R = real per unit rental
H = dwelling stock
HH = number of households
RY = real per capita income
W = real wealth
i = nominal interest rate
π = general inflation rate
a_1 $\cong$ i-π
(.) denotes a time derivative

In (6.2) the determinants of the rental (with their expected signs) are added since, typically, the imputed rental cannot be measured and we have to substitute for the determinants.

Although all empirical models of house prices find lags to be important, a useful first test is whether (6.2) represents a cointegrating relationship. Even though efficiency may not hold in every time period, it may still occur in some long-run sense. A minimum condition for cointegration is that the orders of integration of each series used in (6.2) are consistent. Using the UK as an example, in Chapter 2, we saw that the level of real house prices was non-stationary; its first difference – the dependent variable in (6.2) – is, however, stationary. (a_1), which represents a real interest rate would be expected to be stationary, since a real rate cannot permanently exhibit a trend (although it may appear to do so in small samples). Therefore we require that (R) and (g) cointegrate. Indeed, for the USA, Meese and Wallace (1994) find that prices and capitalised rents are cointegrated in Northern California.

But since (R) is unobservable for the UK, we have to test for cointegration between (g) and (RY, H, HH, W). Initially using Engle-Granger techniques, estimation in logarithms yields (6.3).

$$\ln(g) = -7.44 + 3.49\ln(RY) - 2.19\ln(H/HH) + 0.142\ln(W) \quad (6.3)$$

DF= -4.3; ADF= -2.62

This equation is estimated on quarterly data over the period 1968(2)-1990(4)[2]. Since none of the lagged dependent variables used in the ADF test are significant, the DF test is more appropriate in this case and, indeed, there

[2] See Meen (1996a) for more details. Note also that the estimation period is cut short at 1990. We examine the nineties later.

is evidence of cointegration amongst the variables. But as the parameters derived from Engle-Granger estimation are likely to be affected by small sample bias, the results are compared in (6.4) with those obtained from the long-solution solution to an error correction equation using the same variables. If (6.3) is subject to bias, we would expect to observe differences between the two sets of estimates. The alternative at least provides a range. (6.4) is an updated version of the results presented in Meen (1990).

$$\ln(g) = -9.20 + 3.02\ln(RY) - 2.48\ln(H / HH) + 0.424\ln(W) \quad (6.4)^3$$

With the exception of the wealth coefficients, the results are not too dissimilar. However two points stand out. First, the elasticity with respect to the housing stock appears high in both equations, at more than two. But, in practice, since new construction per annum is only approximately 1% of the stock, the effect of new construction on prices is not dramatic. This becomes important when a two-equation stock/flow model is constructed in the next section. Second, and critically, the income elasticity of house prices is very high indeed and is one of the key differences between UK house price studies and those in the rest of the world. This result appears in almost all UK work. Note, however, that *current* income is the regressor here rather than *permanent* income. The distinction becomes very important when cross-section housing demand studies are discussed below but, in the time-series case, the distinction is of less importance. To see this, suppose that permanent income can be written as a weighted average of past actual levels of income (as often occurs in consumption analysis). Smoothing of income in this way has no effect on its order of integration. Alternatively *transitory* income may be considered as a stationary process. In either case, it makes little difference to the coefficients of the cointegrating vector whether current or an estimate of permanent income is used[4]. A selection of the estimated elasticities from different studies is summarised in table 6.1.

The results from equations (6.3) and (6.4) are, by no means, outside the estimates of other studies. Nevertheless, the elasticity needs to be justified in terms of the underlying theory. Suppose that the equations are also consistent with the reduced form demand/supply framework set out in Chapter 3 – in practice the results are close to being observationally equivalent. In this case, the price equation can be re-inverted to obtain estimates of the price and income elasticities of housing demand. Table 6.2

[3] Johansen estimation also indicates cointegration. In this case, the income elasticity is 3.56.

[4] Pain and Westaway (1997) use consumption as a measure of permanent income, but still find similar results.

provides the estimates from both equation (6.4) and from other recent studies.

Table 6.1. The Income Elasticity of House Prices

Study	Elasticity
Nellis and Longbottom (1981)	1.9
Hendry (1984)	2.6
Meen (1990)	3.0
Giussani and Hadjimatheou (1990)	1.7
Drake (1993)	3.8
Ashworth and Parker (1997)	3.4
Holly and Jones (1997)	2.3
Pain and Westaway (1997)	2.0
Muellbauer and Murphy (1997)	2.6
Mean value	2.6

Table 6.2. Implied Income and Price Elasticities of Housing Demand

Study	Income Elasticity	Price Elasticity
Equation (6.4)	1.2	-0.40
Muellbauer & Murphy (1997)	1.3	-0.52
Pain and Westaway (1997)	1.0	-0.49
Mean	1.3	-0.48

These results are all very similar. The price elasticities are, perhaps, uncontroversial (housing is price inelastic, reflecting limited substitution possibilities[5] and the finding that household formation does not respond strongly to price changes[6]), but the income elasticities may be. However are these findings consistent with micro studies, which estimate income and price elasticities of housing demand directly?

The income elasticity of housing demand is one of the more important parameters in housing economics. As we saw in Chapter 5, this elasticity is particularly important in urban location theory, where a central issue is whether the elasticity is greater or less than one. Residential location models imply that, if the income elasticity is greater than one, then an increase in income leads to households relocating away from cities and towards the suburbs. They demand more space in the suburbs at the cost of more time spent commuting to work in the city centre.

[5] Remember that this refers to substitution with other goods, not between tenures. Substitution between tenures produces much higher price elasticities.

[6] See Bramley *et al* (1997) for a literature review.

Mayo (1981) provides a survey of US estimates on primarily cross-section data, examining the evidence obtained from studies using *current* income data as opposed to *permanent* income estimates. Amongst his conclusions he finds:

- in line with standard consumption theory, estimates using current rather than permanent income will be biased downwards in proportion to the ratio of the variance of permanent to current income;
- estimates that attempt to measure permanent income by grouping over individuals or areas (on the assumption that transitory income will average out) will typically experience major upward aggregation biases, unless the grouping is carried out on some random basis.

Mayo suggested that most of the US estimates, which find an income elasticity in excess of unity, are due to aggregation bias and, compensating for the bias, the elasticity is well below unity. However, there are other explanations. Polinsky (1977, 1979) and Polinsky and Elwood (1979) argue that the main reason for differences in estimates of income elasticities between grouped and ungrouped data concerns the omission or misspecification of price measures in some studies. They show that, correcting for the errors, the differences in the income elasticities are reduced, although the estimates from grouped data are still higher, consistent with the permanent income view. Probit approaches also confirm an elasticity less than unity. Rosen (1979a), for example, finds an income elasticity of 0.76 and a price elasticity of -1.0.

Over time, more emphasis has been placed on the joint modelling of tenure choice and housing demand, because of the biases that may arise from considering each choice independently. Goodman (1988), for example, constructs a joint model of permanent income, hedonic prices, tenure and housing demand. He finds that permanent income is more important in explaining tenure than the level of housing demand. However, even in this extended framework, as shown in table 6.3, housing demand appears to be both income and price inelastic. The recent upsurge in interest in the housing decisions of young households has led to joint models of household formation and tenure choice. Haurin *et al* (1994), for example, construct a bivariate probit model to estimate jointly the probability of leaving home and tenure choice. From this they estimate the income elasticity of housing demand at approximately 0.5.[7]

Although the UK has many time-series studies of aggregate house prices from which we can deduce estimates of the income and price elasticities of

[7] US evidence on time-series data is more limited. Rosen and Rosen (1980) estimate a model of the owner-occupation rate, but direct estimates of the income elasticity are not presented in the paper.

housing demand, there are fewer cross-section studies. As seen in table 6.2, the deduced time-series income elasticities are typically in excess of unity and price elasticities are bunched around the range -0.4 to -0.5[8]. The latter are similar to US cross-sectional estimates, but the former are considerably larger. However cross-section studies do exist. One of the earliest UK studies of housing demand was by Byatt, Holmans and Laidler (1973). The study uses data from building society sample surveys. Byatt *et al* obtained income elasticity estimates in the range 0.6-0.7[9], but since their study includes no price measures, the results may be subject to the biases raised by Polinsky and Elwood (1979) discussed above.

A later study by Rosenthal (1989) used pooled data, again taken from building society surveys, covering the period 1975-81 for each of the standard regions. The use of pooled data allows the estimation of price effects. On grouped data, Rosenthal finds an income elasticity in the range 0.8-0.9 and a price elasticity of approximately -0.5. On individual data the corresponding estimates are 0.7 and -0.45 respectively. Therefore the income elasticity estimates are, again, below unity.

Using a very different methodology, Cheshire and Sheppard (1995) obtain much larger income elasticities. The study is limited to data from Reading and Darlington, where the elasticities of particular housing characteristics (rather than total housing demand) with respect to income are all well in excess of unity in both areas. The elasticities vary between high and low income groups. The price elasticities are also all greater than unity. In the most recent studies, using data for 1988/89, Ermisch (1996) and Ermisch *et al* (1996) estimate bivariate probit models for the probability of both being a mover and an owner-occupier. Given these estimates the conditional demand for housing may be estimated. The studies find an income elasticity of approximately 0.5 and a price elasticity of -0.4. A series of papers by Ermisch and Di Salvo (1996, 1997), Di Salvo and Ermisch (1997) and Ermisch (1999) examine young household formation, tenure choice and the effect of "surprises" [10]. Finally we note that Englund *et al* (1995), for Sweden, find estimates of the income elasticity in the range 0.37

[8] King (1980), however, on FES data, obtains point elasticities of approximately -0.7.

[9] However, they recognise that the estimates may be subject to downward biases and suggest an upper value of approximately unity.

[10] Although not directly interpretable in terms of the income elasticity of housing demand, related work by Åsberg (1999) for Sweden finds that a 10% increase in the wage raises the probability of home-ownership by approximately 7% using a random effects probit model of household formation and tenure choice. For Australia, Bourassa (1995) estimates a logit model for Sydney and Melbourne and finds an income elasticity of home-ownership of 0.29 and a relative price elasticity of –1.96. But, in this case, we are measuring substitution between tenures and, therefore, the results are not comparable to table 6.3.

to 0.41 and the price elasticity in the range -0.25 to -0.35. Table 6.3 summarises the international results.

On cross-section data, therefore, income elasticities are consistently found to be below unity, conflicting with our time-series evidence. But the time-series results cannot be entirely rejected. If, as might be expected, short-run elasticities are less than long-run elasticities, because of transactions and other adjustment costs, estimates derived from cross-section studies may be biased downwards (although panel estimates may not suffer in the same way). In principle, the estimates in table 6.2 avoid this problem, although the evidence is indirect and they may well suffer from the aggregation biases introduced in Chapter 4 or described by Mayo (1981).

Table 6.3. Income and Price Elasticities of Housing Demand

Study	Income Elasticity	Price Elasticity
UK		
Byatt *et al* (1973)	0.6-0.7	-
King (1980)	-	-0.7
Rosenthal (1989)	0.7-0.9	-0.5
Ermisch (1996)	0.5	-0.4
USA		
Rosen (1979)	0.35	-0.67
Polinsky and Elwood (1979)	0.4-0.6	-0.7
Goodman (1988)	0.30	-0.46
Haurin *et al* (1994)	0.50	-0.50
Sweden		
Englund et al (1995)	0.4	-0.25 to -0.35

So far, we have examined only long-run results. But all empirical models and, indeed, the theoretical models of Chapter 3 indicate that lagged adjustment is important. From Chapter 3, the generic model representation in error correction form is given by equations (6.5) and (6.6);

$$\ln(g) = a_1 \ln(RY) + a_2 \ln(W) + a_3 \ln(HH) + a_4 \ln(H) + a_5 \ln(M) + a_6(i) + a_7(\dot{ph}^e) + \varepsilon \qquad (6.5)$$

$$\Delta \ln(g) = \gamma_1 \Delta \ln(g)_{-1} + \gamma_2 \Delta \ln(X) + \gamma_3[\ln(g) - \gamma_4 \ln(X)]_{-1} + \mu$$
$$X' = [RY, W, HH, H, M, i, \dot{ph}^e] \qquad (6.6)$$

In terms of speed of adjustment, the critical parameter is γ_3, although the dynamics are also determined by γ_1 and γ_2. These also affect whether the model exhibits overshooting, as in the stock/flow model of Chapter 3.[11]

There are a very large number of empirical studies in the UK, but there is a remarkable degree of similarity in both the methods and the types of regressors employed. The most commonly quoted studies were set out in Chapter 3. Perhaps, the main exception to the general approach is that by Muellbauer and Murphy (1997).

However the results in table 6.4 are taken from Meen and Andrew (1998), which update an original equation appearing in Meen (1990). In the specification, there are a number of small changes from equations (6.5) and (6.6). First, (*UCC*) is an estimate of the user cost of capital. But from Chapter 3, nominal interest rates are as important as real rates; we find empirically that γ (equation 3.12) takes a value of 0.3. Second, (*M*) is a measure of mortgage rationing, operational until the early eighties in the UK. Its construction is described in Meen (1990a). Third, as a simplification, (*RY*) now refers to total rather than *per capita* income, which allows us to drop the household variable (*HH*). The justification is explained in Meen (1998), but arises from the fact that the coefficients on per capita income and the number of households are insignificantly different from each other.

Consider the first column, which is estimated only to 1990. On most of the diagnostic statistics presented in the table, the equation appears to perform well. The equation standard error is approximately 1.5%. The error correction coefficient at –0.1707 is broadly in line with most results on quarterly UK data, suggesting that only 17% of any disequilibrium is eliminated in each period. But adjustment to any shock is not monotonic. We show in the next section that income shocks typically lead to overshooting *even in the absence* of supply adjustment. Now compare the results with those in the second column, which extends the period to 1996. The equation collapses; the most obvious manifestation is in the error correction coefficient which falls to –0.0592. This could indicate that cointegration no longer holds in the long-run relationship.

This is a key result, which is discussed further later in this section. Historically UK house prices were relatively straightforward to explain using conventional variables. After 1990, there appear to have been structural changes. But it is not true, as is sometimes suggested, that the parameters of house price equations have been particularly volatile compared with other aggregate time-series relationships.

[11] Note that the value of γ_3 will also give an indication of cointegration in the long-run equation.

Error correction models (ECM) dominate the UK empirical housing literature and that in much of Europe - see, for example, Barot (1998) and Hort (1998) for Sweden, Kosonen (1997) for Finland. But methodologies in the USA are more diverse. Malpezzi (1999) employs the error correction approach and the model of Abraham and Hendershott (1996) bears some similarities. But although DiPasquale and Wheaton (1994) construct a price equation, as a part of a stock/flow model, in which prices converge gradually to a long-run equilibrium, the ECM approach is not used.

Table 6.4. Dynamic Models of UK House Prices. Dependent Variable: $\Delta \ln g$

Variable	Coefficient	Coefficient	Coefficient
	69(3)-90(4)	69(3)-96(1)	69(3)-96(1)
Constant	-2.3800	0.2468	-2.1901
	(-5.251)	(0.647)	(-5.056)
$\ln g_{-1}$	-0.1707	-0.0592	-0.1616
	(-8.739)	(-3.638)	(-8.803)
M_{-3}	-0.0110	-0.0183	-0.0110
	(-3.027)	(-4.184)	(-3.087)
$\ln W_{-1}$	0.0556	0.0375	0.0543
	(6.468)	(3.651)	(6.504)
$\ln H_{-1}$	-0.3068	-0.1647	-0.2819
	(-3.516)	(-1.597)	(-3.420)
$\ln RY$	0.4245	0.0891	0.3880
	(5.372)	(1.133)	(5.337)
$\Delta\ln RY_{-1}$	0.2145	0.2754	0.2499
	(2.565)	(2.731)	(3.126)
UCC	-0.00610	-0.00590	-0.00600
	(-9.938)	(-8.078)	(-10.455)
$\ln WSH$	-	-	0.4259
			(3.552)
R^2	0.857	0.744	0.846
SEE	0.0149	0.0188	0.0148
DW	1.72	1.40	1.94
AR	F(5,68)=0.85	F(5,89)=4.51	F(5,87)=0.97
ARCH	F(4,65)=0.35	F(4,86)=1.36	F(4,84)=0.41
Normality χ_2^2	6.98	5.05	3.68
RESET	F(1,72)=13.63	F(1,93)=7.00	F(1,91)=14.18
Chow	F(21,73)=3.68	-	-

t-values in brackets

Equations also include seasonal and other dummies

WSH = share of wages and salaries in total personal income

R^2 = coefficient of determination; SEE = equation standard error; DW = Durbin-Watson Statistic; AR = Lagrange Multiplier autocorrelation test; ARCH = Arch heteroscedasticity test; Normality = Jarque & Bera residual normality test; RESET = Ramsay's RESET test; Chow = Chow post-sample forecasting test.

In looking at US studies, a number of additional issues arise:

- the role of the vacancy rate,
- the relationship between prices and construction costs,
- the income elasticity of house prices,
- the existence of speculative bubbles.

No UK study of prices pays any attention to the vacancy rate but, as discussed in Chapter 3, the vacancy rate takes centre stage in the model of DiPasquale and Wheaton (1996)[12]. Nevertheless, as argued in Chapter 3, there is a relationship between measures of housing market disequilibrium, vacancies, turnover and prices. For the UK, an estimate of disequilibrium and implicitly vacancies can be obtained by comparing the actual owner-occupied housing stock with an estimate of the long-run desired stock. The latter, in turn, can be obtained by solving the equation in the final column of Table 6.4[13] - this is shown as equation (6.7) - and by re-inverting the equation to obtain estimates of the price and income elasticities, (6.8).

$$\begin{aligned}\ln(g) &= -13.552 - 0.0681(M) + 0.336\ln(W) - 1.744\ln(H)\\ &+ 2.401\ln(RY) - 0.0371(UCC) + 2.635\ln(WSH)\end{aligned} \tag{6.7}$$

The long-run price and income elasticities of housing demand are –0.57 and 1.37 respectively.

$$\begin{aligned}\ln(HSTAR) &= -7.771 - 0.5734\ln(g) + 1.376\ln(RY) + 0.1927\ln(W)\\ &- 0.0213(UCC) - 0.039(M) + 1.511\ln(WSH)\end{aligned} \tag{6.8}$$

where $HSTAR$ represents long-run equilibrium housing demand.

Housing market stock disequilibrium may now be defined (in logarithms) as the deviation of desired housing demand from the actual housing stock, that is, $\ln(diseq) = \ln(HSTAR / H)$ and this is graphed in figure 6.1[14]. The

[12] Although not in their 1994 model.

[13] Its relationship to the equations in the first two columns is discussed below.

[14] Note that the figure is defined in thousands of units rather than in logarithms.

figure shows that, for example, excess housing demand takes large positive values in the boom period of the late eighties and large negative values in the subsequent slump of the early nineties.

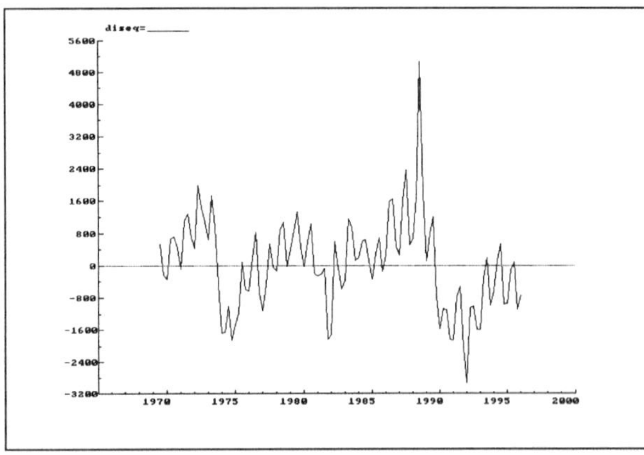

Figure 6.1. Net Excess Housing Demand

Source: Meen (2000)

The simplest version of the stock/flow model of Chapter 3 implies that, in the long run, prices rise in line with construction costs - at least if supply is perfectly elastic. But construction costs typically play a larger role in US than in UK models. Indeed, in the UK, house prices and construction costs do not cointegrate (as discussed in Chapters 2 and 3). However, in Abraham and Hendershott across thirty US cities, the short run elasticity of house price appreciation with respect to construction costs is 0.35, although the elasticity is notably higher for inland cities (0.57) compared with coastal cities (0.16). Indeed the latter is not significant. Abraham and Hendershott (1996) suggest that the differences arise from supply constraints, arising either from limited land availability or from costly local building requirements. Both of these will affect the price elasticity of supply and changes the relationship between prices and construction costs in the long run. Outside the USA, Hort (1998), finds a long-run elasticity of prices with respect to construction costs of 0.5 across twenty Swedish urban areas. Internationally, there appears little evidence that the elasticity is close to unity.

There is little doubt that the income elasticities of house prices in table 6.1 are high by most international standards. Hort finds a value of approximately one for Sweden, Kosonen (1997) a value of 1.4 in Finland. However the results of Malpezzi (1999), using a panel of 133 MSAs between 1979 and 1996 in the US, are particularly interesting. Malpezzi models the ratio of house prices to incomes, but cannot reject a unit root in the ratio. However, the ratio is strongly related to the regulatory environment - those areas with stringent regulations have the highest price to income ratios. This would certainly be consistent with the high elasticities found in UK work. Furthermore in a study of Thailand, Korea and Malaysia, Mayo and Sheppard (1996) find income elasticities 0.1, 2.7 and 2.8 respectively. They argue that these variations are consistent with differences in the degree of development control in the three countries. Since controls are strongest in Korea, the estimated income elasticity of house prices should be the highest. In Thailand, controls are limited, so that income changes will be reflected primarily in output rather than price changes. We return to this issue in the stock-flow models of the next section.

The relative importance of speculative bubbles and fundamentals in determining price changes is clearly an important issue. In equation (6.6) one interpretation of the coefficient γ_1 is as a "bubble-builder" and γ_3 as a "bubble-burster". For the US, Abraham and Hendershott find speculative behaviour to have been important in the coastal regions only. One problem, however, is that these coefficients are consistent with other forms of non-speculative behaviour. In the UK, rather less emphasis has been placed on bubbles. As we saw in Chapter 3, explanations for booms and busts do not need to rely on speculation. Volatility is consistent with the presence of credit constraints and transactions costs. Muellbauer and Murphy (1997) argue for the existence of a housing market "frenzy" which arises from lumpy transactions costs, generating thresholds or hurdles. At times of rapid house price growth, more households are able to cross the hurdle, which feeds the boom. Similarly, in a slump, more households are restrained by transactions costs and credit constraints. However, overall, the jury is still out.

Finally in this section, we return to the issue of aggregation over households. In a world of increasing income dispersion, are aggregate studies of housing demand or house prices meaningful any more? During the eighties, the dispersion of wage income between rich and poor households widened sharply. Similar trends have been observed in the USA and Australia amongst other countries. We saw in Chapter 5 that the incomes of young households have fallen relative to older cohorts during the nineties. Given that the young are the prime first-time buyer groups, from Chapter 4, changes in income trends would be expected to lead to a break down of an aggregate relationship. But we have already seen in table 6.4 that "traditional" house price equations appear to have broken down in the nineties. Meen and Andrew (1998) ask whether the aggregate relationship can be rescued by the inclusion of variables capturing changes in income dispersion.

The income distribution is not the only reason why the aggregate relationship may have changed - some have pointed to tax changes and others to changes in the riskiness of housing as an asset during the nineties. In a lower inflation environment, it becomes less necessary to hold housing as a hedge. Nevertheless, it is hard to believe that changes to labour market conditions are not a part of the story. Although only a proxy measure of dispersion, Meen and Andrew find that the ratio of wage income to total personal disposable income can explain post-1990 price behaviour. Over this period, the wage share fell sharply, but investment income is, disproportionately, received by the older age groups. This change would be expected to reduce house price growth.

There are clearly other variables that potentially capture rather better the complex changes that have taken place in the labour market, although most are not published regularly on a quarterly basis. Nevertheless, the final column of table 6.4 shows how allowance for dispersion has considerable effects on the results. The term (*WSH)* is significant and has a positive sign. The sign has to be positive because housing demand is expected to be less responsive to changes in investment income than to changes in wages. Since total income already appears in the equation, a rise in the wage share will raise housing demand and house prices. Equation fit improves dramatically relative to the second column (which excludes the variable) and the coefficients are very similar to those in the first, estimated only to 1990. The long-run coefficients are shown in equation (6.7). Therefore, allowing for changes in income dispersion, there is little evidence of any fundamental change in UK housing markets during the nineties - the changes are in labour markets rather than in housing.

6.3 Stock-Flow Models of Prices and Construction

Based on the Poterba (1984) framework, we constructed, in Chapter 3, a stock-flow model of house prices and construction. DiPasquale and Wheaton (1994) provide an alternative example. We saw how demand shocks would typically lead to overshooting in prices and to a gradual adjustment towards long-run equilibrium as new construction occurred. Amongst the crucial parameters is the price elasticity of supply as it determines both the new equilibrium and the speed of adjustment. With low elasticities, we are more likely to observe sustained real house price changes. Therefore the first question of this section is whether we can explain different international real house price trends in terms of variations in the supply elasticities. The second question concerns cycles. The Poterba rational expectations model did not exhibit cycles. But can we construct empirical models in which cycles occur?

We attempt, therefore, to estimate a model which is consistent with the stock-flow framework but which allows for cycles through the model dynamics. The model is taken from Meen (2000) and is estimated as a vector error correction model (VECM) covering four variables - house prices, housing activity, construction costs and interest rates. The starting point is a housing starts equation, written as (6.9). A related model for the UK commercial property market has recently been estimated by Nanthakumaran *et al* (2000).

$$st_t = \gamma_0 + \gamma_1(ph)_t + \gamma_2(RSH)_t + \gamma_3(\cos t)_t + \varepsilon_t \qquad (6.9)$$

where :

ST	=	number of private sector housing starts
PH	=	index of house prices
RSH	=	short-term interest rate
COST	=	index of construction costs

lower case denotes logarithms of the variables.

Clearly the four variables could simply be estimated together as a VAR, imposing no identifying restrictions and would not necessarily have an interpretation as a starts equation. But relating construction to prices, interest rates and construction costs is fairly typical of the international literature - see, for example, Whitehead (1971, 1974, 1975), Hadjimatheou (1976), Tsoukis and Westaway (1994), Topel and Rosen (1988) - and this literature provides useful identifying restrictions. Loosely, construction is related to profitability. Note that the rate of change of prices will also be captured through the dynamics of the VECM. The role of the rate of change was explored in Chapter 3. In addition, both Topel and Rosen (1988) and Tsoukis and Westaway (1994) show that equation (6.9) can be nested within an intertemporal optimisation framework, reflecting the role of adjustment costs and construction lags, which introduce further dynamics into the relationship.

In general terms, we can define an *initial* model[15] (6.10), based on equation (6.9), set out as a VECM;

[15] The model is extended later by examining the relationship between house prices and transactions as well.

$$\Delta X_t = \Gamma_1 \Delta X_{t-1} + \cdots + \Gamma_{k-1} \Delta X_{t-k+1} + \psi D_t + \Pi X_{t-k} + \varepsilon_t \qquad (6.10)$$

where $\Pi = \alpha\beta'$ and $\beta' X_t$ are the cointegrating vectors. X_t is an (n = 4) dimensional vector consisting of $X_t = [st_t, ph_t, \cos t_t, RSH_t]$ and D_t is a vector of deterministic dummy variables, $D_t = [Q_1, Q_2, Q_3, 1]$. Q_i are seasonal dummies. ε_t = Niid $(0, \Sigma)$.

But since the VECM is based on the variables in the starts equation, (6.9), there is no reason why any house price equation derived from the VECM should be consistent with those estimated in the previous section. Income, for example, does not appear in the VECM, but is one of the most important variables in table 6.4. The only way in which we can estimate a model based on the VECM, which is consistent with the results in table 6.4, is if house prices can be treated as weakly exogenous in the system. In this case, a joint model of starts, interest rates and construction costs can be estimated conditional on the level of house prices which, in turn, can be taken from table 6.4. But this exogeneity restriction is always likely to be valid in a stock-flow framework. Since the price equation reflects demand for the housing stock, new construction has only a limited effect back onto prices. In the stock-flow framework, the introduction of a price equation from table 6.4 has no effect on the conditional distributions for construction, interest rates and costs as long as the weak exogeneity restriction is valid.

In fact, the argument can be pushed further. We also expect interest rates to be weakly exogenous since interest rates are set with much broader objectives in mind than just the housing market. Therefore, having tested the weak exogeneity assumptions, the final model becomes a joint model for starts and construction costs conditional on house prices and interest rates. But, crucially, none of this is assumed in advance but falls out from the initial VECM. Finally, notice also that, in principle, the stock-flow approach mitigates the problems of simultaneity of house prices, identification and endogeneity of construction costs, raised as major issues by Pryce (1999) and other authors. Here house prices are weakly exogenous, identification conditions can be imposed on the system and starts and construction costs can be jointly modelled.

Since the weak exogeneity restrictions turn out to be valid as expected[16], the final joint model for starts and construction costs conditional on the other variables is shown in table 6.5. Neither equation shows evidence of misspecification from the summary diagnostic statistics in terms of autocorrelation (AR), heteroscedasticity (ARCH), or non-normality (Normality) of the residuals. Notice also that no contemporaneous variable enters the *cost* equation. Construction costs react with a lag to developments

[16] See Meen (2000) for further details.

in the other housing market variables. But contemporaneous difference terms in prices and interest rates do now appear in the starts equation. This change from (6.10) arises from the fact that we are now conditioning the system on these two variables.

Table 6.5. Joint Model of Housing Starts and Construction Costs

Δ st			**Δ cost**		
variable	**coefficient**	**t-value**	**variable**	**coefficient**	**t-value**
$\Delta\, st_{-2}$	0.210	2.4	$\Delta\, st_{-1}$	0.029	2.2
$ECMA_{-1}$	-0.416	-5.3	$\Delta\, cost_{-1}$	-0.128	-1.3
$\Delta\, ph$	1.510	3.8	$\Delta\, cost_{-2}$	-0.247	-2.4
$\Delta\, ph_{-1}$	0.762	1.8	$ECMB_{-1}$	0.0024	7.5
$\Delta\, RSH$	-0.019	-1.9	$\Delta\, ph_{-1}$	0.115	2.1
constant	4.331	5.0	$\Delta\, ph_{-2}$	0.174	3.2
			constant	0.666	7.6
SEE = 0.108			SEE = 0.016		

ECMA, ECMB are two cointegrating equations, defined as:

$ECMA = (st) + 0.0403\,(RSH) - 0.326\,(ph) + 0.326\,(cost)$

$ECMB = (RSH) - 16.05\,(st) + 24.05\,(ph) - 45.34\,(cost)$

Both equations include dummy variables.

Diagnostic Statistics:

$\Delta\, st$	: AR $F(5, 57)$	=	1.2953
$\Delta\, cost$	: AR $F(5, 57)$	=	2.0127
$\Delta\, st$	: Normality χ^2_2	=	2.4726
$\Delta\, cost$	: Normality χ^2_2	=	0.61658
$\Delta\, st$	: ARCH $F(4, 54)$	=	1.0671
$\Delta\, cost$	: ARCH $F(4, 54)$	=	1.2071

The key results are, first, from the cointegrating vector, denoted *ECMA,* that the long-run price elasticity of supply is 0.326. Clearly this is very low, but is similar to that found by other studies. Some UK studies have found evidence of non-linear supply elasticities, which may even be backward-bending (see Pryce 1999). Pryce suggests that non-linearities are consistent with option pricing models, where there are advantages to builders from holding land off the market, even at times of rising house prices if the value of vacant land is even greater. As might be expected, he finds that the supply elasticity appears to be smaller in booms (average elasticity 0.58) than in slumps (1.03). Mayo and Sheppard (1992) provide a theoretical justification in terms of a model of stochastic development controls. But, as noted in

Chapter 3, empirical studies suggest that price elasticities are noticeably higher in many other countries. Topel and Rosen (1988) find an elasticity of approximately three in the USA; using a rather different methodology, as noted above, Mayo and Sheppard (1996) compare elasticities in Malaysia, Thailand and Korea. They show that different regulatory environments have strong effects on supply. Malpezzi (1996) suggests that the long-run UK supply elasticity on post-war data is between 0.9 and 2.1, but pre-war (when controls were weaker) the elasticity was between 4 and 7. For the USA, his comparable findings are between 9 and 16 and 11 and 18 respectively. Whatever the precise figures, it appears clear that the supply elasticity in the UK is low by international standards. However, although this is certainly consistent with the Mayo and Sheppard (1996) view of the world, we cannot necessarily conclude that regulation is the only factor in operation. Labour skill shortages, for example, also engender weak supply responses (Ball 1996).

Second, although the level of prices seems to have only a limited impact, the *rate of change* has a strong effect. From table 6.5, summing the two price coefficients, the elasticity is in excess of two. This is consistent with both the DiPasquale and Wheaton (1996) and Stein (1995) findings discussed in Chapter 3. The former concentrates on the role of vacancies, whereas the latter highlights credit market constraints. Whatever the explanation, since the rate of change of prices is highly volatile, this will mean that housing construction will also fluctuate strongly.

Finally, note that the error correction coefficient in the construction cost equation is 0.0024, although highly significant. The sign and size of the coefficient arises from the nature of the normalisation in the equation. Under the more usual normalisation on costs, the coefficient is –0.1, which is more intuitive.

We are now in a position to provide an explanation of differing long-run real house price trends, because we now have a consistent model of house prices (the final column of table 6.4) and construction activity (table 6.5). The two together constitute a stock-flow model in the Poterba tradition (but not employing rational expectations). In line with most stock-flow models, for the moment, we ignore the construction cost equation and costs are treated as exogenous. Costs are re-endogenised when cycles are considered below.

The argument is that the overall properties of real prices and construction activity depend on both equations. For example, the fact that the elasticity of house prices with respect to incomes (table 6.4) appears to be very high by international standards does not necessarily imply that the price-income ratio rises over time. Indeed many city commentators have argued that there is a constant long-run price-income ratio in the UK. The trend also depends on the supply response (table 6.5).

Although some of this could be demonstrated through a standard impulse response exercise on the prices and starts equations, the economics of the system probably becomes clearer in the following exercise designed to demonstrate the importance of the supply elasticity. Meen (1998) carries out a series of simulations to show how the long-run income elasticity of house prices changes *in a system* under alternative values of the supply elasticity ranging from 0.3 to 10.0. The price equation is as in table 6.4. Figure 6.2 shows the implications.

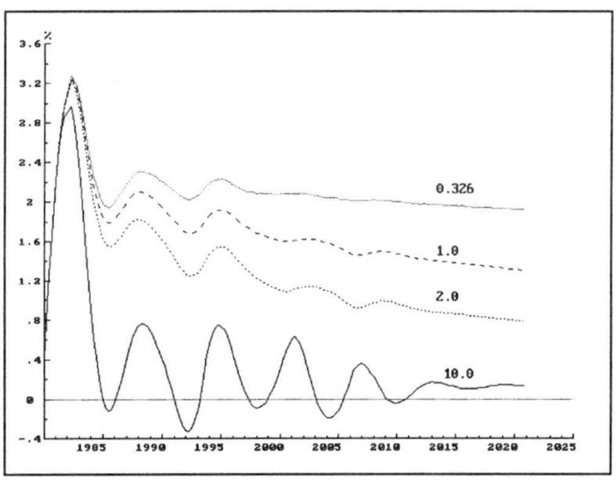

Figure 6.2. Effect on House Prices of Different Supply Elasticities

Source: Meen (1998)

Suppose income in the economy rises permanently by an extra one percent per annum. What would be the expected effect on house prices and construction? As in Chapter 3, if housing supply is perfectly inelastic, then the increase in demand would be choked-off by higher prices. At the other extreme, if supply were fully elastic, output would increase to the point at which prices were unchanged. Under the estimated supply elasticity of 0.326 in table 6.5, we are close to the first position so that new housing supply has little feed-back effect on prices (through changes in the housing stock) and the long-run system income elasticity is close to the original single equation elasticity of 2.4.

Unsurprisingly, higher supply elasticities induce lower long-run income elasticities of house prices; a value of 2.0 induces an income elasticity of house prices of approximately unity. To stress the point, the view that the ratio of house prices to income is constant in the long run is not only determined by the *direct* estimate of the coefficient on income in the house price equation, but is a *systems* property depending also on the effect of the housing stock on prices and the price elasticity of new housing supply. Although the long-run effect of the stock on prices in equation (6.7) appears large at -1.7, if the supply response is weak, then this has little impact as an "automatic stabiliser".

A supply elasticity of ten is sufficient to reduce the income elasticity of prices to approximately zero, the condition we expect to hold if supply is perfectly elastic. But a value of ten is well outside the range of UK findings, although as we saw above it is not outside the range found for other countries.

These simulations suggest that differing real house price movements across countries can be consistent with the same underlying theoretical model. Real house price trends are determined by the system and stronger real trends in, say, the UK than in the US are consistent with weaker supply responses. By itself, the fact that we find a high income elasticity of house prices in the UK is not an indication of stronger long-run real house price trends. Instead the critical factor is the international variation in supply elasticities.

Now, suppose we omit the housing stock term from the house price equation in the first column of table 6.4[17]. This removes the feedback term and any influence from supply. Note that many US empirical price studies do not condition on the housing stock. But within the structure of our model, this is a misspecification and we expect the income elasticity now to be biased downwards. Equation (6.11) shows the long-run solution to the re-estimated equation, which indeed conforms to our priors. The income elasticity is now much closer to unity – implying an approximately constant price-income ratio. The results are also closer to those found internationally. By removing the feedback term, the single equation attempts to proxy the properties of the two-equation system. But since it is only a proxy, the fit is noticeably poorer than in table 6.4. The equation standard error rises to 1.62% from 1.49%, if the stock is excluded. The moral is that systems properties matter, whereas single equation results can be highly misleading.

$$\ln(g) = -16.12 - 0.014(M) + 0.29\ln(W) + 1.21\ln(RY) - 0.045(UCC) \tag{6.11}$$

We can now consider cyclical properties of the model. Even in the two-equation model, figure 6.2 shows considerably volatility in response to a

[17] For the UK, Holly and Jones (1997) estimate equations both including and excluding the housing stock.

constant change in incomes. Prices exhibit a degree of overshooting and the adjustment to the long-run equilibrium is by no means monotonic. Notice that, as the long-run supply elasticity increases, so does the volatility. This is not an accident and arises from the term in the rate of change of house prices in the starts equation. If starts are dependent on credit markets, then they are strongly affected by house price movements but, under high supply elasticities, the feedback from supply to prices is greater. The combination of the two generates greater amplitude in both prices and construction. Therefore it does not appear to be the case that cycles are caused only by factors exogenous to the housing industry, but are an intrinsic feature of the sector although, as Chapter 9 shows, policy can certainly contribute to cycles. As a precursor to Chapter 9, it is useful to turn to the full four variable model, consisting of house prices, starts, construction costs and interest rates.

We already have an equation for construction costs but, in equation (6.10), the VECM consisted of four variables, including interest rates (*RSH*). We found that, unsurprisingly, interest rates were weakly exogenous. In Chapter 9, we shall consider the impact of alternative monetary policy rules but, for the moment, assume that interest rates are derived from the (unsatisfactory) equation estimated in the VECM. The key feature of equation (6.12) is that interest rates are determined only by housing market variables[18]. Both increases in house prices and housing construction raise interest rates. However, since interest rates are weakly exogenous, neither cointegrating vector enters the equation and (6.12) is specified only in first differences.

$$\begin{aligned}\Delta RSH &= 1.693(\Delta st)_{-1} + 1.481(\Delta st)_{-2} + 0.148(\Delta RSH)_{-1} \\ &+ 5.424(\Delta ph)_{-1} + 9.574(\Delta ph)_{-2} - 0.437\end{aligned} \tag{6.12}$$

Source: Meen (2000)

The easiest way to demonstrate the cyclical features of the industry in a consistent framework is to consider the effect of an unexpected one-off 5% house price shock and to show how the four equations adjust over time to a new equilibrium. In a fully efficient market, price changes would be uncorrelated over time, but we can see from the presence of lags that this is not the case. The simulation is run from a base in which the model has settled to its long-run equilibrium. This can be important because of the

[18] See King (2000) for a description of how house prices are only one of a large number of economic variables taken into account by the Bank of England in setting interest rates.

presence of non-linearities, which induce a degree of base dependency. As in Evans and Reichlin (1994), this is achieved by running the model over the future so that the cycles in the model "drop out" leaving only the long-run trend growth path for each variable. In practice this means that the simulation is run over a period to 2020, a period of sufficient length to show the long-run effects for all the variables. The time period itself, however, has no intrinsic significance, given that the variables are on trend. Each graph is expressed in terms of deviations from the base scenario.

Figure 6.3 shows the effects on the four variables. The model has a well-defined equilibrium in which one-off house price shocks have *no* long-run effect on any variable, but the model exhibits noticeable short-run cycles including overshooting. Damped cyclical behaviour would appear to be a minimum requirement of the model. Notice, however, that construction costs do not exhibit the same cyclical behaviour as the other variables. This conforms broadly to historical experience; construction costs certainly have experienced cycles, but not to the same extent as house prices. This is one reason why profitability in the construction industry varies over the cycle. If costs varied to the same extent as prices, there would be no necessary reason why starts should exhibit cycles. Furthermore, in this model, the price shock induces changes in interest rates. Other things equal, a rise in the pressure of demand for housing induces an increase in interest rates. This, of course, ignores external factors that, in practice, affect the setting of interest rates - in particular general inflation targets. The role of inflation targets in contributing to cycles is explored further in Chapter 9. However, here, the simulation, set in a fully consistent model, suggests that both construction costs and interest rates have a role to play in housing market dynamics.

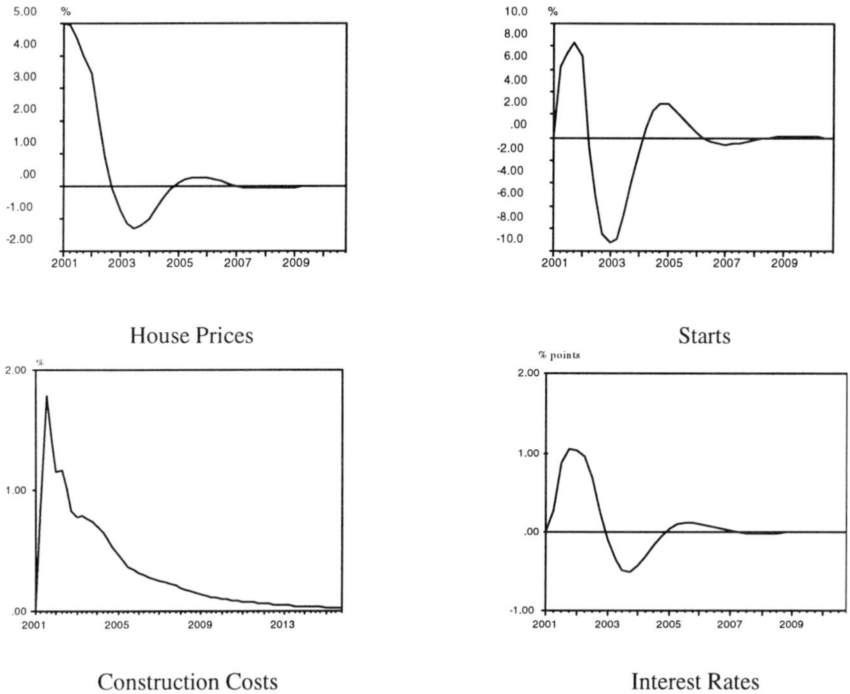

Figure 6.3. Effect of a One-Off 5% House Price Shock

6.4 House Prices and Transactions

We saw in Chapter 3 that, across a range of countries, house prices and property transactions are positively correlated whereas, in an efficient market, no correlation would be expected. There are a number of possible explanations, but the impact of credit constraints has again proved a popular line of enquiry. Ortalo-Magné and Rady (1999, 2000), for example, argue that, at times of rising house prices, credit constraints become less binding and hence transactions rise. They also argue that the exceptional rise in transactions in the UK in the late eighties was primarily caused by financial market deregulation, which reduced downpayment constraints. They suggest that adjustment to the new financial environment has now been completed and, hence, transactions have returned to a more normal level.

Although models of this type provide useful insights, they cannot necessarily explain fully the lower levels of transactions in the nineties. In particular, structural changes in housing or labour markets, which we have already discussed, may have changed the long-run trend. Notably, lower rates of new household formation and the recent tendency of a higher proportion of younger age cohorts to move to the private rented sector, reduce owner-occupier transactions. Ford and Seavers (2000) document in detail changing attitudes to moving and to debt holding in the UK. Their work shows that the proportion of 16-24 year olds expressing a preference for owner-occupancy in the short term has fallen very sharply since the mid eighties. Their survey evidence suggests that the main reason why this age group is less keen on owner-occupancy is strongly related to household financial factors.

But first-time buyers are only a part of the market and, in fact, the boom in transactions in the late eighties was primarily amongst existing buyers. Therefore we need a model that captures the behaviour of both groups. At the aggregate level, section 6.2 showed how changing income dispersion can be captured and we generated a measure of housing market disequilibrium (figure 6.1) that made an attempt to take dispersion into account. One of the aims of this section is to estimate a joint model of prices and transactions in which both are functions of the degree of market disequilibrium. As in Berkovec and Goodman (1996), the propositions that (*i*) transactions change before prices in response to any shock and (*ii*) prices exhibit permanent changes, but transactions only temporary variation, can be tested. This can be seen as an extension to the bivariate model of prices and transactions estimated in Chapter 2. We will find, as expected, that this model is not adequate to explain fully the nineties. Therefore, using a different approach we, then, attempt to quantify some of the factors that caused lower rates of young household formation.

In order to analyse the response of house prices and transactions to shocks, it is convenient to use the Berkovec and Goodman search model introduced in Chapter 4. In this model, the relationship between prices and transactions arises from an asymmetry on the part of buyers and sellers in response to shocks. If for example interest rates rise, typically, sellers are slower to revise their expectations of the equilibrium price downwards than buyers. As a result, the volume of transactions changes before prices. But the fall in transactions implies that the average time that a property remains on the market rises and this acts as an incentive to sellers to reduce prices. Therefore, initially, prices and transactions are positively correlated. Over time, as prices fall to a new equilibrium, transactions are restored to their former position. The model can be seen as an alternative to explanations based on credit market constraints, but relies on asymmetries in behaviour, which not everyone finds attractive.

At the empirical level, Berkovec and Goodman examine the correlation by modelling the rates of change in real house prices, ($\Delta\ln(g)$), and in transactions, ($\Delta\ln(TR)$), as a function of demand indicators:

$$\Delta \ln(g)_t = \alpha_0 + \alpha_1 \Delta \ln Y_{t-1} + \alpha_2 \Delta \ln Y_{t-2} + \alpha_3 \Delta i_{t-1} + \alpha_4 \Delta i_{t-2} + \alpha_5 \Delta \ln(g)_{t-2} + \alpha_6 \Delta CS_{t-1} + \alpha_7 \Delta CS_{t-2} + \varepsilon_{1t} \quad (6.13)$$

$$\Delta \ln(TR)_t = \beta_0 + \beta_1 \Delta \ln Y_t + \beta_2 \Delta \ln Y_{t-1} + \beta_3 \Delta i_t + \beta_4 \Delta i_{t-1} + \beta_5 \Delta \ln(g)_{t-1} + \beta_6 \Delta CS_t + \beta_7 \Delta CS_{t-1} + \varepsilon_{2t} \quad (6.14)$$

$\Delta \ln Y$ represents the percentage change in real disposable income, Δi the change in the nominal mortgage interest rate, and ΔCS the change in consumer sentiment. In fact, Berkovec and Goodman only model the transactions equation in this form - the price equation is rather simpler. But it is useful to write the joint model of prices and transactions as a more general system, allowing the explanatory variables in the house price equation to have longer lags, reflecting the observation that turnover rates appear to be more responsive to changes in housing demand than house prices. The lags in the model are consistent with a non-uniform and non-instantaneous adjustment in the formation of house price expectations but, at best, the relationship to the underlying theory is indirect. Note that the model might be set up as a VECM as in the previous section. Hort (2000) explicitly utilises a three dimensional VAR (the level of house prices, the number of sales and the mortgage interest rate) in her model of the Swedish housing market. She identifies the structural model by imposing a priori exogeneity restrictions. The restrictions involve the assumptions that: (*i*) the nominal after-tax interest rate is weakly exogenous to nominal house prices and the level of sales; and (*ii*) the level of sales is weakly exogenous to house prices.

There are two additional points to be noted from the empirical literature. First, the question of variable differencing arises; in (6.13) and (6.14) prices and transactions are both specified as rates of change. In the Hort model, both variables are in levels. In figure 2.6 the rate of change of prices was graphed with the level of transactions. The choice matters; empirically the orders of integration will differ and have to be consistent in estimation. If real prices are stationary in differences, but transactions are stationary in levels then this might be one indicator of the appropriate dimensionality. In addition, the dimensions have to be consistent with the underlying theory. We cannot test the view that prices are affected permanently, but transactions only temporarily unless the variables are so scaled.

Finally, note that any empirical results are likely to be consistent with more than one hypothesis. Equations (6.13) and (6.14) are consistent with a number of alternative interpretations. The lagged percentage change in real house prices could represent factors such as liquidity constraints, consumer expectations of a capital gain under backward looking expectations, changes to user costs, or could be interpreted as evidence of speculative behaviour, especially if the variable measuring consumer sentiment fails to capture feelings sufficiently about the state of the housing market. It, thus, confounds various effects that may not necessarily act in the same direction, and leads to problems in its interpretation and measurement.

Nevertheless, consider an extension to the bivariate model in Chapter 2 set out as equation (6.15). In this version, transactions are normalised on the size of the housing stock as an appropriate scalar.

$$\begin{bmatrix} \gamma_{11}(L) & \gamma_{12}(L) \\ \gamma_{21}(L) & \gamma_{22}(L) \end{bmatrix} \begin{bmatrix} \Delta \ln(g) \\ \Delta \ln(TR/H) \end{bmatrix} = \begin{bmatrix} \alpha_1 \\ \alpha_2 \end{bmatrix} [\ln(diseq)_{t-1}] + \begin{bmatrix} \varepsilon_1 \\ \varepsilon_2 \end{bmatrix} \qquad (6.15)$$

where $\gamma_{ij}(L)$ are lag polynomials.

In this general form, both prices and transactions respond to housing market disequilibrium, (ln *diseq*) defined in figure 6.1. The joint model is estimated by FIML, treating (ln *diseq*) as weakly exogenous, over the sample period 1969(4) to 1996(1). The first two columns of table 6.6 present the results of the final specification, imposing data-validated restrictions on the general model. We return to the final column below. The important results are:

- the measure of housing market disequilibrium is significant in both equations. Therefore in contrast to a model of perfect price adjustment, *both* variables adjust to shocks.
- In the dynamics, the price equation exhibits short-run positive autocorrelation with some evidence of longer-term mean reversion. This feature of the bivariate model in Chapter 2 remains. Of course, the disequilibrium term also ensures mean reversion.
- From the adjustment coefficients, transactions (0.391) adjust more rapidly than real house prices (0.178) to shocks.
- Although transactions appear to have no impact on the dynamics of house price inflation, price inflation affects transactions. In fact, the negative coefficient aids the return to equilibrium in transactions following any shock.
- Although not shown in the table, a dummy variable is included in the transactions equation after 1990. This approximates the reduction in the

turnover rate in the nineties. Although this, obviously, does not provide any explanation, statistically it is necessary.[19]

Table 6.6. Joint Model of House Prices and Transactions

Variable	$\Delta\ln(g)$	$\ln(TR/H)$	$\ln(TR/H)$
$\Delta\ln(g)_{-1}$	0.305 (3.0)	-	-
$\Delta\ln(g)_{-2}$	0.252 (2.4)	-	-
$\Delta\ln(g)_{-3}$	0.044 (0.4)	-	-
$\Delta\ln(g)_{-4}$	-0.192 (2.0)	-1.012 (3.8)	-1.036 (3.9)
$\Delta\ln(g)_{-5}$	-0.120 (1.4)	-	-
$\ln(TR/H)_{-1}$	-	0.716 (9.8)	0.717 (9.9)
$\ln(diseq)_{-1}$	0.178 (4.1)	0.391 (2.8)	0.534 (3.2)
constant	-0.020 (3.4)	-1.038 (4.0)	-1.039 (4.1)
$\ln(diseq)^3_{-1}$			-4.645 (1.5)
Equation standard error	0.019	0.071	0.070

Equations include seasonal dummies

t-values in brackets

In order to illustrate the properties of the system, suppose that interest rates (a variable common to both the Berkovec and Goodman and Hort models) rise permanently by one percentage point. The rise in the interest rate leads to a reduction in the demand for housing. Given inertia, excess supply occurs which, our model predicts, leads in the short-run not only to a fall in house prices, but also to a reduction in the volume of transactions. Both effects are transmitted through the disequilibrium term. Figure 6.4 charts the movements of each series in response to the shock. Each period is expressed as a quarter. Initially, as expected under inertia, both variables change in the same direction, but transactions change more quickly than prices; transactions reach a minimum point at an earlier stage. Each variable exhibits a degree of overshooting, but transactions return to their base values, whereas prices remain permanently lower, in line with the theoretical predictions. Demand changes have a permanent effect on prices, but no effect on transactions.

[19] If we did not include the dummy, the data would suggest that the dependent variable should be specified in differences. This would be an incorrect conclusion. Rather we have a stationary variable in levels with a possible structural change.

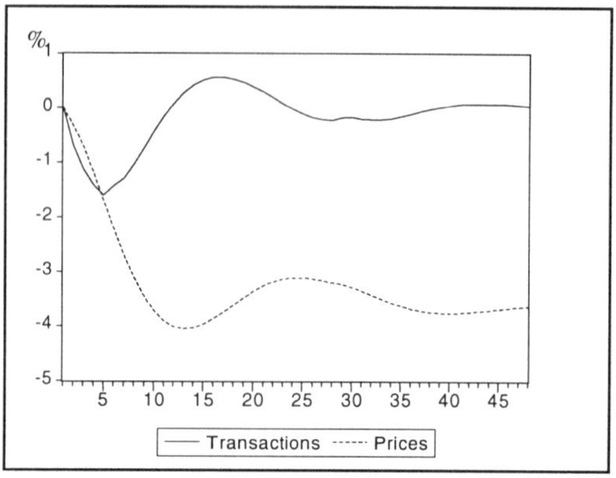

Figure 6.4. Prices and Transactions

(percentage changes in response to an interest rate rise)

In principle, one possible reason for the low levels of transactions in the nineties is the existence of non-linearities. Both Hendry (1984) and Muellbauer and Murphy (1997) point to the existence of "frenzy" effects and model these by the inclusion of cubic terms in their house price equations. The idea is that if markets are a long way from equilibrium, they will adjust more rapidly. But such non-linearities may induce multiple equilibria (see Stein 1995); the nineties might represent a new lower equilibrium.

In the spirit of the Hendry model, assume the following housing demand function, adapted from Fujita *et al* (1999):

$$\dot{H}^{d} = a_1(H - HSTAR) + a_2(H - HSTAR)^3 \qquad (6.16)$$

The rate of change of housing demand ($\dot{H}^{d}$) adjusts to the deviation between the actual and desired stocks. As above, the same equation could be written in terms of house prices and transactions. Stability conditions depend on the values of the parameters a_1 and a_2. A negative value for a_1 ensures stability around the symmetric equilibrium *HSTAR* whereas the shape of the function is influenced by the value of a_2. (a_1) can be interpreted as an error correction coefficient and, in all our empirical results, we have found stability to hold. If a_2 is negative, then the function is as in figure 6.5a. *HSTAR* represents a stable and unique equilibrium at which demand is unchanging and we can see that point (*a*) which is further away from equilibrium than (*b*) has a steeper slope, representing a more rapid rate of change. The other roots of the function are given by;

$$H = HSTAR \pm \sqrt{-a_1 / a_2} \tag{6.17}$$

If both a_1 and a_2 are negative, then these roots are complex and have no ready economic interpretation. Figure 6.5a is consistent with both Hendry's and Muellbauer and Murphy's results (although expressed in terms of house prices rather than housing demand).

But suppose a_2 is positive; from (6.17) there are now three real roots and the graph appears as in figure 6.5b[20]. *HSTAR* is still a stable root, but there are in addition two unstable roots. It is, therefore, possible that if the variables become too far away from equilibrium, i.e. beyond the points (x) or (y), the system will never return to the stable equilibrium at *HSTAR*.

The final column of table 6.6 shows the effect of introducing the cubic term into the transactions equation[21]. Note that the signs on the disequilibrium terms have to be reversed for comparability with equation (6.16). The cubic term is barely significantly different from zero, but the coefficient signs are consistent with figure 6.5b, raising the intriguing possibility that there may be multiple equilibria and that the low level of transactions during the nineties reflects a new equilibrium below *HSTAR*. However, although this is a possibility, the evidence is not fully convincing and the post-1990 dummy variable remains significant.

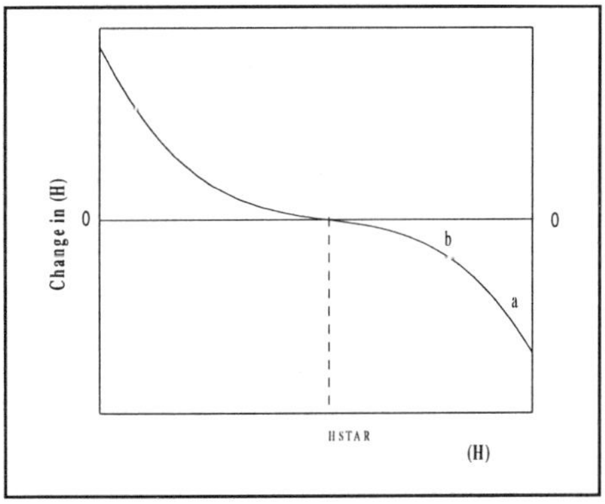

Figure 6.5a. Non-linearities in Demand Adjustment

$a_1 < 0$ and $a_2 < 0$

[20] At least under particular assumed values for the coefficients.

[21] Perhaps surprisingly, given the Hendry and Muellbauer and Murphy results, we found no effect on prices.

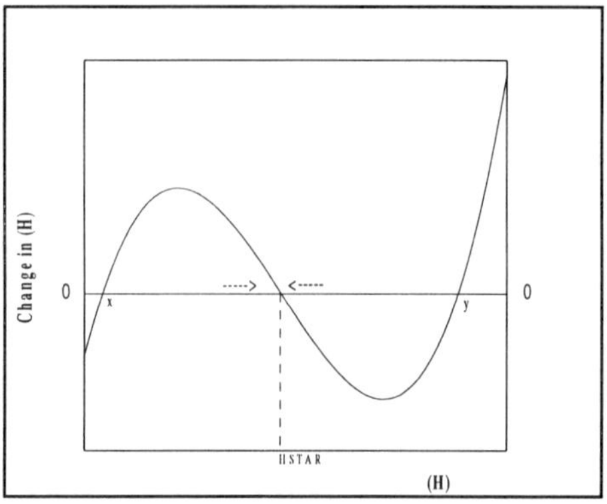

Figure 6.5b. Non-linearities in Demand Adjustment

$a_1 < 0$ and $a_2 > 0$

Although the model can reasonably explain the boom in transactions in the late eighties, the post 1990 dummy still represents the unknown. But at least part of the story is associated with the decline in young household formation and changes in tenure preferences of the young away from owner-occupation. Therefore it is useful to attempt to quantify some of the factors that led to the decline in the rate of young household formation during the nineties, even if we have to use a different modelling framework. In particular, we are interested in the impact of the changes in income dispersion noted in Chapter 5. The estimates come from a dynamic probit study, Andrew and Meen (1999), based on panel data (the British Household Panel Survey) covering the period 1991 to 1996. The method is similar to that used by Ermisch (1999).

The variables chosen to affect household formation are, again, a combination of demographic and economic factors. Amongst the most important are; the individual's age, gender, real gross monthly income, the real housing user cost of capital, the presence of a partner, partner's income and the number of children.

Both demographic and economic factors turn out to be significant. Life-cycle variables - increasing age, the presence of a partner, and the number of children all, unsurprisingly, increase the probability of forming a new household. An increase in housing costs has a negative effect on the propensity to form a household, whereas higher incomes raise the probability[22].

[22] Note, however, that in this study income is not instrumented. The coefficient may well be biased since new household formation and job search may be jointly determined. See Haurin *et al* (1994).

Table 6.7. Random Effects Probit Model: The Probability of New Household Formation

Variable	Coefficient	z-value
Age	0.052	3.1
gender	-0.329	-2.2
income	0.00066	4.2
housing costs	-0.00298	-3.1
existence of a partner	2.891	9.1
partner's income	0.00057	1.5
children	0.485	2.9
constant	-1.272	-2.3

Note that this is only a sample of the regressors included in the study.

The coefficient values are not readily interpretable, but can be translated to look at the marginal effect of a change in each variable on the probability of household formation. The effects are constructed for two reference individuals, (*i*) A 20-year old single female experiencing the sample mean monthly income and housing costs, (*ii*) a 20-year old cohabiting female facing mean housing costs, but each partner receives the mean income. Table 6.8 shows the baseline predicted probabilities of household formation for the reference individuals and associated marginal effects.

Individual 2 is much more likely to form a separate household than 1 - a probability of 99% compared with 20%. The presence of a partner has a very large effect on the probability and, unless economic conditions are particularly weak, couples will form separate households in some tenure.

Table 6.8. Marginal Effects of New Household Formation

Variables	Indiv. (1)	Indiv. (2)
Predicted probability for the reference individual	0.19513	0.99115
Age	0.01468	0.00117
Male	-0.07777	-0.01169
Real Income (£100)	0.01896	0.00148
Notional User Cost (£50)	-0.03838	-0.00425
Partner Present	0.78377	n.a.
Partner Income (£100)	n.a.	0.00129
Sprinc[1*] (£592)	0.79602	n.a.
No. of Children	0.15911	0.00671

1* this is a combined effect of having a partner who also receives the mean income.

The table includes both demographic factors (normally captured by 0,1 dummies, except for age) and economic variables, which are generally continuous. Therefore the table shows the marginal effect of a change in demographic status or a change in income or real housing costs expressed in pounds (units of £100 or £50). At first sight, it appears that the demographic changes dominate. This is in line with the conclusions in Bramley *et al* (1997). The addition of a partner, by itself, raises the probability by 78%. The addition of a child raises the probability of independence for a single female by almost 16%. In general all the effects are larger for the single female. The presence of a partner provides a "cushion".

But the relatively small marginal effects arising from the economic variables, are deceptive. The reference household is assumed to have an income at the sample mean. But the variance is large and a one standard deviation increase in female income would increase the probability of independence by approximately 8% for a single woman and by 0.5% for a woman with a partner. Single individuals are more sensitive to positive income changes since the probabilities are already so high for couples. Similar issues arise with respect to housing costs.

Therefore, the changes in the income distribution experienced in the nineties will have a significant impact on young household formation, particularly amongst single person households. As shown in table 5.3, incomes of the under 25s fell substantially in real terms, whereas incomes of the over 30s rose significantly. But the effect on household formation of the older group will be considerably less than that on the younger group (since the former are more likely already to have partners). Therefore, overall, the rate of new household formation will fall relative to the eighties. Although incomes are unlikely to be the whole story - and the roles of changing demographics, consumer attitudes and credit markets have not been explored - at least part of the fall in housing transactions, therefore, is likely to have been due to changes in the income distribution away from young potential new households.

6.5 Full Models of Housing and the Economy

There are many frameworks within which housing models may be embedded. In Chapter 3, the two-sector growth model of Turnovsky and Okuyama was used. This is an example of one general equilibrium model. Within housing, the micro simulation models of Anas and Arnott (1993, 1994, 1997) are particularly well known. However, in this section, we are concerned with quantitative evidence from aggregate econometric models. In particular, what conclusions can be drawn if the stock-flow model of Section

6.3 is embedded in a wider econometric model? One problem of this approach, however, is that the results are due as much to the properties of the econometric model as to the structure of the housing market model. Nevertheless, drawing on Meen (1995), some points on which there is a reasonable degree of consensus are highlighted. These concern the nature of multipliers and crowding-out - an issue discussed in Chapter 3 at the theoretical level. Housing pressure groups often call for more public funding to be devoted to housing. One of the arguments used is that expenditures raise output and employment in the economy, but is this true?

Table 6.9. Public Housing Investment + £500 million per annum
(percentage differences from base, except where specified as absolute differences)

Year	GDP	Unemployment (000s) (abs.)	Prices	House Prices	Private Starts	Construction Employment (000s) (abs.)
1	0.08	-6.4	0.01	0.03	0.01	5.0
2	0.06	-9.0	0.05	0.06	-0.02	9.5
3	0.04	-5.4	0.09	0.05	-0.07	10.0
4	0.01	-2.2	0.13	0.02	-0.06	10.0

Source: Meen (1995)

As an example, table 6.9 shows the results from simulating the effect of a rise in public sector housing investment of £500 million per annum. Since the short-run effects are not the same as the long-run effects because of inertia, the simulation is conducted over a four-year period, which is sufficient to demonstrate the main impacts. In terms of public investment programmes, this is a large increase. For comparison, the Housing Corporation (the main funder of new social housing in England) capital programme was £642 million in financial year 2000/2001. But although £500 million is a large sum in housing terms, it is not large in proportion to the overall economy. Therefore, the likely impact of public housing for the economy as a whole is often overstated in partial analyses - unless there are indirect effects not considered in standard macro analysis[23]. In table 6.9, the effect on GDP is less than 0.1% even in the first year. By the fourth year, any effect on GDP has almost disappeared, because of forms of crowding-out. Inertia exists not only in housing markets, but also in labour and goods markets. Therefore, in the short run, failure of prices and wages to adjust, allows output to rise. However, as shown in the table, gradually prices start to rise which reduces other forms of private sector expenditure. The effects are reinforced if interest rates rise at higher levels of public indebtedness.

[23] Some of these are considered in Chapter 9.

Although construction employment rises (last column), it is at the expense of employment in other industries. From the second column, although the increased housing expenditures may initially generate positive multipliers - the reduction in unemployment is greater than the increase in construction employment - by the final year, the multiplier is close to zero. The overall fall in unemployment is much less than the rise in construction employment - other industries lose. Finally, note that the rise in public housing may be at the expense of private starts, particularly if interest rates rise.

Overall, therefore, the argument that increased public housing expenditures have positive macroeconomic consequences needs to be treated with some caution, although there may still be a case for extra expenditures in a recession, when the expected price changes are likely to be small. But, as we shall see in Chapter 8, a rather different argument for housing expenditures emerges when spatial factors re-enter the analysis.

Chapter 7

EXPLAINING REGIONAL PATTERNS

7.1 Introduction

One of our themes has been that *aggregate* empirical analysis – typified by much of the work in the last chapter – is often inappropriate in a world of increasing dispersion, both across households and across space. This view is easily testable with regional data since relatively long time series are available at this level. However we saw in Chapter 2 that, in the long run, "regional" trends have not been the same internationally. In the UK, regional prices have moved in a similar manner over time, but this is not true either for the US Census Divisions or the Australian states. Although this could arise simply because the spatial dimensions are not directly comparable, this is probably not the only reason. It appears to be the case that there is no necessary reason why prices should converge across space.

This chapter, therefore, has a number of objectives. First, we review some of the conclusions from the empirical literature on the reasons for regional price and construction differences. This suggests that most of the variation comes from the demand rather than the supply side. But, in our view, some of the conclusions expressed in the literature are not entirely satisfactory. Consequently, second, we establish formally the conditions under which prices converge or diverge. These come directly from the model used in Chapter 4. From these, it can be shown that there is no necessary reason why countries should behave in the same way. Variations can be decomposed into a number of elements, all of which are empirically important. But, third, we concentrate on one component - coefficient heterogeneity between regions. We show how heterogeneity contributes to explaining the ripple effect in the UK. Fourth, we examine the evidence for theories that might explain coefficient heterogeneity. In particular, the role of credit markets is again examined, based on the Stein (1995) model. This suggests that differences in debt gearing around the country contribute to volatility in price movements. Finally, we search for the presence of ripple effects in other countries.

7.2 What Does the Literature Say?

As noted in Chapter 4, the earliest UK study of regional house prices was that by McAvinchey and Maclennan (1982), which explicitly recognised the potential variation in coefficients across space. However, the main stimulus to research was the massive increase in the divide between prices in the South and the North. From Chapter 2, Holmans (1990, 1995) highlighted three central features:

- the geographical percentage differences in house prices are much greater than those in incomes,
- the North/South divide in house prices widened to record levels in the eighties (but narrowed again in the nineties),
- the South appears to lead the house price cycle and its downswing is greater than elsewhere.

These remain the three key features of the data that any UK model of regional house prices must capture. Any equations that fail to model these central features of the data cannot be considered adequate. There are, however, alternative ways in which the features may be modelled - in a purely statistical manner (Chapter 2) and in terms of providing an underlying economic rationale that can explain the observed patterns (Chapter 4). The literature contains examples of both. On the one hand, Muellbauer and Murphy (1994) are concerned with providing behavioural explanations of the three points raised by Holmans. On the other hand, Alexander and Barrow (1994) deal only with the time-series properties of regional house price data, in particular the extent to which they exhibit common trends across the regions.

As noted in Chapter 2, any tendency for regional house prices to change at different rates must, by identity, be caused by *either*;

different changes in the economic influences on house prices - for example, regional incomes may grow at different rates,

or,

differences in the coefficients of the regional house price equations.

Both of these sets of factors play a role in practice, of course, and the relative importance of each may vary over time. We shall have more to say about the distinction in the next section but, broadly, the conclusions of the literature can be classified into one of these two groups. Perhaps, the study that addresses the questions most directly is that by Muellbauer and Murphy (1994). They conclude:

- the geographical percentage difference in house prices is greater than that in incomes, because the elasticity of house prices with respect to incomes is greater than one. This comes as no surprise, given the elasticities found in the last chapter.
- A rise in relative incomes in the South East explains only part of the widening in the eighties. This is augmented by an extrapolative element in expectations so that once prices start to rise in the South East, this will generate even greater increases, widening the gap yet further. The reverse holds in the downturn. In areas contiguous to the South East, particularly the South West and East Anglia, spatial spillovers from the geared rate of return in the South East, generate price increases. Feedback effects from house prices onto regional incomes and consumption growth further reinforce these effects.
- The South East leads the other regions because of the spillover effects. However, because the South East is highly debt geared, changes in interest rates will have their first and strongest effects in the South East. Low interest rates at the current time help to explain why the South East is again leading the recovery.

Under this view of the world, migration is not the major factor leading to the transmission of house price changes through the country. Rather the emphasis is on income differences (although migration may play a role in generating the income differences), backed up by expectational influences, financial market interactions and the effect of differences in debt gearing between the regions.

None of the other studies provides such a comprehensive explanation. Although Giussani and Hadjimatheou (1991) model the ripple effect, their paper concludes that it is difficult "to produce convincing evidence favouring a particular explanation of the ripple effect". They reject differences in regional activity as the major explanation, suggest that differences in the severity of regional land constraints may be a factor (although this is not formally tested) and are doubtful whether migration is quantitatively sufficient to induce the observed price patterns. In their second paper, Giussani and Hadjimatheou (1991a), which is concerned specifically with the North/South divide, the authors are slightly less tentative and suggest that fluctuations result from differences in the speed at which the two regions respond to changes in economic activity. Favourable economic conditions and financial markets have a more immediate effect in the southern regions. Therefore the South will lead the more northern regions. They suggest that speculation and expectations are more important in the southern markets. Giussani and Hadjimatheou's explanation points towards the importance of coefficient heterogeneity.

Ashworth and Parker (1997) reach precisely the opposite conclusion. They argue that the coefficients are relatively homogeneous across the regions so that explanations of house price differences need to be sought in terms of variations in the regressors themselves - in their case mainly regional incomes.

Finally, it is worthwhile summarising Holmans' own explanations of the historical trends. He suggests that the geographical percentage differences in house prices are greater than those in incomes primarily because southern households spend a higher proportion of their incomes in mortgage outgoings. The tendency for house prices to have widened during the eighties can be attributed to differential growth in demand arising from faster increases in population, employment and real incomes, coupled with the failure of housing supply to respond to the differences in demand. The finding that the South leads the house price cycle can be attributed to the demand pattern, arising from changes in interest rates, since mortgages are greater in proportion to incomes in the South. The view coincides with that of Muellbauer and Murphy. Any rise in interest rates is likely to affect the southern regions first. Therefore, low interest rates in the mid eighties led to relative increases in prices in the South and the subsequent increase in interest rates hit the South particularly heavily.

There have been, in the UK, considerable differences in modelling approaches; nevertheless it is useful to draw some conclusions from the literature:

- there is no evidence, on the basis of the existing literature, that regional coefficients exhibit distinct spatial patterns. Coefficients in empirical studies certainly vary regionally, and in some cases to an implausible extent, but the spatial patterns appear to be purely random.
- No formal tests of coefficient homogeneity across the regions have been conducted in any study.
- As in national house price studies, quantitatively, incomes and interest rates are the most important variables explaining house prices, although a wide range of other factors potentially plays a part in the explanation. On the basis of existing work, we cannot reject the view that the income elasticity of house prices is well in excess of unity, in line with national results.
- Existing work does not suggest that housing supply variables such as housing starts are any more important at the regional than the national level.
- Insufficient attention has been paid to the role of demographic factors in most models. This arises from the focus on explaining the increase in the

North/South divide in the late eighties - essentially a short-term phenomenon.

- Most of the equations incorporate terms to capture the ripple effect, usually through forms of spatial lag ranging from the simple to the complex, but none convincingly demonstrates a causal mechanism.

So far we have concentrated heavily on regional demand variation and, indeed, this reflects most of the literature. However, it is possible that variations in prices arise from regional fluctuations in new housing construction. But there is much less empirical evidence on this aspect of the market. A recent study by Pryce (1999), across the English local authorities, finds considerable variation in the price elasticity of supply. For example, in the slump year of 1992, he finds a mean elasticity estimate of 1.03, but a standard deviation of 1.26 and a range of 0.15 to 12.90. However, we might expect more variation between local authorities, where there are bound to be outliers, than regionally. The only regional study, Meen (1996), finds considerable uniformity in elasticities, not only in the long run, but also in the short run. Nevertheless, it does appear to be true – in line with conventional wisdom – that supply elasticities are lower in the South East of England, where planning controls are most stringent. But the study suggested that the elasticities were less than one in all regions, so that demand changes primarily affect prices rather than output[1].

7.3 Convergence and Divergence

In Chapter 4, we considered the deviations of regional house prices from the national average. Equation (4.41) can be rewritten as the following relationship:

$$(Y_i - Y_N) = (\gamma_{0,i} - \gamma_{0,N}) + (\gamma_{1,i} - \gamma_{1,N})X_N + (\gamma_{2,i} - \gamma_{2,N})Z + \gamma_{1,i}(X_i - X_N) + (\varepsilon_i - \varepsilon_N) \tag{7.1}$$

Apart from the error term, regional price changes can be decomposed into three elements:

- a common trend, arising from national price movements.

[1] But remember in the last chapter we found that the rate of change of prices has a strong effect on construction. This is also true for the regions. Therefore, interactions between demand and supply jointly contribute to the generation of short-run price cycles.

- The first three terms on the right hand side; these represent structural differences between regional markets, which are reflected in coefficient heterogeneity in response to common national variables. Regional differences in response to interest rate changes provide an obvious example.
- the last term, which captures regional differences in the determinants – for example, differences in regional income growth rates.

If we wish, equation (7.1) could be expressed as the difference between two regions, e.g. the South and North, rather than in terms of the deviation from the national average; the same relationship still holds.

At this level of generality, there is no reason to assume that the ($Y_i s$) will grow at the same rate. This would require regional incomes to grow at the same rate in the long run and the coefficients to be the same across regions. These are strong conditions and might be expected to be the exception rather than the rule. Comparing the trends in table 2.6, the surprising results are, perhaps, the UK rather than Australia or the USA[2].

Including dynamics, the basic error correction equation – copied from equation (4.43) - becomes:

$$\begin{aligned}\Delta(Y_i - Y_N) &= (\alpha_{0,i} - \alpha_{0,N}) + (\alpha_{1,i} - \alpha_{1,N})\Delta Z + \alpha_{2,i}(\Delta X_i - \Delta X_N) \\ &+ (\alpha_{2,i} - \alpha_{2,N})\Delta X_N - \alpha_{3,i}[(Y_i - Y_N)_{-1} - (\gamma_{0,i} - \gamma_{0,N}) - (\gamma_{1,i} - \gamma_{1,N})X_{N,-1} \\ &- (\gamma_{2,i} - \gamma_{2,N})Z_{-1} - \gamma_{1,i}(X_i - X_N)_{-1}] + (v_i - v_N)\end{aligned} \tag{7.2}$$

As explained in Chapter 4, there is no necessary reason to impose restrictions on the dynamic coefficients, since they have no impact on the long-run movements. However, the existence of spatial coefficient patterns turns out to be particularly interesting.

7.4 Spatial Coefficient Heterogeneity and the Ripple Effect

Typically, estimated regional house price equations are much simpler in structure than their national counterparts. This partly reflects poorer quality data at the lower spatial scale. Income and interest rates are by far the most

[2] Remember, however, Gyourko and Voith (1992), discussed in Chapter 2, who found that national factors were dominant in the determination of US local house prices and also found evidence of growth convergence. Feedback effects across regional US markets are also discussed further below.

common regressors. Fortunately these two variables appear quantitatively to be the most important factors. To these, we add the unemployment rate here as a simple indicator of labour market risk. Assume, therefore, that house prices are determined in the long run by (7.3);

$$ph_N = \gamma_{0,N} + \gamma_{1,N}(R) + \gamma_{2,N}(y_N) + \gamma_{3,N}(up_N) + \varepsilon_N \tag{7.3}$$

where:
ph = index of house prices
y = personal disposable income
R = nominal mortgage interest rate
up = unemployment rate
ε = error term
lower case denotes logarithms

The regional equivalent is (7.4);

$$ph_i = \gamma_{0,i} + \gamma_{1,i}(R) + \gamma_{2,i}(y_i) + \gamma_{3,i}(up_i) + \varepsilon_i \tag{7.4}$$

so that Z=*[R]* and X_i =*[* y_i, up_i*]* and with the exception of *R* all variables are now expressed in logarithms. Note that the variables are defined in nominal terms. Although such models are usually expressed in real terms, in the UK, no explicit regional consumption deflators are regularly published. However, such data as do exist suggest that, excluding housing costs, there is relatively little regional variation in consumer prices.

Including dynamics in an error correction framework and assuming stationarity of regional house price deviations, the equation to be estimated becomes (7.5);

$$\begin{aligned}\Delta(ph_i - ph_N) &= (\delta_{0,i} - \delta_{0,N}) + \delta_{1,i}\Delta(y_i - y_N) \\ &+ \delta_{2,i}\Delta(ph_i - ph_N)_{-1} + \delta_{3,i}\Delta(up_i - up_N) + (\delta_{4,i} - \delta_{4,N})\Delta R \\ &+ (\delta_{5,i} - \delta_{5,N})\Delta y_N + (\delta_{6,i} - \delta_{6,N})\Delta up_N - \delta_{7,i}[(ph_i - ph_N)_{-1} \\ &- \gamma_{2,i}(y_i - y_N)_{-1} - \gamma_{3i}(up_i - up_N)_{-1}] + \mu_i\end{aligned} \tag{7.5}$$

The validity of (7.5) depends on the stationarity assumption. If this does not hold, the *levels* of *R*, y_N and up_N may have to be included. Table 7.1 shows the results of simple ADF tests of the deviations. In each case, the estimates are close to the critical values. Therefore, at most, any trends are weak as we expect if the ripple effect is a valid data representation.

The equations are estimated on annual data covering the period 1973 to 1994. Since these time periods are rather short, we used an initial inspection of the data to group the ten standard regions in Britain into four larger blocs - the South, Midlands, North and Scotland where, as we saw in Chapter 2, house prices have grown at similar rates not only in the long run, but also in the short run. *Within* these blocs, only different fixed effects between the regions are permitted. This allows us to increase the number of observations considerably.

Table 7.1. ADF Tests for Regional House Price Deviations (1970-1994)

Region	**Value of ADF(1)**
North	-2.2
Yorks. & Humberside	-2.9
E. Midlands	-2.9
East Anglia	-2.4
South East	-3.5
South West	-2.7
W. Midlands	-3.0
North West	-2.3
Wales	-2.2
Scotland	-2.7

The equations are estimated as a system of Seemingly Unrelated Regressions (SUR) in order to capture spatial correlation in the error terms. Results are presented in Table 7.2. In the table, data-validated restrictions are imposed on the equations, compared with (7.5), eliminating insignificant terms. However, there are two small changes from (7.5). First, a one-period lag of the change in income is important in some regions as well as the contemporaneous term. Second, rather than using income directly the equation uses consumers' expenditure as a measure of permanent income.

In each of the regions, the error correction coefficient, ($\delta_{7,i}$) in equation (7.5), is highly significant. This introduces a form of spatial lag, in which all regions respond to national trends. Furthermore, in all regions, house prices are highly sensitive to regional consumption (income) deviations. Both of these results are in line with earlier research, but the existing literature pays no attention to spatial patterns in the coefficients. Particularly interesting are the coefficients on the *national* variables - the mortgage interest rate, national consumption and national unemployment. These coefficients determine the short-run differences in regional house prices in response to changes in national factors. The spatial pattern of these coefficients is important in determining which regions change first in response to national shocks. Table 7.2 suggests a distinct spatial pattern. In row (7), for example, the coefficient on national consumption is positive in the South and becomes increasingly negative in a more northerly direction[3] (with the exception of Scotland). This implies that house prices are more responsive to income changes in the South than the national average and less responsive than the average in the North. Notice, however, the results in the final row. The difference between regional and national income in *levels* is only significant in the North. This term implies that the deviation in prices between the North and South is not necessarily stationary. Price differentials can increase in response to differences in regional income levels. Indeed, in Chapter 2, there was some evidence that the North/South divide has increased over time and this is consistent with this coefficient.

Table 7.2. Regional House Prices in Britain. Dependent Variable = $\Delta(ph_i-ph_N)$, 1973-1994

	The South	**The Midlands**	**The North**	**Scotland**
$\Delta(R)$	-	0.0028 (1.2)	0.0096 (2.5)	0.0152 (3.5)
$\Delta(c_i-c_N)$	-	0.341 (3.2)	-	1.928 (6.7)
$\Delta(c_i-c_N)_{-1}$	0.481 (6.3)	0.511 (5.1)	0.555 (3.3)	-
$\Delta(ph_i-ph_N)_{-1}$	-	-	0.390 (6.5)	0.364 (4.5)
$\Delta(up_i-up_N)$	-	-	-0.106 (2.8)	-
$(ph_i-ph_N)_{-1}$	-0.383 (7.4)	-0.226 (5.2)	-0.371 (8.0)	-0.221 (6.2)
$\Delta(c_N)$	0.254 (5.4)	-0.166 (2.8)	-0.428 (4.3)	-
$\Delta(up_N)$	-0.066 (4.5)	-	0.057 (2.9)	0.165 (4.5)
$(c_i-c_N)_{-1}$	-	-	0.409 (3.3)	-

t-values in brackets

The South = South East, (excluding London), East Anglia and the South West.

The Midlands = East Midlands, West Midlands and Wales

The North = Yorkshire and Humberside, North and North West.

Constants are included in all regions to capture fixed effects.

C = consumers' expenditure

PH = index of mix-adjusted second-hand house prices

R = nominal mortgage interest rate

UP = unemployment rate

[3] Note that this does *not* imply that consumption has a negative effect on house prices in the North. The pattern of the coefficients determines the relative effects between the regions. But the common trend ensures that all regions respond positively to income or consumption changes.

Table 7.2a. House Prices - Diagnostic Statistics

Region	R^2	Std. Error	DW
North	0.490	0.043	1.57
Yorks. & Humber	0.676	0.034	1.97
E. Midlands	0.612	0.018	1.84
E. Anglia	0.331	0.030	1.62
South East	0.219	0.028	0.54
South West	0.537	0.020	2.04
W. Midlands	0.247	0.030	0.69
North West	0.512	0.036	1.54
Wales	0.223	0.038	1.20
Scotland	0.667	0.041	2.19

R^2 = coefficient of determination
Std. Error = equation standard error
DW = Durbin-Watson Statistic.

Distinct spatial patterns also emerge in both the interest rate and unemployment coefficients. The interest rate term, (row 1), becomes increasingly positive as we move northwards, signifying that interest rates have a smaller negative effect in the North in the short run. Greater debt gearing in the South - a topic to which we return below - implies that southern households are more vulnerable to changes in interest rates and we might expect, therefore, a quicker response than in the North. For similar reasons, unemployment (row 8) has a larger negative effect in the South. Note, however, that this does not imply that unemployment is more important in the South. Rather, *for a given level of unemployment*, there is a bigger effect on prices in the South.

Table 7.2a presents summary diagnostic statistics. Given that the dependent variables are expressed as regional deviations and have no trend, the R^2s are quite high for most regions. The exceptions are the South East, West Midlands and Wales. This probably indicates that the aggregate groupings are not entirely satisfactory. There may still be some differences between the South East, on the one hand, and East Anglia and the South West, on the other hand, which are not adequately captured by fixed effects. Similarly the categorisation of Wales within the Midlands might be controversial.

Therefore, the key result is that coefficient patterns are spatially non-random, even though no structure has been imposed *a priori*. We can show, as a result, that national shocks such as a change in interest rates will generate a distinct spatial pattern in house price movements in the short run, whereas the common stochastic trend, implied by expressing variables relative to the national average, ensures the existence of a particular form of spatial lag, consistent with observed long-run house price movements. This method of capturing spatial coefficient heterogeneity stands in contrast to the more traditional spatial expansion method discussed in Chapter 4. The extra degrees of freedom arising from the panel allow us to estimate freely the spatial parameters, rather than imposing them on an *a priori* basis. But the spatial coefficient variation also means that standard fixed or random effects models cannot be estimated, since they fall foul of the Pesaran and Smith critique considered in Chapter 4. The only reason that regions can be aggregated into the four larger blocs is because, within these blocs, prices appear to behave in the same manner in both the short and long run.

In order to demonstrate the strength of the spatial coefficient patterns and how they contribute to an explanation of the ripple effect, figure 7.1 looks at the effect on relative regional house prices of raising interest rates permanently by one percentage point. The first panel shows the response of the South relative to the North; the second the South relative to Scotland and the third the North relative to Scotland. Given the common trends, the long-run effects of the change on relative house prices are close to zero over the ten-year period of the simulations. But the short-term effects are very different and reflect the spatial coefficient patterns. A rise in interest rates implies that house prices fall initially in the South relative to both the North and Scotland[4]. Similarly, prices in the North fall relative to Scotland, where owner-occupancy rates are lower. Therefore, the model exhibits a ripple effect. Note that, although the relative price changes look modest in the figures, the assumed one percentage point interest rate rise is small in terms of the volatility in interest rates experienced in the late eighties and early nineties.

Similar spatial patterns emerge with both national unemployment and income shocks (see Meen 1999). In the case of an income change that affects all areas equally, initially, prices in the South rise relative to the North and the Midlands and prices in the Midlands rise relative to the North. Therefore, to emphasise the key point, it is *not* a necessary condition for the ripple effect to occur that regions grow at different rates, although it would be hard to disagree with Holmans (1990) that regional income variations are a part of the full story.

We are now in a position to provide answers to the original questions.

[4] Prices also fall slightly relative to the Midlands, but from table 7.2, the result is not significant.

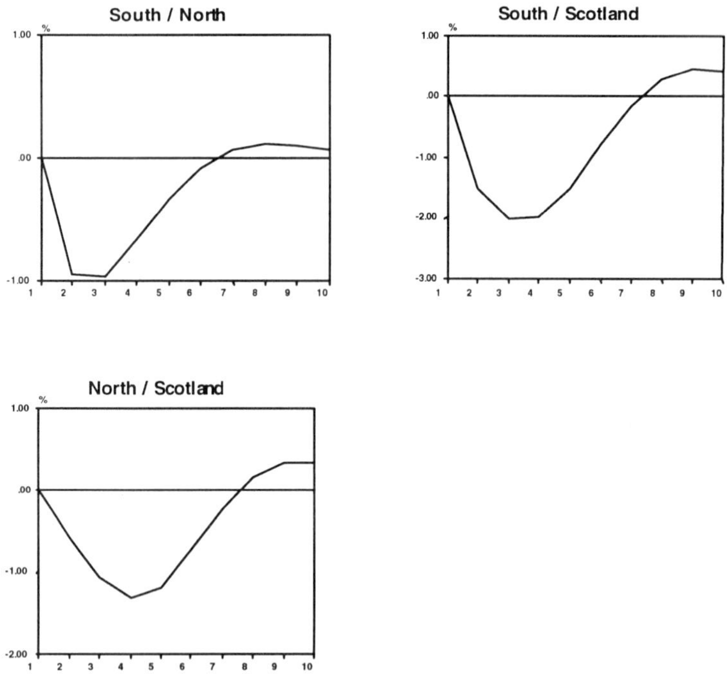

Figure 7.1. House Prices (percentage differences from base)
Interest rates + 1 percentage point

(i) Why has the geographical percentage increase in house prices been greater than that in incomes?

If the income elasticity of house prices is greater than unity, then this result will hold by definition. But high elasticities are not obvious from the coefficients in table 7.2. At first sight the coefficients on (Δc_i-Δc_N) are all less than one, except in Scotland. But this ignores the effect of the common trend introduced by expressing the variables in terms of deviations from the national average. Since the national literature, explored in the last chapter, suggests that national house prices are related to income with an elasticity greater than one, then the same result holds for each of the regions. Table 7.2 is consistent with regional house prices rising more than proportionately to regional incomes.

(ii) The regional difference in house prices rose in the eighties, but fell again in the nineties

In the light of the simulations, the most plausible explanation of the pattern involves a combination of variations in regional economic performance and the effects of different structures, summarised in the form of coefficient heterogeneity. Figure 2.3 shows that most of the increase in the differential took place in the second half of the eighties. However the ratio of consumption in the South East relative to the North rose by only 2% between 1985 and 1989, but by more than 10% between 1980 and 1985. Furthermore the difference between the unemployment rate in the South East and the North *fell* between 1985 and 1989. This suggests that the movements in the *regional* regressors alone are not sufficient to explain fully the change in the house price differential.

However the mortgage interest rate fell from 13.25% in the first quarter of 1985 to less than 10% in the second quarter of 1988; the national unemployment rate fell from 10.8% at the beginning of 1985 to 5.5% mid-1990 and national real personal disposable income grew at an annual average rate of 4.5% between 1985 and 1989. In the light of the simulations, each of these national changes raises the North/South house price divide. Similarly the national economy slump post-1990 reverses the trend.

(iii) The South East leads the house price cycle and its downswing is greater than elsewhere

This follows directly from the previous point. In the short term, the South East is more responsive to changes in, for example, interest rates. The fall in interest rates in the mid-eighties had the biggest effect initially in the South East; similarly the subsequent rise in interest rates led to house prices falling first in the South. The spatial pattern that we observe has little to do with spatial movements *between* regions through migration, for example, but relates to adjustments *within* regions. This contrasts strongly with traditional approaches. Although not always recognised in the literature, national changes have differential effects between the regions in a systematic manner. There is clearly scope for similar tests of spatial coefficient structure in other fields, for example, wages and employment.

7.5 Debt Gearing and Regional Price Changes

So far we have found evidence of regional coefficient differences, but have not fully explained why they occur. Certainly structural differences in the population or in housing supply will generate coefficient heterogeneity, but it is not immediately obvious why these might cause distinct spatial coefficient patterns. Tentatively we suggested that, since the South East is more highly debt geared than the North, it potentially faces greater risks and, therefore, the responsiveness of households in the South East to changes in interest rates, unemployment and incomes would be greater and quicker in order to mitigate risk. However, this is rather imprecise and it is useful to relate this view to the credit market models discussed in Chapter 3. A central feature of the Stein (1995) and Lamont and Stein (1999) models is that volatility depends on the *distribution* of debt. Cities or regions that have a high fraction of households with debt gearing above some critical level are the most likely to experience a housing market crash. Stein argues that this is particularly likely to occur in a city if there is a high level of trading activity during a boom, perhaps as a result of an increase in the number of first-time buyers. But, as a result, the market becomes more fragile and more likely to experience a crash. The story sounds very much like that of London and the South East in the late eighties and early nineties and would be perfectly consistent with our empirical findings. The more fragile southern market would be more sensitive to economic changes whether induced by interest rates, income or unemployment.

But in order for this to be valid as an explanation, we need to know whether (*i*) it is true that the South is more highly debt geared and (*ii*) whether the South has experienced greater volatility in prices.

First, we need to define more precisely debt gearing. This could be defined in terms of either the average mortgage advance relative to income or in terms of the average advance relative to the average house price (the loan to value ratio). Both are important concepts and affect behaviour but, here, we are concerned only with the former. Discussion of the latter is reserved for Chapter 9, although we might note now that the two do not necessarily move in the same way across regions. In particular, the loan to value ratio is higher in the North than the South, but the advance to income ratio is lower. Table 7.3 sets out the average mortgage advance to income ratios for three regions, Greater London, the Rest of the South East and the North over the period 1985 to 1999. There is a small discontinuity in the series before 1993 when the coverage changed[5], but the central conclusions

[5] Prior to 1993, the survey just covered building societies; subsequently the survey included all major mortgage lenders.

are unaffected. As the table indicates, on average over the period, the average advance in the North was 1.86 times income but 2.19 and 2.24 in the South East and London respectively. Since all areas face common interest rates, mortgage repayments, as a proportion of incomes, will also be higher in the South. Notice also that the ratio in the North fluctuates relatively little over the cycle. By contrast, in London and the South East, the ratio rises at cyclical peaks and falls in the slump. For example, the average difference between the ratios for the North and the South East over the 1985 to 1999 period was 0.33. But, at the 1989 peak, the gap rose to 0.55 and narrowed to 0.06 in the 1991 slump. However, there is little evidence of any trend change in the difference in gearing between the North and South. In this case, we might expect that gearing would have no long-run effect on house price differentials; rather gearing has a short-run effect over the cycle. But this is precisely what we observe in the simulations. Prices change initially in the South relative to the North in response to shocks, but the differences are mitigated over time. Following Stein's argument, the South is more likely to experience a crash, due to the volatility of debt gearing.

Table 7.3. Mortgage Advance to Income Ratios – the North, London & South East England

Year	**North**	**South East (excl. London)**	**Greater London**
1985	1.67	2.01	2.03
1986	1.73	2.11	2.13
1987	1.73	2.20	2.27
1988	1.78	2.35	2.37
1989	1.83	2.38	2.33
1990	1.87	2.29	2.23
1991	1.93	1.99	2.23
1992	1.99	2.18	2.16
1993	1.92	2.13	2.12
1994	1.90	2.18	2.22
1995	1.89	2.17	2.20
1996	1.98	2.14	2.21
1997	2.01	2.20	2.24
1998	1.86	2.21	2.34
1999	1.88	2.34	2.48
Mean	1.86	2.19	2.24
Gap at peak		0.55	0.59
Gap at trough		0.06	0.17

Source: Council of Mortgage Lenders, *Housing Finance*

The second condition requires that prices are more volatile in the South than in the North. This can be shown straightforwardly from the data in

Chapter 2. Over the period 1969 to 1999 the standard deviation of annual house price inflation in the South East is 12.7% (12.4% in London) compared with 9.9% in the North. Therefore, prices are noticeably more volatile in the South. Overall, although the evidence is rather indirect, the empirical results of Section 7.4 and the data in this section are both consistent with the Stein view of the world.

7.6 Spatial Interactions in the USA and Australia

In Chapter 2, house price growth rates for the US census divisions and the Australian state capitals were tabulated, showing different long-run trends compared with the UK. Nevertheless, the spatial interactions between these prices can still be explored. Pollakowski and Ray (1997), in fact, conduct a similar exercise for the US, using the Freddie Mac data over the period 1975 to1994. They suggest that interactions may occur from the gradual dissemination of information across space following any shock, both through individual contact and through the news media. Although, in an efficient market, we might expect all areas to react at the same time to a common shock, we have already seen the many reasons why lags may arise. However, we would expect that price relationships between contiguous areas would be stronger since information can be transmitted more quickly.

In fact, at the census division level, Pollakowski and Ray find a relationship between spatial prices, but the relationship is no stronger between contiguous than non-contiguous regions. In further work on the Greater New York area, contiguity appears to be a more important factor. At first sight it appears, therefore, that the ripple effect experienced between prices in the UK regions does not exist between US regions. But there are methodological differences in approach and we can extend Pollakowski and Ray's work. Apart from the trivial extension of the sample period to 1999, we attempt to look for cointegrating relationships between the divisions. Pollakowski and Ray's work examines, in a VAR framework, the relationship between house price *inflation rates*. Equally important is the relationship between the levels of prices. As in the Gyourko and Voith (1992) model, do prices converge or diverge? The cointegration framework bears more relationship to the UK work of MacDonald and Taylor (1993) and Alexander and Barrow (1994) in that statistical relationships may be established, but evidence on the transmission mechanism is not explored.

Nine census divisions are a lot to include in a single Johansen cointegrating system. Therefore we look at the relationship between house prices in contiguous divisions alone. This means that there is a maximum of five variables in any regression. Table 7.4 sets out the estimated number of cointegrating equations for each grouping. In some cases the number of relationships is not entirely clear, depending on the chosen test, and so a range is presented. In general, there is some evidence of cointegration amongst groups of divisions. Nevertheless the pattern is complex. Furthermore, there are few, if any, areas which appear to be weakly exogenous and act as "drivers" for the rest of the country in the manner that the South East does in England. Also, as Pollakowski and Ray found, the coefficients do not show readily interpretable patterns between regions.

Table 7.4. Number of Cointegrating Equations - USA & Australia

Group	No. of Cointegrating Vectors
USA	
NENG, MATL, ENC	1
MATL, NENG, SATL, ENC, ESC	2-3
SATL, MATL, ESC	1
ESC, MATL, SATL, WSC, ENC	3-4
WSC, ESC, WNC, MTN, PAC	1
ENC, NENG, MATL, ESC, WNC	2
WNC, WSC, ENC, MTN, PAC	1
MTN, WSC, WNC, PAC	0-1
Australia	
SYD, MEL, BRIS, ADEL	0
SYD, MEL, CAN	0

NENG	= New England	SYD	= Sydney
MATL	= Mid Atlantic	MEL	= Melbourne
SATL	= South Atlantic	BRIS	= Brisbane
ESC	= East South Central	ADEL	= Adelaide
WSC	= West South Central	CAN	= Canberra
WNC	= West North Central		
ENC	= East North Central		
MTN	= Mountain		
PAC	= Pacific		

Table 7.4 also presents the results of a similar analysis for Australia, concentrating on the eastern states, which are most likely to be related. But in this case, there is no evidence of cointegration between any of the set of state capitals. The state housing markets are highly segmented and operate in isolation from one other. These results confirm the findings of Tu (1999), who conducts cointegration tests for all the state capitals together and on a pairwise basis. At best, she finds any linkages to be weak, although there is some evidence of cointegration between Hobart and Canberra, Adelaide and Brisbane separately.

To conclude, both the US and Australian results are clearly very different from those in the UK. However, we have given no true behavioural explanation for the US or Australian trends and the literature provides little guidance. Pollakowski and Ray suggest that the lack of an obvious relationship between prices in the divisions probably reflects underlying economic conditions and a similar case can be made for the Australian results. From equation (7.5), differing regional economic conditions will generate spatial price differences even if the structural housing market parameters are identical across the regions.

Chapter 8

HOUSING, DEPRIVATION AND URBAN CHANGE

8.1 Introduction

The theme of increasing dispersion continues in this chapter, in this case between urban and suburban areas. In Chapter 5, we suggested that urban structure was at least partly determined by household housing career patterns. The requirements of young, single person households are not the same as those of families with children. In one sense, this generates housing market segmentation. Here we provide quantitative evidence in support and demonstrate how processes of cumulative change lead to conditions of economic polarisation between areas. In order to show this, we need to construct joint models of housing, labour markets and industrial location. Although there are some similarities to models of spatial mismatch, discrimination as such is not, here, the primary mechanism generating polarisation and deprivation. Section 8.2 estimates a nested multinomial logit model of moving and location choice for London and South East England. Section 8.3 constructs a multinomial model of labour market activity, which is then joined to the housing model in order to demonstrate how the population trends described in Chapter 5 can arise. Section 8.4 looks at the relationship between housing and industrial location and suggests that, in a spatial model, crowding-out of industrial investment may not occur. Rather, in some circumstances, crowding-in may be the norm or, at least, the two may be jointly determined. Finally, Section 8.5 briefly considers commuting patterns arising from household location choices. Coupled with the trend in manufacturing job losses in the major manufacturing conurbations, we begin to see how the combination of the different elements generates economic polarisation.

8.2 Moving and Location in London and South East England

Here we present the empirical results of the analysis described in Chapter 5. In that chapter, in addition to demographic factors, we suggested that income was likely to be important in determining moving decisions and, by implication, the final choice of destination. However the location choice would also be dependent on neighbourhood environmental conditions as in the Brueckner *et al* (1999) model. There are no other UK studies that can be used as a basis for comparison, but there is some evidence for other countries, based on estimates of population density gradients. A survey of studies by McDonald (1989) finds that the gradient is negatively related to income. But Mills and Price (1984) and Mills (1992) find that factors such as crime and amenity value appear to have little effect on the gradient and, hence, play a minor role in explaining suburbanisation. Of course, there is no reason why the gradients and the importance of amenities should be the same for all countries. As in Chapter 5, Bourassa *et al* (1999) find that neighbourhood characteristics are important in determining housing sub-markets in Sydney and Melbourne. Furthermore they argue that, in both these cities, there is evidence that wealthy households are attracted to inner urban areas. For Melbourne, Eldridge (1984) finds some evidence of a flattening of the density gradient over time, although the influence of such variables as income is not tested.

Direct tests of location patterns for the UK can be conducted using data from the British Household Panel Survey covering the period 1991-1996. We concentrate on the moving and location decisions of households that were already in existence at the time of the first sample wave. Therefore, this excludes young households who form over the sample period and are more likely to be concentrated at the urban core. Each sample household was initially living in London and the South East and the factors influencing moving and location can be modelled as a nested multinomial logit model. The sample consists of approximately 1000 households of whom about one third moved over the six years. The critical questions are (*i*) what types of households are most likely to move and (*ii*) to which areas are households most likely to relocate? We distinguish between Inner London (IL), Outer London (OL), the Rest of South East England (RoSE) and the remainder of

England.[1] We argued in Chapter 5 that, for short distance moves, housing and environmental factors are typically much more important than employment in explaining moves.

As described in Chapter 5, the model adopts a two-stage hierarchical approach. The first stage determines moving probabilities and the second determines location. The results are presented in table 8.1[2]. The first part of the table concentrates on the decision to move, whereas the second looks at the factors determining location. Most of the factors described in Chapter 5 are found to be significant. The decision to move depends both on the economic and demographic characteristics of each household – including income – whereas location choice depends on the features of each location. Since households typically only move short distances, the previous location is an important determinant of location choice.

In the first part, demographic variables clearly have an effect on the decision to change residence but, here, we are particularly interested in the income variable, which is significant. The model is set up in terms of the probability of *staying*, so that the negative coefficient implies that a higher income increases the probability of moving home. Low-income households are more likely to stay where they are[3]. The second part of the table suggests that the most significant variables determining location are current location, the crime rate, unemployment and housing costs. As expected, households typically avoid areas of high unemployment, crime and deprivation in general. More surprisingly, we found no significant effect from local educational performance, although this may arise from the fact that only a relatively small proportion of our sample had school-aged children

[1] There is a good case for a finer level of disaggregation, since sub-markets exist within each of these wider areas. However, data limitations do not permit a further breakdown.

[2] Note that the use of panel data adds a non-standard estimation problem into the nested multinomial logit model. Because the same individual appears in successive waves, autocorrelation and heteroscedasticity are potentially introduced. The problems only disappear if the serial correlation coefficient is insignificantly different from zero. Further work is required, but initial tests using a dynamic probit model for the decision to move alone found an insignificant coefficient, suggesting that pooling might not be too bad as a simplification.

[3] Note that, in a model stressing credit constraints, the *level* of income matters more than the *change*.

Table 8.1a. Factors Affecting Moving in London and the South East

Variable	Coefficient	z-value
Income	-0.00017	3.0
Marital status change	-2.612	4.2
Age over 40	0.0168	6.5
Job change	-0.482	2.8
Retirement	-1.070	3.0
Spouse employed	0.206	1.4
No. of children aged 0-4	-0.245	1.8
No. of children aged 5-15	0.184	2.1
Previously/private renter	-1.816	6.9
Previously/owner-occupier	0.923	6.0
Previously/not household head	-3.365	6.5
Housing costs	0.022	6.7
Housing costs(-1)	-0.0098	5.7
Inclusive value	0.128	3.5

Table 8.1b. Factors Affecting Location

Variable	Coefficient	z-value
Housing costs	-0.032	2.8
Crime rate	-7.398	2.7
GCSE rate	6.650	1.5
A-level score	-0.297	1.7
Unemployment rate	-118.4	6.5
Deprivation index	-0.023	1.6
Previous location (IL)	2.295	4.4
Previous location (OL)	2.217	4.9
Previous location (RoSE)	2.305	5.9

The equation also includes location specific constants. Note that the two educational variables are interacted with the presence of a child in the household – households without children do not care about the quality of the educational system in an area. The lagged value of housing costs refers to costs in the location inhabited at that time.

Source: Meen and Andrew (1999)

The coefficients, as they stand, cannot be interpreted as marginal effects. It is, therefore, useful to look at the implicit location probabilities and moving probabilities for different household types. The number of households in each location, and hence migration, is dependent on the joint distribution of moving and location choice. This can be written as the product of conditional and marginal distributions. The former determines the location, conditional on the decision to move, whereas the latter determines the probability of moving. Table 8.2 sets out the estimated conditional location probabilities for moving households, disaggregated by origin and destination, whereas table 8.3 gives the moving probabilities for a selection of household types.

Table 8.2. Location Probabilities

	Inner London	**Outer London**	**Rest of South East**	**Rest of England**
Previously IL	0.466	0.106	0.220	0.209
Previously OL	0.033	0.671	0.152	0.144
Previously SE	0.018	0.042	0.859	0.082
Previously England	0.081	0.182	0.378	0.359

Table 8.3. Moving Probabilities

Household Type	**Inner London**	**Outer London**	**Rest of South East**
Income quartile 1; private renting; 0 children; <40	0.870	0.179	0.363
Income quartile 4; private renting; 0 children; <40	0.949	0.377	0.612
Income quartile 1; owner occupn.; 0 children; <40	0.301	0.014	0.036
Income quartile 4; owner occupn; 0 children; <40	0.544	0.038	0.093
Income quartile 1; public renting; 0 children; <40	0.520	0.034	0.085
Income quartile 1; owner occupn.; 1 child; >45	0.206	0.010	0.022
Income quartile 2; owner occupn; 0 children; retired	0.137	0.005	0.013

Table 8.2 (the main diagonal) shows the importance of current location. But, even for those previously living in Inner London, there is a 22% probability that moving households will relocate in the Rest of the South East. By contrast, for those living in the South East, there is a less than 2% probability that they will move to Inner London. For this group, there is an 86% probability that any moves will be to another south eastern location, although there is an 8% chance that they will move out of the South East altogether. Moves by Outer London residents also show relocation outwards

rather than back into Inner London. Note, however, that the final row does not imply that there is a 65% probability that households living outside the South East will move to London and the South East. Rather the interpretation is that, for households who originally start in London and the South East and decide to move outside, there is a 65% chance that, if they move again, they will decide to return to the South East.

Table 8.3 discriminates between income quartiles, tenure, the number of children and the age of the household head[4]. The moving probabilities for households in the upper income quartiles are significantly higher than for households in the lower quartiles. This is, perhaps, most easily seen by comparing rows 3 and 4. Furthermore, moving propensities fall with age and with the presence of school-aged children. These demographic features are important in that they generate asymmetries in behaviour. They imply that, although households may move away from Inner London in search of improved environmental conditions, any future improvements in Inner London will not necessarily reverse the flows since moving propensities for older families are relatively low.

Other important features may be noted. In line with expectations, those in the private rented sector have considerably higher moving probabilities than owner-occupiers but, more surprisingly, public tenants also have higher moving probabilities, *for households of common characteristics*, than those in owner-occupation[5]. This does not readily tally with the influential work of Hughes and McCormick (1981), but there may be at least two explanations. First, estimation is over the period 1991-1996, a period over which the turnover rate of the owner-occupier housing stock, as we have seen, was very low by the standards of the seventies and eighties. Second, Keenan *et al* (1999) record rapid mobility in local authority housing in recent years. Turnover rates have doubled since the late 1970s and this has been attributed to "growing residential instability and a weakening of social cohesion" (p 731). Table 8.3 also shows that mobility rates are greater in Inner London than in the Rest of the South East. This reinforces the asymmetries so that movement out of Inner London is more likely in response to environmental change than the other way round.

We can now begin to see how the population age structure of London and the South East, shown in Chapter 5, might be explained. Table 8.3 shows that mobility is stronger amongst the under 40s, amongst those marrying and amongst households with pre-school children. These demographic factors generate movement independently of income. Furthermore, these moving

[4] Note that >45 means aged greater than 45 but under retirement age.

[5] "common characteristics" is stressed. Since owner-occupiers typically have higher incomes, this raises their probabilities of moving.

households will tend to be attracted to better environmental conditions in suburban locations. Above the age of 40, households are more likely to stay where they are, but these groups will already have typically migrated out-of-town. In turn, the population of London will be "replenished" by young migrating households from other regions, by international in-migration and by natural rates of increase. These differing trends lead to a segmentation of household types by areas.

However, the story so far says little about spatial income distributions. The fact that older households are more likely to be located in the outer suburbs in South East England certainly does not imply, by itself, a declining urban core and economic polarisation. Low-income groups may be, and in some cities e.g. Melbourne, are distributed in the outer suburbs. We have, therefore, to ask which income group is likely to be concentrated in each location. We already have part of the story, since low-income households are less able to move from poor quality locations, but not the whole story. For the complete picture, labour markets and industrial location have to enter the scene. This endogenises income and the locational structure of unemployment.

8.3 Unemployment - Location or Skills?

Therefore, the second part of the model looks at the other side of the coin – how labour market status may or may not be affected by residential location. Is the fact that a household lives in Inner London necessarily a cause of higher unemployment once differences in skills and other demographic characteristics are taken into account? If all labour is mobile within the intra-urban area, then location *per se* might be expected to have little effect on unemployment rates. Urban unemployment rates simply reflect residential patterns. Alternatively, if commuting distances vary by skill/income group, changes in industrial location may have an impact on unemployment rates.

We estimate a multinomial model of labour market status, using pooled data from the BHPS; the sample consists of all individuals in the first wave living in London and the South East and who are of working age in 1991. Over the waves this generates a sample of 6990 observations[6]. The model may be viewed as a reduced form in which individuals are in one of four labour market states – full-time employment, (FT), part-time, (PT), unemployed, (UP), and not participating, (NP). In the sample, the proportions in each category are 58%, 17%, 5% and 20% respectively. Since

[6] Because of lagged variables, estimation only takes place over five waves, 1992-1996.

the number of time periods in the panel is small relative to the number of individual observations, the emphasis is not on the effects of changes in the pressure of demand, which are clearly important[7], but is instead on the influences of the different characteristics of the population, relative to location. The full set of regressors is set out at the end of the chapter, but they may be summarised as follows:

- Gender
- Educational qualifications
- Housing location
- Age
- Health status
- Employment status of spouse
- Number of children
- Previous employment status

Table 8.4. Labour Market Status - Selected Odds Ratios

Variable	Full-Time		Part-Time		Unemployed	
female	0.663	(3.1)	2.059	(4.5)	0.513	(3.7)
degree	4.186	(5.8)	3.003	(4.3)	2.259	(2.8)
hschool	1.864	(3.8)	1.576	(2.8)	1.048	(0.3)
bandu25	1.084	(3.0)	1.028	(1.1)	1.078	(2.8)
band2529	1.066	(3.0)	1.018	(0.9)	1.083	(3.6)
pheal	0.286	(5.7)	0.299	(5.6)	0.466	(2.8)
spjb	1.520	(3.4)	1.666	(4.0)	0.666	(2.4)
fkid5	0.162	(8.3)	0.465	(5.1)	0.258	(4.0)
fkid11	0.497	(5.2)	0.923	(0.8)	0.489	(3.0)
fkid1218	1.010	(0.1)	1.012	(0.1)	0.987	(0.1)
ilon	2.866	(2.9)	3.705	(3.0)	2.423	(2.3)
olon	3.531	(3.6)	5.458	(4.1)	2.371	(2.4)
se	3.614	(3.8)	5.049	(4.0)	2.108	(2.1)
lft	23.44	(14.6)	2.219	(3.2)	0.463	(3.4)
ljbpt	1.213	(0.8)	7.946	(8.7)	0.135	(6.9)
lnonpart	0.049	(12.0)	0.138	(8.1)	0.018	(13.1)

z-values in brackets
Variables are defined at the end of the chapter.

The results from the multinomial logit model are shown in table 8.4, treating non-participation as the "residual" category. Only a selection of the

[7] Year dummies were included to capture changes in the pressure of demand but, perhaps surprisingly, were not significant. Unemployment fell sharply between 1992 and 1996 in both London and the South East. The locational dummies may also be picking up these effects. Note also that, implicitly, the model implies that wages are not fully flexible since, with flexibility, unemployment would be independent of skills.

coefficients from the full model is presented.[8] The probability that an individual will be in each of the four labour market states is given by equation (8.1):

$$\Pr(Y_i = j) = e^{\beta_j' x_i} / \sum_{k=1}^{4} e^{\beta_k' x_i} \tag{8.1}$$

where j= 1...4 are the four labour market states; (x_i) are the individual characteristics given above and β_j are the associated coefficients.

In order to aid interpretation, each of the coefficients is tabulated in terms of the odds ratio i.e. the probability of an event occurring relative to the default case, in this case non-participation. Therefore any coefficient value less than one implies that the option is less likely to occur than non-participation. For example, the first coefficient in the table is 0.663, suggesting that females are less likely to be in full-time employment than non-participating, holding constant all other variables. However, from the second part of the table (for part-time employment), the equivalent coefficient is 2.059. Therefore females are more likely to be employed part-time than non-participating. Furthermore taking the ratio of 2.059 to 0.663 tells us that females are more likely to be employed part-time than full time since the ratio is greater than one. The results lead to a range of further conclusions:

- labour market status is strongly related to educational qualifications. At the upper end of the scale, those with a degree are much more likely to be employed full-time than non-participating. Furthermore they are more likely to be employed full-time than either employed part-time or unemployed. At the other end of the scale, those with more limited qualifications have a higher probability of unemployment. Qualifications, therefore, generate a ranking of labour market status.
- Age, by itself, appears to have relatively little impact on labour market status, at least up to retirement age.
- If the spouse is employed (either part or full-time), the probability of employment rises relative to both non-participation and unemployment. This appears to be a manifestation of the trend to either two or zero worker families. However if the spouse is employed, the individual is slightly more likely to be employed part-time than full-time.
- If a woman has children, the probability of working either full or part-time relative to non-participation falls until the children reach at least age

[8] See Meen and Andrew (1999) for the full results.

12. However the presence of children has no impact on the labour market status of males.

- Labour market status is partly autoregressive. If the individual was employed in the previous period, he/she is likely to be in the same state in the following period.
- Comparing the coefficients on the location variables, there is some evidence that those living in Inner London are more likely to be unemployed (standardising for other variables) relative to non-participation than those living in either Outer London or the Rest of the South East. However those living in the Rest of the South East are more likely to be employed full or part-time (relative to non-participation) than those living in Inner London. This implies that there is a somewhat higher probability of unemployment relative to employment[9] in Inner London than in the Rest of the South East. However this result might be explained by omitted variables. The most obvious is any measure of ethnicity, which the study was not able to include. It is perfectly possible that the residual location effects may be proxying ethnic population structure (see Fieldhouse 1999). If so, there is even less evidence that location *per se* affects labour market status.

Table 8.5 presents the results in a different form, giving the labour market status probabilities for selected individuals. The table indicates that the probability of full-time employment for graduates is similar for males and females, but for the latter (shown in the second half of the table) the probability is affected by the presence of children. The probability of full-time employment for a woman aged 20 with a degree falls by approximately eleven percentage points if she has a pre-school child, although the probability rises again once the child attends school. Note also, from the top half of the table, that males with no qualifications, who were unemployed in the previous time period, have a 7.3% probability of dropping out of the labour force altogether.

[9] The odds ratios for unemployment relative to full-time employment are 0.84 in Inner London against 0.58 for the Rest of the South East. The comparable figures relative to part-time employment are 0.65 and 0.42 respectively.

Table 8.5. Predicted Labour Market Probabilities

	FT	PT	UP	NP
Males				
Degree; age 20; previously FT	0.953	0.013	0.028	0.006
Degree; age 45; previously UP	0.287	0.036	0.648	0.029
No qualifcn; age 45; previously FT	0.895	0.014	0.074	0.016
No qualifcn; age 45; previously UP	0.173	0.030	0.724	0.073
A-level; age 20; previously FT	0.944	0.015	0.020	0.020
Females				
Degree; age 20; previously FT	0.931	0.039	0.022	0.009
Degree; age 45; previously UP	0.304	0.117	0.532	0.046
No qualifcn; age 45; previously FT	0.876	0.044	0.056	0.024
No qualifcn; age 45; previously UP	0.185	0.099	0.599	0.117
A-level; age 20; previously FT	0.910	0.044	0.015	0.032
Degree; age 20; previously FT; 1 child 0-5	0.823	0.099	0.031	0.048
Degree; age 45; previously FT; 1 child 6-18.	0.915	0.045	0.031	0.008

Although the story is still not complete, by endogenising income, we can see further how interactions between housing and labour markets may generate economic polarisation between locations. Formally, the model can be defined in the following way. First, distinguishing by gender, number of children, age and skill level, equation (8.1) defines the probability that an individual will be in each of the four labour market states. Second, for given wage rates, disaggregated by skill, full-time/part-time status and by gender, the expected wage for an individual of type (i) is;

$$E(W_i) = \sum_{j=1}^{4} \Pr(Y_i = j) * W_{ij} \tag{8.2}$$

where (W_{ij}) is the wage rate for an individual of type (i), based on his/her skill characteristics, in each state; the wage for the unemployed is the unemployment benefit rate plus other income support, such as housing benefit, and the wage under non-participation is zero. The labour and housing markets are linked in two ways. Incomes are a major determinant of moving propensities and the unemployment rate is an important influence on location choice. Therefore, the expected unemployment rate, (UR), in each location can be calculated from (8.3).

$$E(UR) = \sum_{i=1}^{n} \Pr(Y_i = 3) * POP_i / \sum_{i=1}^{n} (1 - \Pr(Y_i = 4)) * POP_i \qquad (8.3)$$

where (3) refers to state 3, i.e. unemployment, (4) is non-participation, POP_i is the total population in the (i)th class, and (n) is the number of household types. Finally, the change in population of each class in each location (abstracting from natural rates of increase and interregional migration) depends on net migration between the four areas, which in turn arises from relocation decisions.

$$\Delta POP_{il} = NM_{il} \qquad (8.4)$$

where, NM_{il} is net migration by class (i) to location (l).

Therefore, for any given level of labour demand, the low skilled are more likely to be unemployed and have lower expected incomes. But those on low incomes have a lower probability of moving (or, as we shall see, of commuting to jobs elsewhere). Furthermore as high income, employed households move away from the urban core in the search for better neighbourhood conditions, the unemployment rate in the inner city rises even further which, from table 8.1, makes those locations even less desirable to households who can move. Out-migration, then, increases even further and the end result is a cumulative process of polarisation.

8.4 Housing and Industrial Location

The third element of the story concerns industrial location, which influences labour demand. Of course, if the conventional assumption of residential location theory, that all employment is based at the city centre and employees have to commute to jobs, is adopted then the analytical problems are relatively straightforward. But modelling becomes more complex in the more realistic case where industrial location is, itself, an endogenous process. Indeed, firms may respond to the location decisions of households or both may be jointly determined.

We cannot assume, therefore, that industrial location is an exogenous factor to which population responds. Models, such as those of Muth (1971), suggest joint movements, so that models of employment and population change have to be constructed in a simultaneous framework. Core-Periphery models under increasing returns to scale (Krugman 1991) also imply that firms and households will tend (if transport costs are low) to locate together to take advantages of scale economies in both factor and goods markets.

The assumption that employees move to jobs is therefore, by no means, universal in the literature although, as Thurston and Yezer (1994) suggest, formal tests of industrial location are more limited than those for household location.[10] However a number of US studies have attempted to distinguish whether "workers follow jobs" or "jobs follow workers". Early studies by Steinnes (1977, 1982), for example, conduct causality tests in a joint model of population change and employment in the manufacturing, retail and service sectors. He finds that, in manufacturing, jobs typically move to workers. Tests by Cooke (1978), which reformulated the Steinnes model in terms of population and employment gradients, also found evidence in favour of jobs following population in manufacturing. The main counter evidence comes from Thurston and Yezer (1994), who disaggregate to finer industrial sectors and use annual changes in the variables, rather than the more usual 5-10 year horizons. They find evidence that employment decentralisation in some industrial sectors subsequently influences population suburbanisation, but little evidence that jobs follow population except in the retail and service sectors.

Our own tests are slightly different from those previously employed. First, rather than concentrating on population and employment, we look at the relationship between new housing construction and industrial construction investment, which are directly related to population and employment change respectively. This alternative set of variables has a number of advantages. First, the periodicity of the data is more frequent than population data. We can, therefore, use quarterly observations; this can be important if the lags between population and industrial changes are short. Using data at longer frequencies may, mistakenly, suggest that both are simultaneously determined. Second, the approach allows us to consider, at the same time, issues of crowding-out. If jobs follow workers, then business investment and housing will be *positively* related. Third, tests of causality are based on weak exogeneity restrictions set in a cointegration framework. Earlier Granger causality tests have generally been specified in terms of rates of change in order to induce stationarity. But this does not permit the testing of long-run relationships between the variables in levels. Since we are primarily concerned with the long run, cointegration is a more appropriate framework.

[10] Fingleton (1991) estimates a model of industrial firm relocation between London and other counties. However the work concentrates on cost differences and does not explicitly include such factors as labour availability and residential quality.

The three questions are (*i*) is there any long-run relationship between housing and industrial construction investment? This is an issue of cointegration (*ii*) if any relationship exists, is it negative (crowding-out) or positive (crowding-in)? This depends on the coefficients of any cointegrating relationship (*iii*) what is the direction of the relationship? This depends on Granger causality and weak exogeneity restrictions.

There is no necessary reason why the relationship between housing and business location should be the same for all sectors. In particular, the relationship might differ according to the strength of commuting patterns. If employees are prepared to commute long distances, there is no reason why firms should be constrained in their location choice by labour availability, since labour is in elastic supply. But in the absence of commuting, labour supply is inelastic and existing firms may be forced to relocate or new firms will locate in areas of plentiful labour with appropriate qualifications. Here we concentrate on industrial (mainly factories and warehouses) construction. Ideally tests for the commercial and retail sectors should also be conducted. However, appropriately disaggregated commercial construction data are unavailable. Nevertheless the industrial sector is still important in determining unemployment in cities. Turok and Edge (1999) and Bailey and Turok (2000) show that job losses from the conurbations have been concentrated primarily in manufacturing.

Two further tests arise if firms are attracted primarily by labour availability - particularly skilled labour. First, we expect to observe a relationship only with private housing, since social housing has become an increasingly residualised sector with approximately 70% of tenants now receiving social benefits. Second, we might expect any relationship to be stronger in the South East than in other regions, since this is where the most innovative firms, requiring highly skilled labour, have tended to concentrate in Britain.

Table 8.6 begins by estimating the relationship between housing construction output and industrial construction for Britain as a whole on quarterly data over the period 1966-1995. More precisely, the equation considers the long-run relationship between four variables, using Johansen estimates of the cointegration vectors. In fact, tests indicated the presence of only one vector. The four variables included are constant price industrial new orders (*NOIND*), private housing output (*QPRD*), public housing (*QPBH*) and manufacturing output (*QMF*). The housing variables are measured in terms of construction *output* whereas industrial construction is measured by *new orders*; this is in order to aid identification of the timing of any relationship since new orders precede output. Manufacturing output is included in order to capture the type of variables traditionally used in modelling industrial and commercial construction through accelerator models. Since lags are included for each variable (order 3), the variables could be reparameterised in difference form, as an accelerator model, should the data so suggest. Table 8.6 imposes data-validated restrictions on the coefficients.

There are a number of features to note. First, in the long run, manufacturing output has an insignificant effect and, hence, its coefficient may validly be constrained to zero; importantly, changes in manufacturing output may explain cyclical movements in industrial construction as accelerator models suggest, but they do not explain any long-run trend in new orders. Second, private sector housing (and to a lesser extent public housing) have significant *positive* effects on industrial new orders[11]. The private sector effect is approximately four times larger than the public sector effect. This may, therefore, suggest that the low skilled are less important in determining location. The conclusion becomes stronger below. Third, (*QPBH*) and (*QMF*) are weakly exogenous to the system. This can be tested through over-identifying restrictions on the adjustment (alpha) matrix, which determines the speed of adjustment of the system to equilibrium following any shock. This implies that these variables are not Granger-caused by the cointegrating vector. Fourth, the adjustment parameter on (*NOIND*), which takes a value of (-0.362), implies that any disequilibrium in the long-run relationship is primarily eliminated by changes in new orders rather than in housing output. This suggests that private housing is either jointly endogenous or, perhaps, weakly exogenous[12] and that industrial new orders are caused by changes in housing construction. This result is consistent with the view that existing firms in this sector relocate or newly- forming firms locate in places where more highly skilled workers desire to live. Fifth, since the relationship between housing and industrial construction is positive, housing appears to crowd-in industrial investment[13]. There are, of course, other explanations of a positive association, particularly since we are dealing with reduced forms.

For example, first, the positive long-run correlation could be generated by a common supply shock. For example, a technological improvement, which requires new factory space, could raise the economy's long-run growth rate. This, in turn, raises the demand for housing. But, under this view, changes in industrial construction would precede changes in the housing market and this does not appear to be consistent with the evidence.

[11] In order to interpret the effects of each variable on new orders the signs have to be reversed.

[12] Other versions of the equation suggested that the adjustment coefficient on housing was barely significant.

[13] Not, however, that this does not necessarily imply that productive capacity in the economy as a whole is enhanced. If the investment is carried out by relocating existing firms rather than newly-forming firms, existing premises become obsolete.

Alternatively, both industrial construction and housing might respond to common external factors such as land availability. So, for example, a relaxation of binding planning constraints would increase both housing and industrial construction. However there is evidence that housing and industrial development are not equally constrained by the planning process. Typically in the South East, controls are more lax for industry than for housing. It is not necessarily the case that the provision of extra jobs is automatically accompanied by the release of extra land for housing.

Table 8.6. Housing & Industrial Construction

Cointegration vector			
noind	**qmf**	**qprd**	**qpbh**
1.000 (0.0)	0.000 (0.0)	-0.573 (0.174)	-0.153 (0.050)
Adjustment matrix			
noind	-0.362 (0.037)		
qmf	0.000 (0.0)		
qprd	-0.049 (0.020)		
qpbh	0.000 (0.0)		

Standard errors in brackets. Lower case denotes logarithms.

Data sources. *Housing and Construction Statistics, Economic Trends.*

Table 8.7 looks at sub-sample estimates in order to see whether any relationship has changed over time. Perhaps the most interesting results arise from the relative importance of the two housing variables shown in the table. In each of the sub-periods, at least one (if not both) of the housing coefficients is significant, but the full period results disguise an important change in the relative coefficients; the private sector variable became much more important after the 1960s - indeed it was insignificant during the sixties - whereas the public sector variable was most significant during the sixties and had a much larger effect than private housing. However, in the most recent period, public housing appears to change sign - an inverse relationship with industrial new orders (although we need to bear in mind that new social housing construction has become very small in recent years). These changes in the relative importance of the two coefficients are precisely what we expect to observe on the basis of the changes in the composition of tenants in the social sector. In earlier years, the sector contained a high proportion of skilled workers, but this has become increasingly uncommon. If anything, industrial investment now appears to be deterred by the presence of social housing.

Table 8.7. Sub-Sample Estimates of the Housing Coefficients[14]

	qprd	qpbh
66(4)-95(2)	0.573 (0.174)	0.153 (0.050)
73(1)-95(2)	0.597 (0.122)	0.065 (0.037)
80(1)-95(2)	0.505 (0.080)	-0.146 (0.042)
66(4)-80(4)	-0.047 (0.386)	0.724 (0.300)

Standard errors in brackets

Testing the relationship at the regional level is more difficult because constant price construction output data are not available below the national level and hence current price data have to be used. Furthermore available time spans are much shorter, beginning in 1980. Nevertheless, table 8.8 presents a selection of the regional results.

Table 8.8. Regional Industrial Construction & Housing 1980(4)-1996(1)

Region	qprd	qpbh
South East (ex. London)	0.738 (0.063)	-0.074 (0.065)
East Anglia	0.901 (0.120)	0.089 (0.079)
South West	0.931 (0.127)	0.291 (0.109)
North West	-0.917 (0.380)	-0.474 (0.073)

Standard errors in brackets

The table suggests that the finding of a positive relationship between industrial new orders and private housing is not uniform across the country. The results indicate that the relationship only holds in the three southern regions and that the coefficient is strongly negative in the North West. By contrast, public housing generally has an insignificant effect in the southern areas. Therefore, the national results disguise very distinct spatial patterns, which are consistent with the skill requirements of high technology companies, disproportionately distributed in the South East. Such companies need to be in locations where skilled labour can be found.

In summary, in terms of the original questions, it appears that there is a positive long-run relationship between industrial construction and housing - housing does not crowd-out industrial construction. The direction of causality suggests that jobs move to workers - although joint endogeneity cannot be ruled out. The relationship is at its strongest with private housing,

[14] Note that the signs are reversed from the previous table.

particularly in recent years and the relationship is dominated by the South of England.

Finally, although we cannot test the relationship in the same way, it is useful to speculate on the relationship between housing and commercial and retail developments. In particular, commercial developments might have little relationship with housing because of strong commuting patterns by employees in financial services. But the connection is likely to be stronger for retail developments, which require concentrations of relatively low-skilled local employment and rely on local population centres for their markets. To look at this issue, a different approach is required by analysing the commuting patterns of different types of households.

8.5 Commuting Behaviour

The two main questions briefly examined in this section are (*i*) do low-income households commute shorter distances? This provides evidence of the size of labour market areas for different groups, (*ii*) do commuting distances vary by industry? If there is evidence that workers in financial services commute longer distances, then there is no necessary relationship between housing and business location for this sector in the manner that we found in the last section.

Standardising on individual characteristics we examine, therefore, how commuting times vary by industry and income using panel data again taken from the British Household Panel Survey, over six waves from 1991 to 1996. Table 8.9 shows estimates of travel to work times (in minutes). Because of sample truncation, a full information maximum likelihood version of the Heckman selection model is used (this is more efficient than the two-stage method). Estimation by this means is necessary because of the truncation arising from non-participation in the workforce by part of the sample. By definition, non-participants or the unemployed have zero travel to work times. The resultant biases are overcome by estimating jointly a travel-to-work and a labour force participation equation. However the table concentrates only on the results of the travel-to-work equation.

The factors expected to affect travel to work times comprise economic variables (wage rates, labour market status and local vacancy rates), demographic variables (age, gender, number of children) and housing influences (housing costs and time since the last move). In models of this form potential endogeneity problems arise from the inclusion of wage rates and housing costs since these are both determined by the travel-to-work decision. In order to overcome the problem, wages were not taken for each household from within the BHPS. Rather skill-specific wage rates for the

South East as a whole were constructed from the New Earnings Survey. Therefore the potential wage rate facing each individual in the sample depends on his or her level of skills rather than on location. As noted in Chapter 5, higher wages might increase or decrease commuting, although in the UK, our expectation is of a positive effect. This is also consistent with the view that high-income individuals have larger labour market areas. The measure of housing costs is also a notional construct, based on regional house prices, rather than on the actual housing costs faced by each household. The results suggest:

- those in the 25-34 age band are prepared to commute longer distances, but distance declines with age.
- Those in part-time employment commute shorter distances than full-time workers, but if the worker is on a short-term contract he/she will be prepared to commute longer distances.
- Women travel shorter distances, but an individual of either gender will travel further if he/she has an employed spouse. This represents the difficulties of optimising location for two worker households. The presence of children reduces commuting distances for females but not males.

However the important points are (*i*) that low-income groups spend less time travelling and (*ii*) that both male and female workers in manufacturing face lower travel to work times than those in financial services. The differences are not particularly large for females (who travel smaller distances in any case), but are significant for males. Those in financial services travel an extra 12.5 minutes in each direction compared with those in manufacturing. It is, however, possible that this effect reflects partly skill factors not fully picked up in the wage variable.

Table 8.9. Travel to Work Times (minutes) - London & South East

Variable	Coefficient	z-value	Variable	Coefficient	z-value
ln (wage)	11.397	7.3	Fdk2	-6.433	3.7
rnwhp	0.00047	5.1	Fdk3	-7.166	4.2
Band2534	0.144	2.6	Fdk4	-9.317	3.6
Band3544	0.088	2.0	manf	6.467	2.5
Band4559	0.033	1.1	finf	9.229	3.9
jbten	-0.0017	3.0	manm	-8.242	4.3
jbten2	1.87 e-7	3.3	finm	4.355	1.5
ptime	-6.674	5.5	lmove	-5.617	2.7
jbterm	3.274	2.0	qvrate	-1.018	0.9
female	-3.533	2.0	caruse	-4.736	7.5
spjb	2.419	1.2	constant	-13.02	2.1
Fdk1	-0.670	3.2			

See end of chapter for variable definitions

8.6 Conclusions

Some of the policy implications of these empirical results are picked up in Chapter 10. But, to recap, in this chapter the empirical results imply that cumulative economic polarisation and urban/rural drift arise from interactions between housing and labour markets and the location decisions of firms. Low-income households typically experience both lower moving propensities and shorter travel-to-work times, which imply that labour market search areas are smaller. But low-income households are also more likely to be those lacking labour force skills. Lower moving propensities are generated by poor housing and credit market access.

High-income households, by contrast, will typically be concentrated in areas of high neighbourhood quality. At least in manufacturing there is some evidence, from our empirical results, that firms will follow highly skilled workers into the suburbs, generating a positive correlation between housing and industrial investment. But if low-skilled workers are recruited from the local labour market (because of a weakness in wider information networks and high commuting costs in proportion to incomes), the continuing loss of male, manual, manufacturing jobs from cities is bound to fall disproportionately on the low skilled in the conurbations. However, we re-examine in Chapter 10 whether these patterns are inevitable or whether different patterns of location emerge in other countries.

Definitions of variables used in table 8.4

Dependent variable
Full-time employment = 1 – the hours of work are greater than 29 per week
Part-time employment = 2 – the hours of work are less than 30 per week
Unemployment = 3 – if the individual states that he/she is unemployed and/or on a government sponsored training scheme
Non-participant = 4 – if the individual is retired, involved in family care, on maternity leave, in full-time education or ill

Gender
female = 1 if gender is female

Qualifications
degree = 1 if has degree or higher degree
hschool = 1 if has a high school qualification (O-level, GCSE, CSE, or Scottish equivalent)

Location
ilon = 1 if residence is in inner London
olon = 1 if residence is in outer London
se = 1 if residence is in South East (excluding London)

Age Band
bandu25 = < 25
band2529 = 25-29

Health
pheal = dummy for poor health

Employment status of spouse
spjb = dummy for spouse being employed

Children
fkid5 = female dummy * number of children aged 0 to 5
fkid11 = female dummy * number of children aged 6 to 11
fkid1218 = female dummy * number of children aged from 12 to 18

Previous Employment Status
lft = previously in full-time employment
ljbpt = previously in part-time employment
lnonpart = previously a non-participant.

Definitions of variables used in table 8.9

Age & gender

female = 1 if gender is female

Band2534 = actual age if 25< age < 34, otherwise 0

Band3544 = actual age if 35< age < 44, otherwise 0

Band4559 = actual age if 45 < age < 59, otherwise 0

Wage rate

wage = real wage rate

Housing costs

rnwhp = real regional house prices

Tenure in employment

jbten = number of days spent in the state of employment

jbten2 = $(\text{jbten})^2$

ptime = 1 if part-time employee

jbterm = dummy if employed on a short term contract

spjb = dummy for spouse being employed

Industry

man = dummy for being in manufacturing sector

fin = dummy for being in the financial services sector

manf = female*man

finf = female*fin

manm =male*man

finm = male*fin

Children (only effective for females)

Fdk1 = dummy for youngest child aged under 5

Fdk2 = dummy for youngest child aged 6 to 11

Fdk3 = dummy for youngest child aged 12 to 15

Fdk4 = dummy for youngest child aged 16 to 18

Job access measures

caruse = dummy if individual has access to a car

qvrate = (local authority vacancy rate/ regional vacancy rate)

lmove = dummy for having moved in the last 2 years.

Chapter 9

SELECTED ISSUES IN NATIONAL HOUSING POLICY

9.1 Introduction

Housing policy is, of course, an enormous subject in its own right. Rather than attempting to cover the whole field, we discuss only those elements that naturally arise from the types of model constructed over the last eight chapters. This chapter deals with the ever-expanding literature on the relationship between housing and the national economy, whereas Chapter 10 considers the regional and urban dimensions.

The literature has always recognised that the macroeconomy affects housing markets and both monetary and fiscal policy are key influences, but the idea that housing has an effect on the macroeconomy disproportionate to its share in GDP is a more recent idea and still remains controversial. Four areas of policy are considered:

- housing, consumers' expenditure and financial market liberalisation,
- monetary policy and housing cycles,
- housing and European Monetary Union,
- housing models, planning and household projections.

The first of these topics originally arose during the UK boom in the late eighties, where Muellbauer (1990) argued that a causal relationship exists between house price growth and excessive growth in consumers' expenditure in the liberalised mortgage market conditions of that time. Some other countries, notably Scandinavia and the Netherlands, appear to have found similar evidence, but there has always been a contradiction between macroeconomic time-series evidence and microeconomic findings.

Our second topic looks at volatility in housing markets and cycles. We consider three possible causes – excluding bubbles or forms of irrational behaviour. The first returns to the topic of downpayment constraints, originally raised in Chapter 3. Although these constraints are not generally caused by government action, we show that volatility is still likely to occur whatever action government takes in the other two areas. These other areas are monetary policy and planning regulations. These two are considered together because it is the interactions between them that contribute to cycles. The fact that housing markets are sensitive to changes in interest rates should cause no surprise - and was recognised in the very earliest empirical studies – but we are concerned with the more recent moves towards inflation targeting, using interest rates as the main policy instrument. If, as generally occurs in Europe, short-term interest rates are geared towards meeting general inflation targets, what are the implications for housing? We suggest that inflation targets can increase the volatility of housing markets, particularly if planning controls reduce housing supply elasticities.

Third, it has been argued that differences in housing markets across Europe may, in some circumstances, slow down processes of economic convergence. Chapter 2 certainly suggested that differences in housing trends remain substantial. But, again, the arguments are controversial and centre on differences in owner-occupancy rates, debt gearing and the proportion of variable rate mortgage debt.

The final section turns to a rather different question - the issue of planning for future housing needs and demand. At least in the UK, traditionally, household projections, which are used as a basis for local and regional housing plans, have been based entirely on demographic projections. We examine the role that economics can play in the process.

9.2 Housing, Consumers' Expenditure and Financial Liberalisation

As noted above, it has always been recognised that macroeconomic conditions are important in determining movements in house prices and construction but, until the mid-eighties, little attention was paid to the view that housing itself could have a major impact on the macroeconomy. The immediate stimulus to a revision of the view was the house price boom in the second half of the eighties - noted in Chapter 2 - which coincided with a boom in consumers' expenditure. Consumption grew in excess of 5% in each of the three years 1986-1988. No-one questions that the two took place, but considerable dispute concerns causality. However more traditional consumption functions failed to predict the consumption boom, which led to an over-relaxation of monetary policy at that time (see Meen 1996a). House price booms had, of course, taken place before in the early and late seventies, but no corresponding boom had occurred in consumption. However, the difference between the periods was the liberalisation of mortgage markets in the early eighties. Under the rationed conditions of the seventies, an increase in house prices could not be translated into higher consumption through borrowing. But the removal of rationing meant, under this view of the world, that households could borrow against the accumulated equity in their houses to finance consumption - a housing wealth effect. This view is summarised in Muellbauer (1990) and lies behind their house price modelling work at both the national and regional levels (Muellbauer and Murphy 1994, 1997). Furthermore, as we saw in Chapter 3, liberalisation of credit markets increases the sensitivity of housing markets and, indirectly, consumption to changes in interest rates. As shown in figure 9.1, equity withdrawal - the propensity to borrow on mortgage more than is required to finance the purchase of a home – rose dramatically in the late eighties. Equity withdrawal reached almost 7% of household income in 1988. Similarly, Boelhouwer (2000) reports that, in the Netherlands, rapidly increasing house prices have been responsible for sharply increasing consumers' expenditure in 1999 through the same route of equity withdrawal.

But, although equity withdrawal has begun to re-emerge in the UK in the late nineties, the volume has not approached that in the late eighties. Furthermore, the figure shows how equity withdrawal disappeared altogether in the early nineties as house prices collapsed. Rather the phenomenon of negative equity occurred, concentrated on the South East of England, caused by the first sustained fall in house prices since the early fifties. Negative equity refers to a condition where the value of the mortgage exceeds the value of the property. Henley (1998) has argued, reasonably, that negative equity lowered labour mobility in the nineties.

However although equity withdrawal, negative equity and their underlying cause – movements in house prices – correlate well with the consumption boom and subsequent slump, the boom of the second half of the eighties has also been attributed to other explanations. King (1990) argues that, instead, the boom represented a re-assessment of permanent income in the light of the "Thatcher Productivity Miracle" in the eighties. Since the demand for housing and, hence house prices, would also be affected by the revision to expectations, the correlation between consumption and house prices may represent a proxy effect. In terms of policy which explanation (if either) is true is important. The explanation in terms of a wealth effect might suggest tax measures explicitly targetted at the housing market to prevent price booms - a measure that would be irrelevant if expectations were the true causal mechanism.

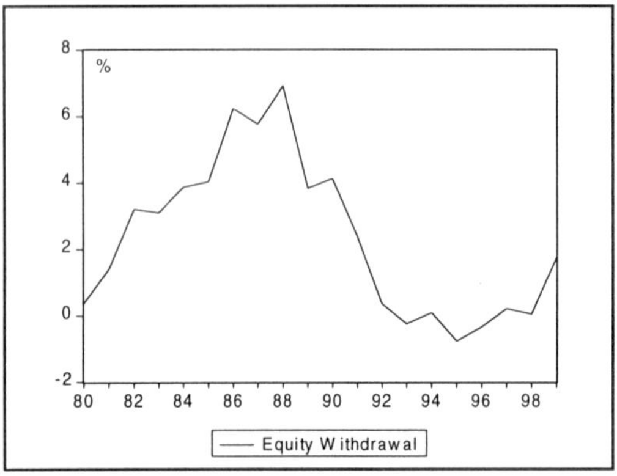

Figure 9.1. Equity Withdrawal (% of household income)

However standard life-cycle models suggest that the removal of credit rationing would raise current consumption, irrespective of the existence of a housing wealth effect in the consumption function. For example in Muellbauer (1983), Miles (1992) and Patterson (1993), the existence of credit constraints implies that some households may not be able to borrow against future expected income; therefore their consumption patterns will be determined primarily by current income. The removal of a constraint can shift the consumption stream towards the current period.

As Hort (1997) points out, macroeconomic and microeconomic data yield conflicting evidence. On microeconomic data, both Attanasio and Weber (1994) and Miles (1997) are not supportive of explanations of the consumption boom in terms of house price changes. But on macroeconomic data, Muellbauer and Murphy (1990) find significant effects in the UK. In a comparative exercise, Muellbauer (1994) finds major structural differences between the UK and Germany. Berg (1994), Berg and Bergstrom (1995) and Koskela and Viren (1992) find that in the Scandinavian countries, which have experienced house price movements similar to the UK, there are significant effects. In the USA, the evidence is generally unsupportive of any direct link although, as we shall see in the next section, indirect links consistent with life-cycle behaviour can occur.

9.3 Downpayments, Monetary Policy and Cycles

9.3.1 Downpayments and Volatility

Downpayment constraints played an important role in the models of Chapter 3 and still exist even in liberalised financial markets because of adverse selection. The predominantly US literature shows that constraints have wide-ranging effects. Notably, they affect the tenure choices of young households; Haurin *et al* (1997) show that constraints raise the proportion in private renting. Furthermore, they influence the savings behaviour of renters, (Engelhardt 1994), and they also increase the volatility of house prices. This last line of research implies that the strong cycles that characterise housing markets do not necessarily arise from speculative bubbles and that government policy can only have limited mitigating effects. In this sub-section, the three issues that are explored are:

- the effects of downpayment constraints on national housing volatility,
- their effects on regional price differentials,
- their influence on aggregate savings and consumers' expenditure.

The simplest way to illustrate the effect of constraints on volatility is to consider the following financial market multiplier model, based on an extension to the export base model, used in Fujita *et al* (1999). This can be used to demonstrate that house prices will typically be more sensitive to income changes in the presence of downpayment constraints.

$$PH = \gamma Y/(1-DC) \tag{9.1}$$

$$DC = \alpha PH \tag{9.2}$$

where; PH = house price
Y = income
DC = downpayment ratio

In equation (9.1), we assume a simple relationship between prices and (permanent) income. Although we saw in Chapter 6, that there is no simple long-run cointegrating relationship between the two variables alone, it is the case that income is the single most important determinant of prices in the UK[1]. The relationship may reflect demand or an income limit imposed by the

[1] Note that city analysts in the UK generally assume that there is a long-run relationship between house prices and income to which the economy returns. As Meen (1996a) argues

lender. If the downpayment ratio is equal to zero ($DC = 0$), there is a simple proportionality between prices and incomes so that the income elasticity of house prices is equal to one. But, as shown in Chapter 6, all empirical evidence for the UK suggests that the elasticity is greater than one. If ($DC \neq 0$), however, and if households *can* meet any downpayment constraint[2] then, as incomes rise (or at the national level, the economy expands), house prices rise more than proportionately. However, this result is dependent on equation (9.2) – the downpayment ratio is assumed to rise with the level of house prices. We present empirical evidence on this below, but there are a number of reasons why this might occur. First, at higher house prices, the risk to lenders may rise and they may require a higher downpayment ratio. Second, for existing owner-occupiers, at higher prices, their own property will have increased in value, reducing the size of the required advance. Substituting (9.2) into (9.1), yields a quadratic equation with two roots determined by (9.3).

$$PH = 1 \pm \sqrt{1 - 4\alpha\gamma Y} \,/\, 2\alpha \tag{9.3}$$

In fact, one of the roots has no economic meaning since it implies that prices are *decreasing* in income. The equation is also only defined for real roots up to the point $\gamma Y = 1/4\alpha$. As an example, for $\gamma = 2.0$, $DC = 0.2$ (for $Y=1.0$), $\alpha = 0.08$, the relationship between house prices and incomes is plotted in figure 9.2. In this simple model, the ratio of mortgage repayments to incomes always remains constant. Higher incomes generate a proportionately higher demand for mortgage loans, but since prices rise more than proportionately to income, the downpayment ratio has to rise in line with (9.2). Under this arbitrary set of parameter values, the implied income elasticity of house prices over the range for which the function is defined turns out to be approximately 2.7. This is not dissimilar to the findings in Chapter 6 although, as we have seen, the elasticities are also dependent on supply conditions in a more general model.

Therefore, at ($DC = 0$), the income elasticity of house prices is one, but at ($DC = 20\%$), the elasticity rises to 2.7. Variations in the downpayment ratio – whether imposed by lenders or resulting from the individual decisions of households – increase the volatility of house prices considerably relative to income changes.

---

this is a dangerous forecasting rule-of-thumb. As we saw in Chapter 6, the relationship between prices and incomes changed in the nineties.

[2] The effects of a failure to meet downpayment constraints on aggregate saving are discussed below.

Now assume that $\alpha = 0.04$, i.e. the downpayment ratio is less dependent on house price changes. This becomes important when we discuss regional differences. Figure 9.3 now shows that the function becomes approximately linear and the elasticity of house prices with respect to income falls. Therefore the lower the value of α, the weaker is house price volatility.

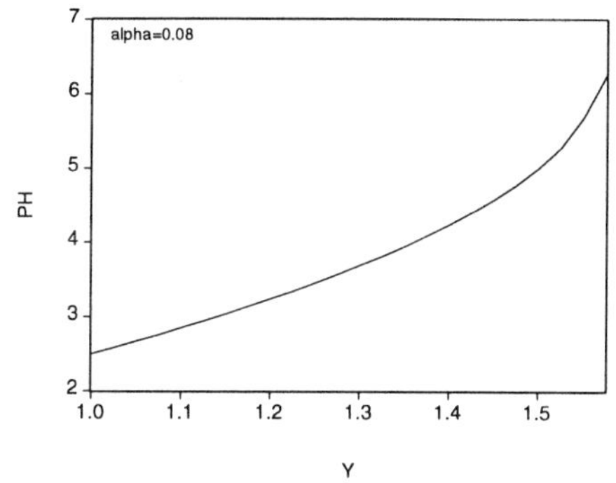

Figure 9.2. House Prices & Incomes (α=0.08)

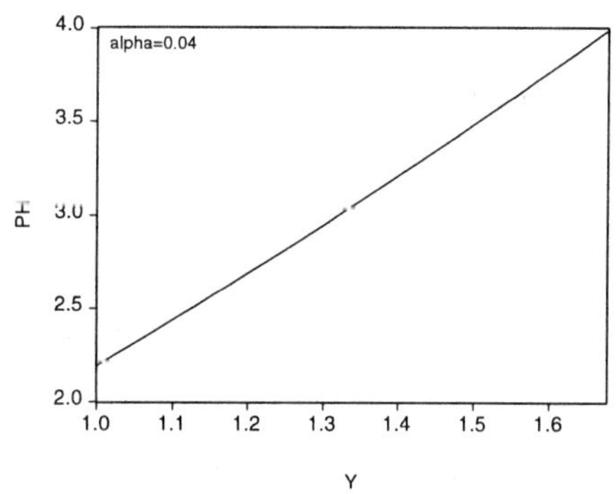

Figure 9.3. House Prices & Incomes (α=0.04)

To complete the story, we need to justify equation (9.2) – the fact that the downpayment ratio is positively related to house prices. This can be shown empirically from the error correction regression in table 9.1, explaining the average loan size taken out by first-time buyers. The equation implies that, in the long run, the average loan as a proportion of income depends on the level of house prices. Rewriting the equation in terms of the loan to house price ratio (which equals one minus the downpayment ratio), equation (9.4) is obtained.

Therefore the loan to value ratio (*LVR*) is negatively related to house prices or, alternatively, the downpayment ratio is positively related, which is in line with (9.2).

Table 9.1. The Average Loan for First-Time Buyers in the UK (£)

Dependent Variable: $\Delta\ln$ (RLNFTB)

Variable	**Coefficient**	**t-value**
Constant	0.131	2.9
$\ln (LY)_{-1}$	-0.150	3.1
$\Delta\ln RYFTB$	1.116	17.3
$\Delta\ln RYFTB_{-1}$	0.151	2.3
$\ln g_{-1}$	0.050	2.3
$REBM_{-1}$	-0.002	1.5
$\Delta REBM_{-1}$	-0.015	5.0
Adjusted R-squared	0.824	
Std. Error of regression	0.015	

where:

RLNFTB	=	real average loan for first-time buyers
LY	=	loan to income ratio
RYFTB	=	real income of first-time buyers
g	=	real house prices
REBM	=	mortgage interest rate

$$\ln (LVR) = 1.0 \ln (RYFTB) - 0.666 \ln (g) + \ldots \tag{9.4}$$

One further issue arises. As noted above, in this simple version of the model, the repayment to income ratio is constant (for given interest rates) but at the cost of an expanding downpayment ratio. In fact, in figure 9.1, the downpayment ratio reaches a maximum of approximately 50% under the assumed set of parameters. This is probably unreasonable for most first-time purchasers, although not for many existing owner-occupiers. If the constraint becomes binding, then, the purchaser could (*i*) increase repayments by taking out a larger loan (but repayment constraints will eventually bind) (*ii*) reduce housing demand by purchasing a smaller home (*iii*) remain as a renter for a longer period of time[3]. Some of these options are considered further below. But in terms of figure 9.2, the imposition of a fixed downpayment percentage implies a proportional relationship between prices and incomes.

[3] Remember, in Chapter 3, we indicated that downpayment constraints extended the period of sub-optimal housing consumption. Since the earlier model did not include tenure choice, the options are greater here, although the general principles are the same.

This is the same as assuming that α = 0.0, i.e. similar to figure 9.3. Therefore, superimposing the two graphs gives figure 9.4 so that the house price function kinks at the point where the constraint binds. The locus of the lower points represents the highly non-linear price function[4].

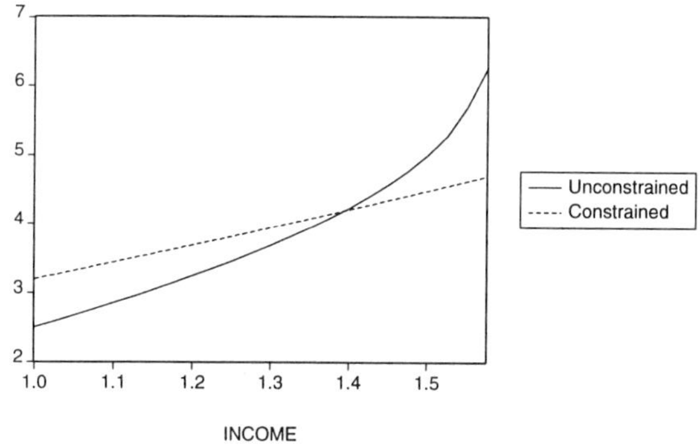

Figure 9.4. Constrained & Unconstrained Prices

Turning to regional patterns, as noted in Chapter 7, loan to value ratios are lower in the South East of England than in the North. Excluding London, in 1999, the average loan to value ratio (for all buyers) was approximately 67% in the South but 75% in the North. Although the differential varies over the cycle, the ratio is always higher in the North and, in both regions, the ratio falls at times of increasing house prices in line with equation (9.4). At first sight, the relative positions of North and South might seem strange since we have already seen, in Chapter 7, that households in the South are more highly debt geared in terms of loan to income ratios. However it is perfectly possible for households to spend a greater proportion of their income on housing but, at the same time, take out as a loan a lower proportion of the property's value. This simply reflects the fact that prices are higher in the South.

A similar position appears to exist in the US. Engelhardt (1994), compares median house prices, average downpayment percentages for first-time buyers and an estimate of the average time taken to save to meet the downpayment, across a range of US cities. Two points stand out from his results. First, in the very expensive coastal cities of California and the North East, the average saving period is much longer than in lower priced cities.

[4] The constrained function could, of course, lie at all points below the unconstrained function in which case there is no kink.

Second, in line with the UK regional findings, the average downpayment is positively correlated with the level of house prices

From the model above, we expect the region with the lowest loan to value ratio (highest downpayment ratio) to experience the strongest fluctuations in house prices. This is precisely what we observe. As noted in Chapter 7, over the period 1969 to 1999 the standard deviation of annual house price inflation in the South East was 12.7% compared with 9.9% in the North. Therefore, prices are noticeably more volatile in the South.

A further question is whether the analysis extends the explanation of the ripple effect discussed in Chapter 7. We saw that the parameters of regional price equations showed a distinct spatial pattern. The parameters in the South were typically larger than in the North and we suggested that differences could be due to variations in debt gearing around the country. This is consistent with the model espoused here.

However, there is a proviso. The model in this section refers primarily to a long-run position rather than the cycle. But a feature of the ripple effect is that prices in the long run tend to return to some long-run fixed relationship. Nevertheless, the model can potentially explain cyclical regional price variations. In *both* the North and South, the loan to value ratio falls in the upturn. But since the downpayment ratio is higher in the South, the percentage change in house prices will be correspondingly greater. As "trend" loan to value ratios are restored over time, so will long-run regional price relativities[5].

We can now return to the question of the relationship between house prices and consumers' expenditure, but from a different perspective. One of the criticisms of the Muellbauer hypothesis of the relationship between consumption and house prices is that it does not readily tally with life-cycle models. Furthermore micro evidence (Attanasio and Weber 1994) suggests that the marked increase in consumption by younger households in the late eighties (who have less accumulated housing equity) is not consistent with housing-based explanations.

But, again, US work on downpayment constraints suggests an alternative route – consistent with life-cycle theory - whereby house prices may have a positive influence on consumers' expenditure. The presence of a binding downpayment constraint may have a number of effects on renters who wish to become owner-occupiers (remembering that a high proportion of young households in the US do not go directly into owner-occupation). First, there is considerable evidence that constraints delay entry into owner-occupation; second, households may demand smaller houses but, third, they may alter

[5] The pattern will be reinforced by the fact that changes in loan to value ratios in the North lag those in the South.

their savings behaviour. One response may be to *increase* savings (reduce consumption) in order to meet the constraint more quickly. Alternatively, households may *reduce* savings (increase consumption), because of a discouragement effect. This effect will be strongest when prices are rising rapidly (because it becomes more difficult to meet the constraint) or if the individual's discount rate is high, i.e. households do not like to forgo current consumption. Essentially, households give up on the goal of owner-occupation in these circumstances and simply consume more other goods. In this case, a positive relationship between house price changes and consumers' expenditure occurs. Engelhardt (1994) argues that the discouragement effect dominates in the US.

9.3.2 Monetary Policy, Planning and Housing Cycles

At first sight the idea that monetary policy and planning policy interact in their effects on housing is not obvious. But the result arises directly from Chapter 6. It is, however, obvious in simple demand/supply models that inelastic supply causes demand shocks to be reflected in large price changes. In rational expectations stock-flow models we saw that prices typically overshoot. If it is the case that planning controls reduce supply responses – and this is a common perception (although rather more difficult to demonstrate empirically), then it is straightforward, at one level to see how planning contributes to volatility. In the US, the finding by Malpezzi (1999) that price-income ratios are positively related to the strength of the regulatory environment is particularly interesting. The analysis becomes slightly more complex when we recognise, as in Chapter 6, that supply is related not only to the level of prices, but also to the rate of change. In this case, volatility in house prices feeds back to supply volatility. This was demonstrated in our simulations.

But how does monetary policy enter the picture? Our simulations on a four-equation model showed that interest rates can play an important policy role. Since both house prices and construction are sensitive to interest rate changes, this is hardly surprising. The simulations suggest that changes in interest rates may help to stabilise the housing market in response to random shocks. But the need for alternative stabilising instruments arises from the existence of weak supply elasticities. Therefore, interest rates provide a useful second-best solution for market stabilisation if governments are not willing to relax planning constraints. But interest rates are, of course, not primarily set with the housing market in mind. Although the Bank of England takes housing market conditions into account, interest rate policy is set in the light of wider inflationary conditions (see King 2000). However if interest rates can help to stabilise housing markets under appropriate instrument settings, by the same argument, interest rates set with wider goals in mind can destabilise housing markets.

To show that broader macroeconomic objectives can *increase* the volatility of housing markets under certain interest rate policy rules, the four-equation model of Chapter 6 is embedded in the full macroeconomic model used earlier to examine crowding out. The results may, therefore, be to some extent model specific, but they still point to a potential policy problem. The nature of the problem becomes clear from simply repeating the simulation in which the model is subjected to a one-off 5% house price shock. In this augmented framework, the critical factor is the choice of interest rate rule and we select three (*i*) the earlier equation (6.12), i.e. an equation related directly to housing conditions (*ii*) a rule that maintains a constant real interest rate (*iii*) a version of the Taylor Rule, which Stuart (1996) suggests is a reasonable approximation to actual UK monetary policy in recent years. This takes the form of (9.5);

$$i_t = p_{t-1} + \alpha_1 (cu)_{t-1} + \alpha_2 (p - p^*)_{t-1} + r^* \tag{9.5}$$

where:

i = nominal interest rate
cu = gap between actual and capacity output
p = rate of inflation
p^* = target rate of inflation
r^* = equilibrium real interest rate

The rule implies a rise in interest rates if either inflation is above target or if demand is above capacity output. The coefficients reflect the weights attached to each target, here assumed to be equal. One drawback of this version of the equation is that it is backward looking, whereas actual policy would consider the expected future values of the variables. In practice, modellers have found that interest rate rules need to be model specific and so the Taylor rule may not be ideal in all circumstances. A further issue concerns the choice of inflation indicator. Here the underlying inflation rate is chosen as the variable on which the Bank generally concentrates. However, this implies that the impact of the housing market on interest rates is small and indirect. By definition, the underlying rate excludes mortgage interest payments and house prices only have a low weight in the Retail Prices Index (RPI). Any further influences stem from the effect of housing on the pressure of demand in the economy as a whole. This includes Muellbauer and Murphy's (1990) view, discussed in the previous section, that house prices affect consumers' expenditure via a wealth effect.

Figure 9.5 shows the effect of the shock on prices under each of the three rules. The question is how quickly the shock dies away and whether cycles are generated. The one-off price shock is expected to fade away over time and, indeed, under the interest rate rule taken from Chapter 6, this fairly quickly happens. In other words, embedding the four-equation housing model in the full macroeconometric model, by itself, has little effect. However, this no longer holds under either of the two other interest rate rules. In each case house prices return to the zero axis much more slowly and, indeed, heavily overshoot. Over the five-year horizon (in quarters), there is little evidence of the shock dying away. There are two problems in using rules not directly aimed at the housing market; first, the initial change in interest rates is not large enough to mitigate the house price shock. Second, since any effect of house prices takes time to feed into the RPI, the timing of the interest rate change is inappropriate for the housing market. The induced interest rate change exacerbates fluctuations in the housing market. We are not, of course, suggesting that interest rate rules should always be aimed at house prices. But, potentially, there is a conflict and the same policy rules are not necessarily suited to all types of shock. Neither can we categorically state that it is impossible to find a rule to stabilise all markets; only that given the structure of the model, we have been unable to find such a rule. It is possible that the introduction of forward-looking expectations, for example, might help to solve the timing problems.

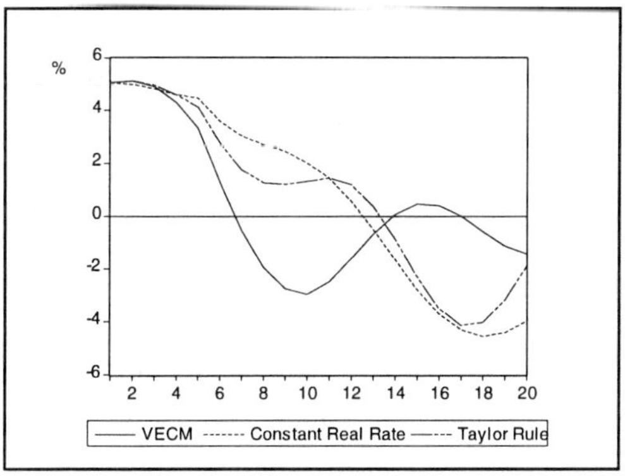

Figure 9.5. 5% House Price Shock - Effect on House Prices of Different Interest Rate Rules

9.4 Housing and Monetary Union

If inflation targetting *within* a country can add to housing volatility, we might think that European-wide monetary policy could make matters even worse since individual country housing conditions will have even less impact. In Chapter 2, we saw that considerable differences in housing volatility still exist across Europe in both construction and prices. Germany and France, for example, are relatively stable compared with the UK and Scandinavia. However, we did not discuss the structural market differences that contribute to the variation in conditions.

Since the beginning of 1999, monetary policy for most European Union members has been set centrally. At the time of writing, only the UK, Sweden, Denmark and Greece have opted out. In the UK, one of the reasons for not entering put forward by some, concerns differences in housing conditions. The most important differences across Europe are:

- variations in owner occupation rates,
- differences in mortgage debt as a percentage of GDP,
- in some countries mortgage debt is primarily at fixed rates but, in others, debt is mainly variable rate[6].

The main arguments are rehearsed in Maclennan *et al* (1998)[7]. The first reason why conditions differ concerns owner-occupation rates. In the UK, it is sometimes argued that owner-occupier rates are high and this is certainly the case compared with Germany and France. The owner-occupancy rate in Britain stands at 68%, but only approximately 40% and 55% in Germany and France respectively. But this is relatively modest compared with Ireland and Spain at around 80% and Greece and Italy at approximately 75%. However, high owner-occupancy rates are not necessarily correlated with high levels of outstanding debt. The ratio of outstanding mortgage loans to GDP stood at 57% in 1995 in the UK, only exceeded in Europe by the Netherlands at 60% and Denmark at 65%. But of the high owner-occupancy countries, the debt ratio was only 27% in Ireland, 22% in Spain, and 6% in Greece and in Italy (Stephens 2000). Clearly a high degree of development in financial markets is not a necessary condition for high levels of owner-occupation. Therefore, in low debt countries, volatility in interest rates is not going to be important despite high owner-occupancy rates.

However, even at high debt ratios, variations in market interest rates would not be important if a high proportion of the mortgage debt were at fixed rates. However, around 70% of mortgage debt is variable rate in the

[6] Planning systems also vary across Europe but these are not discussed.

[7] Maclennan *et al* also consider differences in degrees of financial market liberalisation and differences in transactions costs.

UK, but only 10% in the Netherlands, 20% in France and 40% in Germany. The United Kingdom, therefore, experiences a combination of circumstances unique amongst the European countries - high owner-occupation rates, high debt levels and high proportions of variable rate debt. The trend in recent years in the UK towards mortgages with interest rates fixed for 1-5 year periods has, so far, had only a limited impact on the overall debt stock. In these circumstances, it would be unsurprising to find that (*i*) activity in mainland Europe is less elastic in response to changes in interest rates[8] and (*ii*) the same level of interest rates may not be suitable to all European countries. We might imagine a situation in which the European Central Bank raises interest rates to combat expected inflation, but this would have very different impacts around Europe.

But the view that housing has wider consequences for monetary union is, still, considered controversial. Clearly, if mortgage markets converge in structure across Europe, many of the problems disappear. However, Stephens (2000) argues that, although some features may converge, non-financial aspects of mortgage systems, such as legal frameworks, will prevent the development of a fully integrated European mortgage market. Other arguments, both theoretical and empirical, are summarised in Britton and Whitley (1997). First, they point out that, although *gross* debt may be higher in the UK, there is little difference between the UK, Germany and France in the level of *net* indebtedness and it is the latter which is likely to have the strongest influence on spending decisions. Second, they argue that housing markets have little effect on demand. In the simplest version of the life-cycle model, consumption depends on current and future incomes and, if households are not credit constrained, then consumption is not affected by home-ownership patterns or the extent of variable rate debt[9].

9.5 Planning for Household Growth[10]

For many years, projections of social housing need in Britain have been based on a detailed analysis of demographic trends. Recent projections using this methodology are given in Holmans (1995a), (1996a) for England and Wales respectively, in Forrest *et al* (1995) and in Breheny and Hall (1996). The most recent official household projections, which suggest that the

[8] Note, however, that even this is controversial. Britton and Whitley (1997) estimate simple IS/LM models for different European economies and find no evidence that the IS curve is less elastic with respect to interest rates in Germany.

[9] However we have already seen in more complex life-cycle models, that consumption patterns can depend on the mortgage market and rates of change of house prices.

[10] This section is adapted from Meen (1998).

number of households in England will increase by 3.8 million by 2021, are based on this approach. Broadly the approach takes exogenously determined population projections and applies detailed estimates of future headship and owner-occupancy rates, disaggregated by age and gender, based on past trends. Since relatively small numbers of households are in the private rental sector, the need for social housing is determined by "residual", subtracting the expected increase in owner-occupation from the expected rise in the total number of households. The method has merits; it allows a much finer level of age/gender disaggregation than would be feasible with, say, purely econometric approaches. Furthermore, given the history of UK housing, once households of any age have entered owner-occupation, departures from the tenure have been limited, although there was a significant rise in repossessions of owner-occupied houses in the late eighties and early nineties. Therefore, with the exception of first-time buyers, it has been relatively straightforward to project forward owner-occupancy rates for each group.

However there are a number of implicit assumptions, two of which are particularly important. First, the level of housing demand generated by the owner-occupancy projections represents effective demand. In other words, demand is backed-up by the ability to pay. But there is no necessary reason why this should be the case. At the aggregate level, increases in effective demand depend on changes in the economy's long-run growth rate and on the price at which housing is offered. We have already seen that there have been important changes in the structure of housing demand in the nineties, particularly amongst first-time buyers, induced by labour market changes that have affected both household formation and tenure choice. Traditional demographic methods, based on extrapolating past trends will fail to capture these changes. Second, the approach assumes that the construction industry can meet demand. But, we have found that supply elasticities are typically low. The fact that we observe *ex post* that supply approximately equals demand (although, of course, there have been housing shortages), does not imply that *ex ante* the two are equal at the current price.

The two implicit assumptions and the changes in the nature of the market suggest that the traditional approach needs to be augmented. Our analysis of housing careers in Chapter 5 implies that demographic analysis remains central, but market mechanisms can also be incorporated so that both housing price and output determination are endogenous. In the UK, official projections have already begun to move in this direction (see DETR 1997). However, we can also use the models developed in Chapter 6 to shed light on the issues.

Any sustainable equilibrium for the market requires two conditions. First, for consumers, housing must be "affordable". Although a much used concept in the social housing literature, its definition is not always entirely straightforward. Although we could adopt the usual approach that housing payments should not exceed a certain proportion of income, at least for owner-occupation, we prefer to use the user cost of capital – a measure of the real price of owner-occupier housing services. Meen (1996a) argues that, historically, the user cost has shown little evidence of a strong trend[11]; therefore we expect projections of future housing demand to be consistent with this property. If the user cost rises without bound, housing demand and, hence, prices will simply fall. Note also that structural changes in demand, e.g. because of the labour market, will be reflected in the user cost.

Second, housing construction must be profitable for builders. Clearly without this, extra supply will not be forthcoming. But, from the housing starts equation in Chapter 6, profitability depends on house prices, construction costs and interest rates. In a similar manner to the user cost, an index of builder profitability can be constructed combining the three elements (see Meen 1998).[12]

Moving away from purely demographically based projections, therefore, the three key factors affecting owner-occupancy rates (and subsequently social housing demand) are:

- the capacity of the construction industry and the planning system, which in turn affect the price elasticity of supply,
- growth in the economy which affects incomes and, consequently, affordability and effective housing demand,
- structural changes in home-ownership demand as a result of labour market change.

Bearing these points in mind, we are now in a position to present sample projections of owner-occupancy rates under a range of assumptions; the idea is to demonstrate that economic factors matter in addition to demographic variables. The most important macroeconomic influences are GDP growth, inflation and short-term interest rates. In the baseline projections, over the period 1996-2016, these are set at approximately 2.3%, 2.8% and 8% respectively. The implied affordability and profitability indices are graphed in figures 9.6 and 9.7. The strong rise in the user cost in the late eighties, when the mortgage rate rose to approximately 15%, is apparent along with the increase in affordability subsequently as interest rates fell again. More importantly, the index shows little change over the projection period. Similarly, figure 9.7 shows no fall off in builders' profits (high profits imply a low value of the index). It is important to appreciate, however, that these estimates are not forecasts of profitability and user costs. Rather they

[11] As we might expect for a variable that is based on a real interest rate.

[12] The measure is defined as $(RSH - \dot{P}H)(COST / PH)$.

represent the required values for the system to be in equilibrium. Under these assumptions, the level of housing starts is approximately 160,000 per annum and annual house price growth averages around 6.5% over the period. The estimates imply that the owner-occupancy rate reaches 72% by 2016 (69% excluding sales of public sector dwellings).

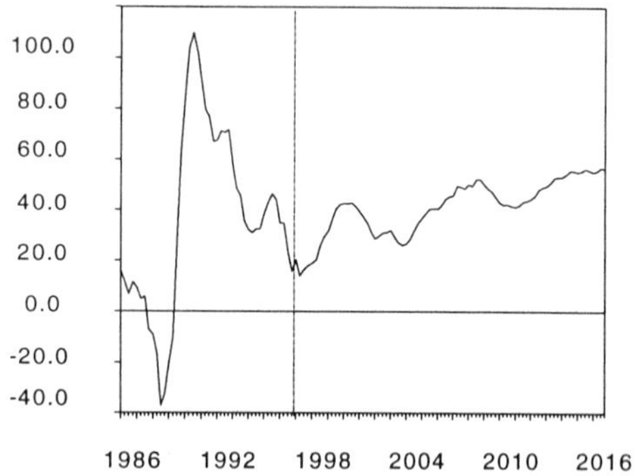

Figure 9.6. Affordability (1990=100)

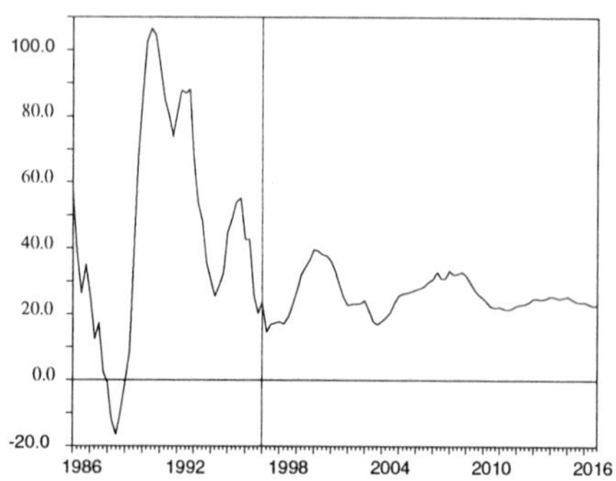

Figure 9.7. Profitability (1990=100)

Now suppose that long-run growth in the economy is significantly higher. We assume that GDP grows by approximately 0.27% per annum more than in the base scenario. In the standard demographic approach, this can only be simulated in an *ad hoc* manner. Here we can trace through the model the effects on construction, house prices and the owner-occupancy rate. However the effects depend crucially on the price elasticity of supply. The lower the elasticity, the greater the effect on prices and the smaller the effect on construction output and owner-occupancy. By implication, if higher incomes increase the number of households, then a greater proportion has to be housed in the rental sectors. Therefore, the simulation is run on both the estimated supply elasticity of 0.3 and an assumed value of 10, which we saw, in Chapter 6, was an approximation to a perfectly elastic supply. The results, in this case run over a ten-year period, which is sufficient to illustrate the main points, are shown in table 9.2. In each scenario, results are shown in terms of differences, either in percentages or absolute terms, from the baseline scenario.

The first half of the table uses the low price elasticity. As expected, the price effects are much larger than those on housing output. The induced increase in the owner-occupancy rate is modest, rising by only 0.5 percentage points in the final year, but house prices are approximately 20% higher than in the base. By contrast, in the second half of the table at the higher supply elasticity, the balance between house prices and construction changes significantly. The higher price elasticity allows the owner-occupation rate to expand by 1.5 percentage points. But to achieve that rate requires new housing to be expanding by almost an *extra* 300,000 in the peak year relative to the baseline projection, which is not feasible under current policies. Note that, at the end of the period, starts do not remain permanently higher, but return approximately to the initial level. This comes about because of a catch-up in construction costs in a high output environment, lowering builders' profits.

Table 9.2. Higher Growth & Supply Elasticities (% changes from base, except where stated)

	Low Elasticity			High Elasticity		
Year	**Starts (000s)**	**House Prices**	**Owner-Occupation Rate (% points)**	**Starts (000s)**	**House Prices**	**Owner-Occupation Rate (% points)**
1	1	0.1	0.00	1	0.1	0.00
2	5	1.5	0.01	10	1.5	0.02
4	15	7.0	0.10	125	6.5	0.20
6	20	14.0	0.25	290	10.5	0.80
8	25	20.0	0.40	160	11.0	1.40
10	20	20.5	0.50	0	9.5	1.50

To conclude, projections of home-ownership rates have usually been based on an analysis of demographic trends under the implicit assumption that supply is perfectly elastic. But this is inadequate since the economic environment and the structure of house building and planning influence the outcomes. Whereas demographic studies have usually allowed for economic factors in an *ad hoc* manner through arbitrary changes to projections of owner-occupancy rates, economic influences can be consistently treated in our framework. Our simulations implied:

- on the basis of current policies and economic performance, in our baseline case, home-ownership rates reach 72% nationally by 2016, allowing for further sales of public sector dwellings. Since the rate is currently 68%, this represents slow growth compared with the seventies and eighties.
- Simulations under alternative assumptions concerning the economy's growth rate indicate that the scope for increasing this figure is limited *unless* the nature of the construction industry and the land use planning system changes substantially. Under present arrangements, increases in the economy's performance will lead to higher house prices rather than higher owner-occupation rates.

Chapter 10

SELECTED ISSUES IN REGIONAL AND URBAN HOUSING POLICY

10.1 Introduction

This chapter continues in a similar vein to the last by examining a selection of policy issues – in this case at the regional and urban levels - on which light can be shed by the use of formal models. At the regional scale, the central issue to be tackled is the extent to which regional economic convergence is aided or hindered by housing market structure and the role that policy plays in the process. There is, of course, now a voluminous literature on international and regional growth convergence, but relatively little of this explicitly takes into account housing markets. In the UK, the work of Bover *et al* (1989), Cameron and Muellbauer (1998, 2000) and subsequent work arising from these studies provide major exceptions and place strong emphasis on housing as a destabilising influence. By contrast, for the USA, the influential work of Blanchard and Katz (1992) on *Regional Evolutions* pays only limited attention to housing issues.

The urban analysis is also partly concerned with convergence and divergence, but in a different context. We suggested earlier that urban areas are potentially subject to cumulative processes of growth and decline, where housing and environmental conditions play a central role. In this chapter, we are concerned with urban/suburban population dynamics. We ask whether the loss of high-income households from city centres is an inevitable process, as our empirical work on London might suggest. However we show that, internationally, different population patterns can emerge. But just because wealthier households inhabit central locations in some countries does not necessarily solve the problems of low-income households. The problem is simply displaced. Cumulative processes of decline can occur just as much in outer areas as in cities.

10.2 Regional Evolutions

The term *Regional Evolutions* is taken from Blanchard and Katz's (1992) work on regional adjustment in the US states. They pose the question of how each state adjusts to demand shocks. In particular, in response to a state specific shock, do wages or employment change? Blanchard and Katz point to the fact that, over a forty-year period, state unemployment differentials have shown no trend and relative wages have converged, despite the fact that states have shown very different employment and output growth rates. The model that they construct implies that, starting from a position of full employment, a positive demand shock in any state raises wages in the short run but this, in turn, generates an increase in in-migration to the state until wages fall back to the original level. Therefore, a permanent demand shock generates permanently higher levels of employment, but both relative wages and unemployment return to their initial levels. This, of course, implies a highly elastic supply of labour in each region caused by migration. In practice, as suggested in Chapter 4, male manual labour appears to be more mobile in the US than in the UK.

In terms of housing, Blanchard and Katz make two points. First, their model assumes that land is not a scarce factor. But in the presence of fixed land supplies, their model loses its property of constant returns to scale. Regions cannot grow at permanently different rates, although they may experience differences in employment levels and relative land prices. Second, Blanchard and Katz estimate a joint model of employment and house prices on the grounds that migrants should take account of the effect of housing costs on relative real wages. They suggest that the influence of demand shocks on employment is not affected strongly by the introduction of house prices to the model, although negative demand shocks initially lower house prices. However prices eventually return to their original level as the supply of housing and land adjust to the lower level of demand[1].

Overall therefore, the main adjustment mechanism in response to demand shocks is through labour mobility, which, in turn, is primarily a response to differences in unemployment rates. Relative real wages, of which house prices are a component, appear to play a secondary role. Many of these conclusions would not be supported by UK research. In particular, migration would play a smaller role. The UK literature suggests that housing can have

[1] Blanchard and Katz emphasise the tentative nature of this result because of poor data quality.

an impact on regional growth rates, wages and unemployment through a number of routes.

First, tenure structure (particularly an over-reliance on owner-occupation) influences mobility and migration. Those in the private rental sector are more likely to be mobile. The results in Chapter 8 supported this conclusion, although there is an element of self-selection. But the proportion of households in the private rental sector is much lower in the UK than in the US. Traditionally, individuals in the social rented sector, which has a higher unemployment rate, have a low degree of mobility. Oswald (1996), in an international comparative study, argues that unemployment rates are positively related to the owner-occupation rate.

Second, relative house prices have a direct impact on migration. The literature suggests that relative employment differences have a strong effect on regional migration (in line with Blanchard and Katz for the US), but regional house prices also appear to have an influence for most areas.

Third, relative house prices affect wages both directly and through the user cost of capital, which is a component of the cost of living. The initial influential work by Bover *et al* (1989) used national data, but the main results were subsequently confirmed on regional data by Blackaby and Manning (1992). Most recently, Cameron and Muellbauer (2000) try to capture house price effects in a reduced form model of earnings and unemployment. In contrast to Blanchard and Katz, they find greater persistence in UK unemployment differentials. Furthermore, a rise in relative house prices raises wages for both full-time men and women, although the effect for males is only significant for non-manual workers.

Fourth, planning operates with a different degree of intensity between areas. Constraints are particularly strong in the South East where housing demand is strongest. This changes relative house prices, feeding back onto each of the above. If the supply of housing were perfectly elastic, then any relative price effect disappears.

Fifth, the system of local property taxation (the Council Tax) is regionally regressive. The average tax rate in the South East is noticeably lower than in the North. These differentials will be capitalised into property prices.

Finally, house prices may affect regional demand via wealth effects on consumers' expenditure. Carruth and Henley (1993), estimating consumption functions for each of the UK standard regions, find no consistent effect, although, using panel data across the regions, Green and Hadjimatheou (1990) reach the opposite conclusion. The significance of housing wealth in regional consumption functions is also confirmed in Muellbauer and Murphy (1994a). Further evidence on the effects of house prices on aggregate demand at the regional level can be found in Evans and

McCormick (1994); they look at the effects of housing wealth and the ability to repay debt on unemployment directly, and find significant effects. Their conclusions are supported by similar work at the county level by Taylor and Bradley (1994).

In the UK literature, therefore, housing plays a stronger role in influencing the degree of regional economic convergence, both through relative price and tenure effects.

10.3 Relative Prices, Planning and Policy

From Chapter 4, most of the UK regional housing literature concerns the so-called North/South divide although, as shown in Chapter 5, the patterns of deprivation are in fact more complex with major pockets of deprivation, particularly in London. For policy, the regional dispersion in prices became a major issue in the late eighties when the gap widened to record levels. Despite higher unemployment in North, the cost of housing in the South East became a major disincentive to migration.

The reasons why prices are higher in the South East have attracted considerable attention. Why has the supply of housing not responded to the increase in demand, leaving relative prices unchanged? The nature of the planning system has inevitably come under criticism since it restricts the supply of new housing. Evans (1988, 1989), for example, has been particularly critical of the economic costs imposed by the nature of planning controls. The costs of planning are, of course, not confined to the UK. From Chapter 6, Abraham and Hendershott (1996) found that evidence of speculative bubbles is greater on the west coast of the USA, where land shortages are strongest. Malpezzi (1999) provides evidence for the USA that house price to income ratios are positively related to the extent of development controls. In a comparative study of Thailand, Malaysia and Korea, Mayo and Sheppard (1996) find that there is a direct relationship between controls and supply elasticities.

The literature on land use planning is enormous in its own right - see, for example, the survey by Monk *et al* (1991). Here, we concentrate on the more limited modelling literature and, in particular, on how land constraints affect house prices. One criticism of modellers raised by Bramley (1993) is that few economists have a detailed knowledge of the intricacies of the planning system - a charge that is, no doubt, true - and this should influence the nature of the models to be estimated. In macro time-series models, as we have seen in Chapter 6, the planning system influences the price elasticity of supply. Low elasticities are cited as evidence that the planning system must be binding. At best, this is indirect evidence and there are other possible interpretations of the result. For example, low elasticities may arise from constraints on the supply of skilled construction workers or, simply, from deficiencies in the organisation of the industry itself.

Direct evidence on the costs of the land use planning system in terms of house prices is limited. Indirect evidence is provided by the fact that, even in the long run, house prices do not rise in line with construction costs. For the UK, direct evidence of the costs primarily comes from two well-known studies using very different methodologies. The first by Cheshire and Sheppard (1989) uses a hedonic approach, based on cross-section information for two towns, Reading and Darlington. The former is an area where controls are thought to be binding and the latter is an area of relatively relaxed controls. The study examines the impact of introducing the Darlington system into Reading. However, their results do not suggest that the North/South differential can be fully explained in terms of planning.

The second study by Bramley (1993, 1993a)[2] constructs a small, three-equation model, covering housing output, house prices and land with planning permission; the endogeneity of the latter is a novelty, but recognises that land availability is, at least partly, determined by market conditions and the decisions of builders in addition to policy factors. The data cover ninety districts, approximating local housing market areas. In contrast to time-series studies of housing starts, the output equation includes land supply explicitly as a regressor. The non-linearities in the equation mean that the elasticities vary between locations, but the mean supply elasticity remains low and similar to those estimated on time-series data. Bramley concludes that the effect of planning on house prices is limited, although there is a bigger effect on new construction. In Bramley's model two issues are central (*i*) the openness of housing markets, i.e. the extent to which planning controls simply divert production to other locations and (*ii*) the size of the "implementation gap" - since it is developers rather than planners who decide on construction, a decision to provide more land is not necessarily translated into higher output. Bramley argues that housing markets are, indeed, open so that the price effects of land controls are limited and that the implementation gap is large.

Such conclusions are bound to be controversial and Evans (1996) makes a number of suggestions as to why Bramley only finds limited evidence of an effect on house prices. The criticisms mainly concern the use of a cross section sample as a basis for drawing policy conclusions of this form. The cross section is unlikely to capture the long-run equilibrium. For example, the large implementation gap may simply reflect the fact that changes in

[2] The work is extended further in Bramley and Watkins (1996) to cover a wider locational area and different time periods. The main conclusions of the earlier study remain, however, intact.

planning are unlikely to be reflected in new permissions in the same year. There is a time lag involved, even though the estimation period (the late eighties) was one of housing market boom, which might be expected to shorten the lags somewhat. Similarly the weak responsiveness of housing output to land availability may also reflect a disequilibrium phenomenon.

In conclusion, therefore, the question of the quantitative effect of land use controls on regional price differentials remains unsettled in the UK. In empirical models it has proved difficult to identify large effects, although the economic theory suggests that the effects should be substantial. More direct evidence comes from Evans (1988) who points to the huge difference in value between agricultural land and land with planning permission in the South East.

10.4 Urban Population Dynamics

Urban-suburban drift has become a key policy issue in Britain. Although this is a phenomenon facing metropolitan areas in general, the problem has attracted most attention in London and the South East. The problem has two dimensions. First, population movements have led to an increasing concentration of low-income households in parts of the urban core with associated problems of deprivation, social exclusion and economic polarisation. Second, out-migration to the suburbs has put increasing strain on Green Belt land in the counties surrounding London. A central feature of policy is now to ensure that 60% of new house building is on Brownfield sites in order to ease the burden. The two questions that we address are (*i*) whether these population patterns are inevitable, (*ii*) whether reversing the patterns would benefit low-income households.

We noted in Chapter 5 that standard location models do not provide an entirely satisfactory explanation of economic polarisation. From a British or American perspective, there is, perhaps, a tendency to think that wealthy households are always concentrated in the suburbs and this could be consistent with the view that the income elasticity of housing demand is high (although empirical evidence in Chapter 6 certainly does not provide convincing evidence). The problem is that, taking a wider international perspective, the distribution of wealthier households is more complex. Brueckner *et al* (1999) show that household incomes are noticeably higher in the Paris metropolitan area than in the suburbs and suggest that this pattern is not uncommon in Europe. We have shown already that wealthier households in Australia also tend to favour central locations.

Although it might be argued that these international patterns simply reflect differences in income elasticities and the valuation of travel time, this is not satisfactory since we would have to explain why the elasticities themselves vary. Alternatively, we might ask whether there are other directions in which location theory might be extended. A full explanation requires a general equilibrium framework, encompassing residential location choice, labour markets and firm location. We showed in Chapter 8 how, in principle, the combination of these factors can generate economic polarisation through cumulative causation. In our model, neighbourhood amenities played a central role. Recently, partial models of residential location have also considered the role of amenities. Brueckner *et al* (1999) argue that differences in location patterns between Paris and Detroit can be ascribed to amenity differences at the core. In general, those cities providing a high level of amenities will attract wealthier households. These conclusions are very much in line with our own empirical findings.

Three general observations aid our later analysis. *First*, the idea of cumulative causation has gained ground in housing economics in recent years, having become more fashionable in economics as a whole again, due to the work of Krugman (1991)[3]. Amongst the central ideas of Krugman's work is the conflict between centripetal and centrifugal forces. Depending on the relative strength of these forces, economic activity will be either concentrated in a small number of locations or dispersed.

Although housing does not enter into Krugman's models, the ideas of cumulative causation can be found in housing models. Population flows may, in some circumstances, generate cumulative processes of decline in urban areas. Recently Galster (1998) has modelled, for a sample of a hundred US cities, the linkages between housing, mortgages, labour markets, the public sector, crime rates and education and shows how these factors are mutually reinforcing through feedback loops. As a result, processes of cumulative urban decline can be generated. Less formally, for the UK, the following quotation from Keenan *et al* (1999) dramatically captures the main concerns.

> "Once a few properties are boarded up confidence in the area begins to be undermined and the life-blood of the community begins to seep away. Corner shops close down, people that can choose to move drift away and housing abandonment intensifies. Property values quickly ebb away and rental housing becomes difficult to let. Petty criminals, pimps and serious crime, often associated with drugs, soon move in,"

The quotation is hinting at processes of cumulative causation. Price movements are unable to bring about a spatial equilibrium, where all areas are growing at the same rate.

[3] The idea of increasing returns and cumulative causation, of course, has a much longer history dating back to Marshall (1920), Myrdal (1957) and Kaldor (1972) for example.

Power and Mumford (1999) and Power (2000) also describe the cumulative processes of urban decline leading to neighbourhood collapse. They argue that the most disadvantaged areas experience:

- a skewed tenure distribution with large concentrations of social housing,
- rapid depopulation over long time periods,
- concentrated deprivation as in-comers are more deprived than out-goers.

This leads to:

- a rapid turnover of tenants and high vacancy rates,
- a decline in local demand,
- pressures to build outside the city, so that households can escape the worst inner areas.

But, in contrast to the USA, Power argues that concentrated poverty is frequently not connected with race. White populations as well as ethnic minorities can experience deprivation.

Second, at least in the UK, the geographical pattern of employment growth has not matched the pattern of housing provision. The collection of papers in Breheny (1999) describes the continuing concentration of employment growth in South East England. But housing shortages, fuelled by planning constraints, have led to a worsening of housing affordability, measured in terms of house price to income ratios. Monk (2000) describes the problems that this has engendered for the recruitment of "key workers", particularly in the public sector. Lower income workers have become excluded from high-quality areas in the counties that border London.

Third, the model of Brueckner *et al* (1999) considers amenities within the context of residential location theory and it is worth highlighting some of the main conclusions. Suppose that conventional factors (based on income elasticities) mean that high-income households prefer to locate in the suburbs, but the city centre has better amenities. In this case, if the amenities are valued highly enough by wealthy households, these will override the more conventional forces. Amenity could come to dominate location patterns. Furthermore, if amenities are endogenous, i.e. high-quality environments are, themselves, caused by the presence of the wealthy, the possibility of multiple equilibria exists. Either the city or the suburbs could be an equilibrium depending on where the rich decide to reside. Amenities become self-reinforcing and the wealthy become reluctant to leave wherever they originally decide to locate.

From a policy perspective, this can be important since it implies that the problem is not location *per se*, but the location of low-income households. Inner city improvements, which add to amenities, may attract the wealthy, but the poor simply become displaced to other locations.

10.5 Urban Structure

Some of these points can now be used to address our two original questions concerning population patterns. As noted in Chapter 5, within urban areas, population changes are determined primarily by short distance moves across local authority boundaries and, at this level, moves result primarily from housing considerations with the labour market playing only a subsidiary role. Over time, employment patterns may adjust so that employees work closer to home but, typically, work place and housing changes do not occur simultaneously. Recently, Bate *et al* (2000) have shown that the increase in population in the South of the country (excluding London) has been dominated by short distance migration from London. International migration, natural increase and migration from the northern regions play a much smaller role. Therefore the strong pressures on housing markets and land provision in the South East have arisen not from North/South migration related to employment, but from out-migration from London. This is, of course, consistent with the empirical findings in Chapter 8. London itself, by contrast, has maintained its population through a combination of high rates of natural increase, international immigration and in-migration from the northern regions by young households. This is the only age group for which London experiences net in-migration.

In order to answer our two original questions, it is useful to compare Britain with another country, which has managed to preserve a higher concentration of wealthier households close to the urban centre. Australia, or more precisely Melbourne, is chosen for the comparison, since the city's experiences have wider applicability.

There are three key issues, arising from the models of Chapters 5 and 8, which determine migration patterns.

(*i*) *within* any labour market area, housing sub-markets will exist differing in terms of their neighbourhood characteristics, since certain features are not always reproducible. Therefore households will not be indifferent between residential locations, standardising on distance to the city centre. Sub-markets also exist in terms of tenure since the proportions of the housing stock in each tenure vary both within and between countries.

(*ii*) Different household types value neighbourhood characteristics in different ways at various points in their housing careers. For example, the quality of local schools may not be important to young, single person households, but could be crucial to couples with children. Therefore sub-markets are also defined in terms of household types, based on demographic characteristics.

(iii) The process of matching household and housing sub-markets generates the observed patterns of migration and the changes in urban/suburban residential structure.

A corollary is that simply building extra dwellings in city centres will not necessarily bring back residents, since dwellings in different locations are not perfect substitutes. In summary, the matching processes, and hence population movements, will depend on four factors:
- the housing careers of inhabitants,
- neighbourhood conditions in each location,
- the tenure structure in each location,
- work patterns and the distribution of employment opportunities.

10.5.1 Housing Careers and the Neighbourhood

The importance of a framework that analyses housing careers and neighbourhood conditions in order to explain spatial structure has been emphasised at length in Chapters 5 and 8 and, hence, the arguments do not need repeating. But two further comments are in order. First if, as appears to be the case, young, newly forming households are more likely to be attracted to the urban centre, changes in new household formation rates have particular consequences for cities. We have seen that, during the nineties in both the UK and Australia, there has been a marked decline in the rate of new household formation and owner-occupancy, related to changes in the income distribution. Second, for existing households, neighbourhood conditions are an important determinant of location choice. But, as we shall see in more detail below, there are major differences in neighbourhood conditions in the inner urban areas of Australia compared with Britain. Melbourne has been successful in retaining wealthy households partly because of the attractiveness of its inner area neighbourhoods.

10.5.2 Tenure Structure

Both Australia and Britain have similar owner-occupancy rates at approximately 70%, but tenure structures differ between urban and suburban areas. In London, the owner-occupation rate is 56% compared with 72% in the Rest of the South East. Unsurprisingly, private renting in Greater London is higher than in the rest of the country at 17% of the stock. But a big difference between Britain and Australia is the social rented share - 27% in London, 15% in the Rest of the South East, but only approximately 5% in Melbourne. Low-income households are housed primarily in the private rented sector in Melbourne. The point of highlighting these differences is that housing availability (whether directly or indirectly through price) will determine the location of *low-income* households. Crudely, low-income households in the worst inner areas of London become trapped in those areas because of the absence of alternatives. Affordability and poorer access to credit markets rule out a move by social sector tenants into owner-occupation. The absence of a viable private rental sector prevents migration to other areas by this route, whereas an excess supply of social housing in city centres and an excess demand in suburban areas limit intra-tenure transfers. By contrast, in Australia, although low-income households are concentrated in private renting, Australia still suffers from a shortage of low-cost private rentals, (Yates and Wulff 2000). As a result, excess demand has raised rents so that low-income households are relegated to cheaper outer areas. There is no necessary reason why low-income households are concentrated in inner areas – it depends partly on availability in the different tenures.

10.5.3 Work Patterns and the Distribution of Employment

Here the key issue is the distribution of employment and unemployment within urban areas and how this affects residential patterns. If workers are highly mobile, then changes in the distribution of employment from urban to suburban locations, should have little effect on residential location – commuting patterns adjust. But we saw in Chapter 8 that local labour market areas are positively related to income levels – the more highly skilled have wider travel-to-work areas. It is in fact true for both the South East and for Melbourne that a high correlation exists between workplace and residential locations. This has been put forward to support the view that labour market areas are small, are not "seamless" within the urban area and policy needs to be aimed at increasing jobs in high unemployment areas. But these correlations do not necessarily imply that labour market areas are limited; they might also indicate that firm (re)location itself is sufficiently flexible to adapt to residential preferences. In Chapter 8, we argued that firm location could not be taken as an exogenous variable and the extent to which "jobs move to workers" potentially varied according to industrial sector. What this indicates, however, is that in a full general equilibrium model, housing, labour markets and industrial location have to be considered jointly.

10.6 Is Population Loss from Cities Inevitable?

Cheshire (1995) shows that urban losses are not inevitable. But we have to look closely at why some cities have recovered. The reasons are unlikely to be identical in each case, but our case study raises a number of issues, which imply that a general recovery in city populations cannot be taken for granted. Cities that re-populate have a number of distinct advantages.

Melbourne reached a population peak in the years immediately after the First World War, but lost population fairly continuously over the following seventy years as inhabitants moved outwards, towards the suburbs. Melbourne became one of the lowest density cities in the world; it is approximately 50% larger in area than urban Paris, but has around 50% of Paris' population. But, from the beginning of the nineties, the city's population loss was arrested and, in 1999, the City was the strongest growing local government area in the state of Victoria, with its population rising by 6.6% (Department of Infrastructure 2000). Fears expressed in the seventies and eighties that the city centre would become depopulated with continuous movement towards the suburbs have proved groundless.

Before 1992, the inner part of Melbourne was not a major location for new construction activity. Most new housing was on the urban fringes and consisted of detached dwellings. But, since then, inner area building has risen substantially and, at the centre in the City of Melbourne, the share of metropolitan building activity rose to almost 6% in 1996, compared with 2% in 1992, (Department of Infrastructure, 2000). However, it is important to recognise that most new houses are still built on the urban fringes.

The reasons behind the changes are multi-faceted. They are partly related to changes in planning regulations in 1993, which encouraged higher building densities within established areas, leading to the sub-division of existing plots. Within the City, the redevelopment of large areas, such as the docklands, had a significant impact. But equally important have been changes in work practices, lifestyles and demography. In particular, in common with many other countries, Australia has experienced a reduction in average household size, with increasing numbers of single person households and couples without children. Sub-markets have developed; larger families still, typically, demand detached houses in the outer suburbs, whereas new City developments have been dominated by young households (with fewer children) in the 20-29 age group. In 1996, 25% of inner city residents were in this age group compared with 16.5% in the Melbourne Statistical Division as a whole. Furthermore, inner city residents are more highly qualified, work in managerial and professional occupations, typically in service industries, and earn more than the Statistical Division average. For example, 20% have higher degrees (9% for the Statistical Division) and 10% (5.9%) earn more than A$1,000 per week (Department of Infrastructure, 2000). Melburnians, at the urban core, are highly mobile with 75% of residents in the City of Melbourne having moved between 1991 and 1996 (compared with 43% in the metropolitan area as a whole).

In contrast to London, educational performance is markedly better in the inner areas. Failure rates in school examinations vary across the metropolitan area, but the wealthy Inner East labour force region has a much lower failure rate than the poorer Outer West region. Similarly, in November 1999, the highest unemployment rate was to be found in the North Western region at 9.7%, followed by the Outer Western at 9.3%. In terms of the Brueckner *et al* (1999) model, neighbourhood characteristics of this form are "endogenous amenities". Neighbourhood conditions and the location of wealthy households build upon each other. On the other hand, the size and location of the public sector housing stock are exogenous, determined by the historical decisions of state and commonwealth housing authorities. Both endogenous and exogenous amenities are crucial in explaining differences in population patterns between Melbourne and London.

In summary, there are, perhaps, four main explanations of Melbourne's recovery. First, traditionally, construction in Melbourne has been at low densities, But changes in planning regulations in the early nineties to encourage medium density building and the subdivision of existing plots has led to an increase in land availability in inner areas. The same opportunities are not available in London without building at even higher densities.

Second, differences in tenure and in the nature of housing support encourage the concentration of low-income households in inner areas in Britain, but in outer areas in Australia. Therefore, deprivation in inner areas is reduced, but at the cost of greater deprivation in outer areas. Based on the Australian Bureau of Statistics Index of Socioeconomic Disadvantage, Wulff and Evans (1999) show that households in the public sector are still concentrated in areas of disadvantage as in Britain, but the proportion of public housing in the overall stock is much smaller. However the spatial distribution of low-income private tenants is more diverse than for public sector tenants. Private tenants live in areas with broader social patterns. This tendency is reinforced by the fact that small landlords dominate the private rental market. Large-scale estates of deprivation are less likely to occur.

Third, Melbourne enjoys higher environmental standards, in many inner areas, than in Britain. These have acted as an attraction to higher income households. Nevertheless, there is still a strong degree of market segmentation. Although the City of Melbourne is amongst the fastest growing local government areas, larger families with children are still following traditional patterns, demanding detached housing in the suburbs. Quantitatively, building of this form still dominates and, in this respect, is no different to Britain. Pressures on Greenfield sites remain. This brings us to the final point. Central Melbourne growth is in a narrow, although expanding market. The market caters for young, small, high-income households.

10.7 Housing and Low-Income Households

Australia has not solved the problem of low-income housing. But the difference is that the problem areas are in different locations, primarily in outer rather than in inner suburbs[4]. Both unemployment and weak educational performance are concentrated in these areas. What Melbourne does suggest, however, is that deprivation is not intrinsically related to location, but to the type of households that live in any area. Locational disadvantage is primarily a *result* of concentrations of low income/low skill households, which do not necessarily have to be at the urban core.

This is consistent with the idea of multiple equilibria. If amenity advantages are endogenous and arise primarily from the characteristics of the resident population, high-income households become reluctant to move away from others of similar socio-economic status. But those locations could be in either the city or in the suburbs. If Britain manages to improve its urban areas, bringing back high-income families, the likelihood is that low income/low skilled households currently living in the outer areas would suffer. The problem is simply displaced.

10.8 Cumulative Growth and Decline – Some Conclusions

The last two sections have suggested that cumulative processes of urban-suburban growth and decline can occur from the housing market alone, particularly if amenities are endogenous, generated by the nature of the resident population. But one of the lessons of Chapter 8 is that full explanations of urban structure require general equilibrium approaches, encompassing both labour markets and industrial location. Since full general equilibrium approaches are uncommon, we have to be speculative at some points and cautious in our conclusions.

The model in Chapter 8 came to the following conclusions. First, in terms of the housing market, mobility is stronger amongst the under 40s, amongst those marrying and amongst households with pre-school children. Britain and Australia share these characteristics; moreover, families with children are more likely to demand larger houses in the outer urban areas in both countries. But high-income households have a greater probability of moving. In Britain, this reinforces population out-movements for families with children although, as in Melbourne, higher incomes widen the housing choices of single person households within inner London areas. But, in general, moving households will tend to be attracted by better environmental conditions in suburban locations. Moreover, since mobility falls above the

[4] This is a simplification since sub-markets exist within both inner and outer areas.

age of forty, it becomes difficult to attract families back to cities even if government action leads to an improvement in environmental conditions. There is, therefore, an asymmetry in behaviour. Improvements in environmental conditions may, perhaps, limit the losses of current young households from cities in the future, but the probability of attracting older families back to British cities is low in our judgement. In general, the greater mobility of high-income households tends to exacerbate polarisation between housing sub-markets.

From our analysis of labour markets, we found that:

- labour market status is primarily related to educational qualifications. This conforms to the so-called "characteristics approach" to unemployment.
- There is a tendency towards either zero or two workers families in Britain. This reinforces polarisation even further.

Therefore, the low skilled are more likely to be unemployed or to be on low incomes. But those on low incomes have a lower probability of moving. Furthermore, as high income, employed households move away from the centre, the unemployment rate in the inner city will rise even further, which makes those locations even less desirable. Two income households are particularly likely to move. Note, however, that skills improvement programmes, by themselves, can actually make the position worse since those whose skills improve are likely to join the general exodus. The widening gap in unemployment rates between London and the Rest of the South East, shown in figure 5.1, can be seen in this light, reflecting the relative worsening of the skills base in London.

Since unemployment in cities has often been ascribed to job losses, industrial location decisions need to be examined to complete the picture. Our time-series results in Chapter 8 suggested there is evidence, in manufacturing, that firms follow workers. Although the determinants of industrial location are multi-faceted, surveys also suggest that the availability of white-collar labour is one of the most important factors determining firm location across a broad range of industrial sectors (see Gordon 1999). Gordon also suggests that firms away from Central London typically place greater emphasis on the availability of skilled labour. But skilled labour is attracted to areas of better housing. Therefore, both firms and the skilled workforce tend to be co-located.

Under this view of the world, the low skilled are of less importance to firm location since they can be recruited from local labour markets. Relocating firms are much more likely to take their senior staff with them if they can. If this is correct, then the large scale losses of manual, manufacturing jobs from cities, described by Turok and Edge (1998) and Bailey *et al* (2000) are predictable, but it does not follow that the solution is to encourage firms back to cities. Firm location is endogenous. The disadvantage of encouraging firms back to inner cities is that the firms may no longer be able to attract the highly skilled and may suffer competitive losses. The extent to which this is achievable depends on the willingness to commute. Porter (1995) provides case studies of firms that have failed because of an inability to maintain key staff in deprived areas of US cities. Overall, the disadvantages of such policies may outweigh the advantages.

There is a similarity to spatial mismatch models (see Holzer, 1991 or Ihlanfeldt and Sjoquist, 1998 for surveys). However the story is not identical. Here, mismatch arises primarily from skill differences, which lead to housing market constraints, occurring either in credit markets or resulting from the tenure structure. This, of course, does not rule out mismatch arising from racial discrimination as well.

Finally, a major policy concern is the co-existence of excess housing demand in some parts of the country and excess supply in others. This partly reflects differences in the pressure of demand around the country, but is exacerbated by policy. There has been little coordination in planning between expected job growth and housing provision. Strong employment growth in the South of England has led to house price pressures and to a worsening of affordability. As in Section 10.2, this generates higher wages, at least for highly skilled staff, but the main sufferers have been "key workers" in the public sector, such as teachers and nurses, whose salaries are set primarily by national pay scales, and newly-forming households from the children of local residents, who are squeezed out of the market. These trends have arisen from a combination of planning controls on new housing development and the cumulative growth processes described above.

But excess supplies of dwellings simultaneously exist in mainly urban areas around the country. Bramley *et al* (2000) describe the geographical patterns of the excess stocks. These arise, again, from cumulative processes of decline. As Power (2000) describes, turnover rates in difficult to let public sector estates are considerably higher than elsewhere. In policy terms, these twin issues have typically been considered separately from one another. What our analysis shows is that both are features of common processes, cumulative growth in some areas accompanied by cumulative decline in others.

Chapter 11

... AND FINALLY

Almost all problems known to theoretical economics and econometrics crop up in some guise or other in housing analysis. This is both the beauty and the frustration of the subject. Furthermore, the field is multi-disciplinary. Sociologists or political scientists, for example, who are also heavily involved in housing, would probably be horrified by the approaches and models adopted in this book.

To make life more complex, the literatures in North America and Europe are not fully consistent or concerned with the same topics. This partly reflects general methodological differences – approaches to applied econometrics in general are rather different on each side of the Atlantic – and partly reflects differences in policy concerns and institutional frameworks. UK policy is still heavily concerned with public housing, since more than 20% of the housing stock remains in this sector. Therefore public sector rent and subsidy policies remain a central concern. Differences in tenure structures between countries influence the balance of research. The UK and most of Europe have only a limited secondary mortgage market (see Coles and Hardt 2000), but the dominance of this market in the USA again influences the focus of attention.

Nevertheless, we have attempted to emphasise issues that we consider central and which straddle the international divide. First, with increasing income dispersion in many countries, caused by labour market reform, standard quantitative time-series analysis of housing markets has become less relevant. Aggregate relationships will typically break down, except under very limited conditions, which typically will not hold.

Second, spatial analysis matters. In recent years there has been a tendency to treat housing in the finance literature simply as another asset to be modelled in the same way as shares or government bonds. Housing, of course, has a strong investment dimension but, as noted in Chapter 1, it also has a number of other distinctive characteristics that distinguish it from financial assets. These mean that random walk models and arbitrage pricing relationships, for example, do not immediately hold. Spatial fixity is key amongst these characteristics.

The problem is that a fully consistent framework that integrates each of the main spatial scales - national, regional and urban – does not exist. Traditionally, each of these dimensions has been treated in isolation. Nevertheless, we have attempted to show that some progress can be made.

Finally, we have stressed that, for analysing many housing issues, a general equilibrium framework is required. Issues of urban-suburban population drift, spatial housing shortages and excess demand are general equilibrium problems that can only be partly analysed by looking at housing markets in isolation.

References

Abraham, J.M., and P.H. Hendershott. (1996). "Bubbles in Metropolitan Housing Markets". *Journal of Housing Research* 7(2): 191-207.

Alexander, C., and M. Barrow. (1994). "Seasonality and Cointegration of Regional House Prices in the UK." *Urban Studies* 31(10): 1667-1689.

Alonso, W. (1964). *Location and Land Use: Toward a General Theory of Land Rent.* Cambridge Mass: Ballinger.

Anas, A., and R.J. Arnott. (1993). "Development and Testing of the Chicago Prototype Housing Market Model." *Journal of Housing Research* 4(1): 73-129.

Anas, A. and R.J. Arnott (1994). "The Chicago Prototype Housing Market Model with Tenure Choice and Its Policy Applications." *Journal of Housing Research* 5(1): 23-90.

Anas, A. and R.J. Arnott (1997). "Taxes and Allowances in a Dynamic Equilibrium Model of Urban Housing with a Size-Quality Hierarchy." *Regional Science and Urban Economics* 27: 547-580.

Andrew, M., and G.P. Meen. (1999). "An Explanation of Declining Rates of Young Household Formation in the Nineties". *University of Reading Discussion Paper in Urban and Regional Economics No. 138.*

Anselin, A. (1988). *Spatial Econometrics: Methods and Models.* Kluwer Academic Publishers.

Artle, R., and P. Varaiya. (1978). "Life Cycle Consumption and Home-Ownership." *Journal of Economic Theory* 18: 38-58.

Åsberg, P. (1999). "Housing Decisions of Young Swedish Adults." *Journal of Housing Economics* 8(2): 116-143.

Ashworth, J., and S. Parker. (1997). "Modelling Regional House Prices in the UK." *Scottish Journal of Political Economy* 44(3): 225-46.

Attanasio, O.P., and G. Weber. (1994). "The UK Consumption Boom of the Late 1980s: Aggregate Implications of Microeconomic Evidence." *Economic Journal* 104(427): 1269-1302.

Baffoe-Bonnie, J. (1998). "The Dynamic Impact of Macroeconomic Aggregates on Housing Prices and Stock of Houses: A National and Regional Analysis." *Journal of Real Estate Finance and Economics* 17(2): 179-198.

Bailey, M.J., R.F. Muth., and H.O. Nourse. (1963). "A Regression Method for Real Estate Price Index Construction." *Journal of the American Statistical Association* 58(304): 933-942.

Bailey, N., and I. Turok. (2000). "Adjustment to Job Loss in Britain's Major Cities". *Department of Urban Studies: University of Glasgow.*

Ball, M. (1996). *Housing and Construction, a Troubled Partnership?* Joseph Rowntree Foundation.

Ball, M., and A. Wood. (1999). "Housing Investment: Long Run International Trends and Volatility." *Housing Studies* 14(2): 185-210.

Barkham, R.J., and D.M. Geltner. (1996). "Price Discovery and Efficiency in the UK Housing Market." *Journal of Housing Economics* 5: 41-63.

Bar-Nathan, M., M. Beenstock., and Y. Haitovsky. (1998). "The Market for Housing in Israel." *Regional Science and Urban Economics* 28(1): 21-49.

Barot, B. (1998). "An Econometric Model for Private House Prices and Stock. The Demand and Supply Sides for the Household Sector in Sweden". *National Institute of Economic Research: Sweden.*

Barrow, M., and A. O'Sullivan. (1984). "The Empirical Determination of House Prices, Error Correction Mechanisms and Correction of Errors." *Urban Studies* 21(1): 89-91.

Bate, R., R. Best, and A. Holmans. (2000). *On the Move: The Housing Consequences of Migration.* Joseph Rowntree Foundation: York.

Berg, L. (1994). "Household Savings and Debts: The Recent Experience of the Nordic Countries." *Oxford Review of Economic Policy* 10(2): 42-53.

Berg, L., and R. Bergstrom. (1995). "Housing and Financial Wealth, Financial Deregulation and Consumption - The Swedish Case." *Scandinavian Journal of Economics* 97(3): 421-439.

Berger, T., P. Englund, P.H. Hendershott, and B. Turner. (2000). "The Capitalization of Interest Subsidies: Evidence from Sweden." *Journal of Money, Credit and Banking* 32(2): 199-217.

Berkovec, J.A., and J.L. Goodman. (1996). "Turnover as a Measure of Demand for Existing Homes."*Real Estate Economics* 24(4): 421-440.

Blackaby, D.H., and D.N. Manning. (1992). "Regional Earnings and Unemployment – A Simultaneous Approach." *Oxford Bulletin of Economics and Statistics.* 54: 481-502.

Blanchard, O.J., and S. Fischer. (1989). *Lectures on Macroeconomics.* MIT Press: Cambridge, Massachusetts.

Blanchard, O.J., and L.F. Katz. (1992). "Regional Evolutions." *Brookings Papers in Economic Activity* 1: 1-61.

Blanchard, O.J., and D. Quah. (1989). "The Dynamic Effects of Aggregate Demand and Supply Disturbances." *American Economic Review* 79(4): 655-673.

Blanchard, O.J., and D. Quah. (1993). "The Dynamic Effects of Aggregate Demand and Supply Disturbances: Reply." *American Economic Review* 83(4): 653-658.

Boelhouwer, P.J. (2000). "Convergence in European Mortgage Systems Before and After EMU." *Journal of Housing and the Built Environment* 15(1): 11-28.

Borsch-Supan, A., and J. Pitkin. (1988). "On Discrete Choice Models of Housing Demand." *Journal of Urban Economics* 24: 153-172.

Bourassa, S.C. (1995). "A Model of Housing Tenure Choice in Australia." *Journal of Urban Economics* 37(2): 161-175.

Bourassa, S.C., F. Hamelink., M. Hoesli., and B.D. MacGregor. (1999). "Defining Housing Submarkets." *Journal of Housing Economics*. 8(2): 160-183.

Bover, O., J. Muellbauer., and A. Murphy. (1989). "Housing, Wages and UK Labour Markets." *Oxford Bulletin of Economics and Statistics* 51(2): 97-136.

Bramley, G. (1993). "The Impact of Land Use Planning and Tax Subsidies on the Supply and Price of Housing in Britain." *Urban Studies* 30(1): 5-30.

Bramley, G. (1993a). "Land Use Planning and the Housing Market In Britain: The Impact on Housebuilding and House Prices." *Environment and Planning A* 25(7): 1021-1051.

Bramley, G., M. Munro., and S. Lancaster. (1997). *The Economic Determinants of Household Formation: A Literature Review*. Report for the Department of the Environment, Transport and the Regions.

Bramley, G., H. Pawson., and H. Third. (2000). *Low Demand, Housing and Unpopular Neighbourhoods*. Edinburgh College of Art/Heriot-Watt University.

Bramley, G., and C. Watkins. (1996). *Steering the Housing Market: New Building and the Changing Planning System*. The Policy Press, Joseph Rowntree Foundation.

Breedon, F.J., and M.A.S. Joyce. (1993). "House Prices, Arrears and Possessions: A Three Equation Model for the UK." *Bank of England Working Paper No. 14*.

Breheny, M. (1999). *The People: Where Will They Work?"* TCPA: London.

Breheny, M., and P. Hall. (1996). *The People: Where Will They Go?* TCPA: London.

Britton, E. and J. Whitley. (1997). "Comparing the Monetary Transmission Mechanism in France, Germany and the United Kingdom: Some Issues and Results." *Bank of England Quarterly Bulletin* May:152-162.

Brown, J., H. Song, and A. McGillvray. (1997). "Forecasting UK House Prices: A Time Varying Coefficient Approach." *Economic Modelling* 14(4): 529-548.

Brueckner, J. (1986). "The Downpayment Constraint and Housing Tenure Choice: A Simplified Exposition." *Regional Science and Urban Economics* 16: 519-525.

Brueckner, J., J-F. Thisse., and Y. Zenou. (1999). "Why Is Central Paris Rich and Downtown Detroit Poor? An Amenity-Based Theory." *European Economic Review* 43: 91-107.

Buckley, R., and J. Ermisch. (1982). "Government Policy and House Prices in the United Kingdom: An Econometric Analysis." *Oxford Bulletin of Economics and Statistics* 44(4): 273-304.

Buckley, R., and J. Ermisch. (1983) "Theory and Empiricism in the Econometric Modelling of House Prices." *Urban Studies* 20(1):83-90.

Burbidge, A. (2000). "Capital Gains, Homeownership and Economic Inequality." *Housing Studies* 15(2): 259-280.

Burrows, R. (1998). *The Dynamics of the Owner-Occupied Housing Market.* CML Research Report.

Burrows, R., and S. Wilcox. (2000). "Half the Poor? The Growth of Low-Income Home-Ownership." *Housing Finance*, 47: 47-54.

Byatt, I.C.R., A.E. Holmans., and D.E.W. Laidler. (1973). "Income and the Demand for Housing: Some Evidence for Great Britain." in M. Parkin and A. Nobay (eds), *Essays in Modern Economics.* Longmans, London.

Cameron, G., and J. Muellbauer. (1998). "The Housing Market and Regional Commuting and Migration Choices." *Scottish Journal of Political Economy* 45: 420-446.

Cameron, G., and J. Muellbauer. (2000). "Earnings, Unemployment and Housing: Evidence from a Panel of British Regions". *CEPR Discussion Paper No. 2404.*

Can, A. (1992). "Specification and Estimation of Hedonic Housing Price Models." *Regional Science and Urban Economics* 22(3): 453-474.

Can, A., and I. Megbolugbe. (1997). "Spatial Dependence and House Price Index Construction." *Journal of Real Estate Finance and Economics* 14(1,2): 203-222.

Capozza, D.R., R.K. Green, and P.H. Hendershott. (1998). "Tax Reform and House Prices: Large or Small Effect?" *Paper presented at the National Tax Association meeting*: Austin, Texas.

Carruth, A., and A. Henley. (1993). "Housing Assets and Consumer Spending: A Regional Analysis." *Regional Studies* 27(7): 611-622.

Case, B., H. Pollakowski., and S. Wachter. (1991). "On Choosing Among House Price Index Methodologies." *AREUEA Journal.* 19(3): 286-307.

Case, B., H. Pollakowski, and S. Wachter. (1997). "Frequency of Transaction and House Price Modelling." *Journal of Real Estate Finance and Economics* 14(1,2): 173-187.

Case, B., and J.M. Quigley. (1991). "The Dynamics of Real Estate Prices." *Review of Economics and Statistics* 73(3): 50-58.

Case, K.E,, and R.J. Shiller. (1989). "The Efficiency of the Market for Single Family Homes." *American Economic Review* 79(1): 125-137.

Case, K.E., and R.J. Shiller. (1990). "Forecasting Prices and Excess Returns in the Housing Market." *AREUEA Journal* 18(3): 253-273.

Casetti, E. (1997). "The Expansion Method, Mathematical Modelling, and Spatial Econometrics." *International Regional Science Review* 20(1,2): 9-32.

Champion, T., D. Atkins., M. Coombes., and S. Fotheringham. (1998). *Urban Exodus.* CPRE: London.

Cheshire, P. (1995). "A New Phase of Urban Development in Western Europe: The Evidence for the 1980s." *Urban Studies* 32(7): 1045-1063.

Cheshire, P., and S. Sheppard. (1989). "British Planning and Access to Housing: Some Empirical Estimates." *Urban Studies* 26(5): 469-485.

Cheshire, P., and S. Shepherd. (1995). "On the Price of Land and the Value of Amenities", *Economica* 62(246): 247-267.

Cheshire, P., and S. Sheppard. (1998) "Estimating the Demand for Housing, Land and Neighbourhood Characteristics." *Oxford Bulletin of Economics and Statistics* 60(3): 357-382.

Cho, M. (1996). "House Price Dynamics: A Survey of Theoretical and Empirical Issues." *Journal of Housing Research* 7(2): 145-172.

Clapp, J., and C. Giaccotto. (1992). "Estimating Price Indices for Residential Property: A Comparison of Repeat Sales and Assessed Value Methods." *Journal of the American Statistical Association* 87: 300-306.

Clapp, J.M., and D. Tirtiroglu. (1994). "Positive Feedback Trading and Diffusion of Asset Price Changes: Evidence from Housing Transactions." *Journal of Economic Behaviour and Organization* 24(3): 337-355.

Clark, W.A.V., and F.M. Dieleman. (1996). *Households and Housing: Choice and Outcomes in the Housing Market.* Center for Urban Policy Research: Rutgers.

Clark, W.A.V., and R. Flowerdew. (1982). "A Review of Search Models and their Application to Search in the Housing Market." in W.A.V. Clark (ed.) *Modelling Housing Market Search* Croom Helm: London: 4-29.

Coles, A., and J. Hardt. (2000). "Mortgage Markets: Why US and EU Markets Are So Different." *Housing Studies* 15(5): 775-783.

Cooke, T. (1978). "Causality Reconsidered: A Note." *Journal of Urban Economics* 5: 538-542.

Crone, T., and R. Voith. (1992). "Estimating House Price Appreciation: A Comparison of Methods." *Journal of Housing Economics* 2:324-338.

DETR (1997). *An Economic Model of the Demand and Need for Social Housing.* Department of the Environment, Transport and the Regions. London.

Department of Infrastructure. (2000). *Housing Ourselves: The Story Behind Housing in Victoria.* Victoria: Australia.

Dieleman, F.M., W.A.V. Clark, and C. Deurloo. (2000). "The Geography of Residential Turnover in Twenty-Seven Large US Metropolitan Housing Markets, 1985-95." *Urban Studies* 37(2): 223-245.

DiPasquale, D., and W. Wheaton. (1994). "Housing Market Dynamics and the Future of House Prices." *Journal of Urban Economics* 35(1): 1-27.

DiPasquale, D., and W. Wheaton. (1996). *Urban Economics and Real Estate Markets.* Prentice Hall: Englewood Cliffs, NJ.

Di Salvo, P., and J. Ermisch. (1997). "Analysis of the Dynamics of Housing Tenure Choice in Britain." *Journal of Urban Economics* 42: 1-17.

Dombrow, J., J.R. Knight., and C.F. Sirmans. (1997). "Aggregation Bias in Repeat-Sales Indices." *Journal of Real Estate Finance and Economics* 14(1,2): 75-88.

Dougherty, A., and R. Van Order. (1982). "Inflation, Housing Costs and the Consumer Price Index." *American Economic Review* 72(1): 154-165.

Drake, L.M. (1993). "Modelling UK House Prices Using Cointegration: An Application of the Johansen Technique." *Applied Economics* 9: 1225-1228.

Drake, L.M. (1995). "Testing for Convergence Between UK Regional House Prices." *Regional Studies* 29(4): 357-366.

Dubin, R.A. (1998). "Spatial Autocorrelation: A Primer." *Journal of Housing Economics* 7: 304-327.

Duffy, M. (1970). "A Model of UK Investment in Dwellings." *London Business School Discussion Paper No. 18.*

Early, D.W. (1999). "A Microeconomic Analysis of Homelessness: An Empirical Investigation Using Choice-Based Sampling." *Journal of Housing Economics* 8: 312-327.

Ebrill, L.P., and U.M. Possen. (1982). "Inflation and the Taxation of Equity in Corporations and Owner-Occupied Housing." *Journal of Money, Credit and Banking* 14(1): 33-47.

Eichholtz, P. (1997). "A Long-Run House Price Index: The Herengracht Index, 1628-1973." *Real Estate Economics* 25(2): 175-192.

Eldridge, N. (1984). "Melbourne: Population Density; Distance; the Relationship." *Journal of Urban Economics* 15(3): 310-316.

Engelhardt, G. (1994). "House Prices and the Decision to Save for Down Payments." *Journal of Urban Economics* 36: 209-237.

Engelhardt, G.V., and J.M. Poterba. (1991). "House Prices and Demographic Change, Canadian Evidence." *Regional Science and Urban Economics* 21(4): 539-546.

Englund, P., Gordon, T.M., and J.M. Quigley. (1999). "The Valuation of Real Capital: A Random Walk Down Kungsgaten." *Journal of Housing Economics* 8(3): 205-216.

Englund, P., P.H. Hendershott., and B. Turner. (1995). *The Tax Reform and The Housing Market.* Tax Reform Evaluation Report No. 20, National Institute of Economic Research, Sweden.

Englund, P., and Y. Ioannides. (1997). "House Price Dynamics: An International Empirical Perspective." *Journal of Housing Economics* 6(2): 119-136.

Englund, P., J.M. Quigley, and C.L. Redfearn. (1998). "Improved Price Indexes for Durable Goods: Measuring the Course of Swedish Housing Prices." *Journal of Urban Economics* 44: 171-196.

Englund, P., J.M. Quigley, and C.L. Redfearn. (1999). "The Choice of Methodology for Computing Housing Price Indexes: Comparison of Temporal Aggregation and Sample Definition." *Journal of Real Estate Finance and Economics* 19(2): 91-112.

Ermisch, J. (1996). "The Demand for Housing in Britain and Population Ageing: Microeconomic Evidence." *Economica* 63(251): 383-404.

Ermisch, J. (1999). "Prices, Parents and Young People's Household Formation." *Journal of Urban Economics* 45: 47-71.

Ermisch, J., and P. Di Salvo. (1996). "Surprises and Housing Tenure Decisions in Great Britain." *Journal of Housing Economics* 5: 247-273.

Ermisch, J., and P. Di Salvo. (1997). "The Economic Determinants of Young People's Household Formation." *Economica* 64: 627-644.

Ermisch, J.F., J. Findlay., and K. Gibb. (1996). "The Price Elasticity of Housing Demand in Britain: Issues of Sample Selection." *Journal of Housing Economics* 5: 64-86.

Evans, A.W. (1976). "Economic Influences on Social Mix." *Urban Studies* 13: 246-260.

Evans, A.W. (1988). *No Room ! No Room !,* Institute of Economic Affairs, London.

Evans, A.W. (1989). "South-East England in the Eighties: Explanations for House Price Explosion." in M.J. Breheny and P. Congden (eds) *Growth and Change in a Core Region.* London: Pion.

Evans, A.W. (1990). "The Assumption of Equilibrium in the Analysis of Migration and Interregional Differences." *Journal of Regional Science* 30(4): 515-531.

Evans, A.W. (1993). "Interregional Equilibrium: A Transatlantic View." *Journal of Regional Science* 33(1): 89-97.

Evans, A.W. (1996). "The Impact of Land Use Planning and Tax Subsidies on the Supply and Price of Housing in Britain: A Comment." *Urban Studies* 33(3): 581-585.

Evans, A.W., and R. Richardson. (1981). "Urban Unemployment: Interpretation and Additional Evidence." *Scottish Journal of Political Economy* 28(2): 107-124.

Evans, G., and L. Reichlin. (1994). "Information, Forecasts and Measurement of the Business Cycle." *Journal of Monetary Economics* 33: 233-254.

Evans, P., and B. McCormick. (1994). "The New Pattern of Regional Unemployment: Causes and Policy Significance." *Economic Journal* 104(424): 633-647.

Fieldhouse, E.A. (1999). "Ethnic Minority Unemployment and Spatial Mismatch: The Case of London." *Urban Studies* 36(9): 1569-1596.

Fielding, A.J. (1992). "Migration and Social Mobility: South East England as an Escalator Region." *Regional Studies* 26(1): 1-15.

Fingleton, B. (1991). "Industrial Location and Policy: A Spatial Statistical Analysis." *Papers in Regional Science* 70(3): 267-285.

Fleming, M.C., and J.G. Nellis. (1984). *The Halifax House Price Index Technical Details.* Published by the Halifax Bank.

Follain, J.R., and O.T. Velz. (1995). "Incorporating the Number of Existing Home Sales in a Structural Model of the Market for Owner-Occupied Housing." *Journal of Housing Economics* 4: 93-117.

Ford, J., and J. Seavers. (2000). *Attitudes to Moving and Debt: Household Behaviour in the 1990s.* Council of Mortgage Lenders Research Report.

Forrest, R., P. Leather., D. Gordon, and C. Pantazis. (1995). "The Future of Home-Ownership." *Housing Finance* 27(August): 9-15.

Fujita, M., P. Krugman, and A. Venables. (1999). *The Spatial Economy: Cities, Regions and International Trade.* MIT Press: Massachusetts.

Galster, G.C. (1998). *An Econometric Model of the Urban Opportunity Structure: Cumulative Causation Among City Markets, Social Problems, and Underserved Areas.* Fannie Mae Foundation Research Report.

Garrod, G., and K. Willis. (1992). "The Environmental Impact of Woodland: A Two-Stage Hedonic Price Model of the Amenity Value of Forestry in Britain." *Applied Economics* 24: 715-728.

Gatzlaff, D., and D.R. Haurin. (1997). "Sample Selection Bias and Repeat-Sales Index Estimates." *Journal of Real Estate Finance and Economics* 14(1,2): 33-50.

Gatzlaff, D., and D. Ling. (1994). "Measuring Changes in Local House Prices: An Empirical Investigation of Alternative Methodologies." *Journal of Urban Economics* 35: 221-244.

Gatzlaff, D., and D. Tirtiroglu. (1995). "Real Estate Market Efficiency: Issues and Evidence." *Journal of Real Estate Literature* 3(2): 157-192.

Giussani, B., and G. Hadjimatheou. (1990). "Econometric Modelling of UK House Prices." *The Cyprus Journal of Economics* 3(1): 36-57.

Giussani, B., and G. Hadjimatheou. (1991). "Modelling Regional House Prices in the UK." *Papers in Regional Science* 70: 201-219.

Giussani, B., and G. Hadjimatheou. (1991a). "Modelling the North/South Divide in House Prices." *University of Reading Discussion Paper No.* 66.

Goodman, A.C. (1981). "Housing Sub-Markets within Urban Areas: Definitions and Evidence." *Journal of Regional Science* 21(2): 175-185.

Goodman, A.C. (1988). "An Econometric Model of Housing Price, Permanent Income, Tenure Choice, and Housing Demand." *Journal of Urban Economics* 23(3): 327-353.

Goodman, A.C., and T.G. Thibodeau. (1998). "Housing Market Segmentation." *Journal of Housing Economics*. 7(2): 121-143.

Gordon, I. (1990). "Housing and Labour Market Constraints on Migration Across the North-South Divide." in J. Ermisch (ed.) *Housing and the National Economy*. Avebury.

Gordon, I. (1999). "London and the South East." Chapter 10 in M. Breheny (ed.), *The People Where Will They Work*. TCPA.

Green, F., and G. Hadjimatheou. (1990). "Regional Differences in Personal Savings." *Applied Economics* 22(7): 933-945.

Green, R., and P.H. Hendershott. (1996). "Age, Housing Demand and Real House Prices." *Regional Science and Urban Economics* 26(5): 465-480.

Groenewold, N. (1997). "Does Migration Equalise Regional Unemployment Rates? Evidence from Australia." *Papers in Regional Science* 76(1):1-20.

Gyourko, J., and P. Linneman. (1996). "Analysis of the Changing Influences on Traditional Households' Ownership Patterns." *Journal of Urban Economics* 39(3): 318-341.

Gyourko, J., and P. Linneman. (1997). "The Changing Influences of Education, Income, Family Structure and Race on Homeownership by Age over Time." *Journal of Housing Research* 8(1): 1-26.

Gyourko, J., and R. Voith. (1992). "Local Market and National Components in House Price Appreciation." *Journal of Urban Economics* 32(1): 52-69.

Hadjimatheou, G. (1976). *Housing and Mortgage Markets: The UK Experience*. Saxon House, Farnborough, Hants.

Hall, R.E. (1978). "Stochastic Implications of the Life Cycle-Permanent Income Hypothesis: Theory and Evidence." *Journal of Political Economy* 86: 971-987.

Hall, S., S. Lazarova, and G. Urga. (1999). "A Principal Components Analysis of Common Stochastic Trends in Heterogeneous Panel Data: Some Monte Carlo Evidence." *Oxford Bulletin of Economics and Statistics* Special Issue 61: 749-767.

Hall, S., Z. Psaradakis., and M. Sola. (1997). "Switching Error-Correction Models of House Prices in the United Kingdom." *Economic Modelling* 14(4): 517-528.

Hamilton, B.W. (1991). "The Baby Boom, The Baby Bust and the Housing Market: A Second Look." *Regional Science and Urban Economics* 21(4): 547-552.

Hamnett, C. (1988). "Regional Variations in House Prices in the United Kingdom, 1969-1988." *Royal Bank of Scotland Review* 159: 29-40.

Harsman, B., and J. Quigley. (1995). "The Spatial Segregation of Ethnic and Demographic Groups: Comparative Evidence from Stockholm and San Francisco." *Journal of Urban Economics* 37(1): 1-16.

Haurin, D.R., P.H. Hendershott, and D. Kim. (1994). "Housing Decisions of American Youth." *Journal of Urban Economics* 35: 28-44.

Haurin, D., P. Hendershott, and S. Wachter. (1997). "Borrowing Constraints and the Tenure Choice of Young Households. *Journal of Housing Research* 8(2): 137-154.

Heckman, J.J. (1974). "Shadow Prices, Market Wages and Labour Supply." *Econometrica* 42(4): 679-94.

Hendershott, P.H. (1991). "Are Real House Prices Likely to Decline by 47%?" *Regional Science and Urban Economics* 21(4): 553-564.

Hendershott, P.H., and S.C. Hu. (1981). "Inflation and Extra-ordinary Returns on Owner-Occupied Housing: Some Implications for Capital Allocation and Productivity Growth." *Journal of Macroeconomics* 3(2): 177-203.

Hendershott, P.H., and S.C. Hu. (1983). "The Allocation of Capital Between Residential and Non-Residential Uses, Taxes, Inflation and Credit Market Constraints." *Journal of Finance* 38(3): 795-812.

Hendershott, P.H., J. Slemrod. (1982). "Taxes and the User Cost of Capital for Owner-Occupied Housing." *AREUEA Journal* 10(4).

Henderson, J.V., and Y. Ioannides. (1983). "A Model of Housing Tenure Choice." *American Economic Review* 73(1): 98-113.

Hendry, D.F. (1984). "Econometric Modelling of House Prices in the United Kingdom." in D.F. Hendry and K.F. Wallis (eds). *Econometrics and Quantitative Economics*. Oxford: Basil Blackwell.

Henley, A. (1998). "Residential Mobility, Housing Equity and the Labour Market." *Economic Journal* 108(447): 414-427.

Hill, R.C., J.R. Knight., and C.F. Sirmans. (1997). "Estimating Capital Asset Price Indexes." *Review of Economics and Statistics* 79(2): 226-233.

Holland, A.S. (1991) "The Baby Boom and the Housing Market: Another Look at the Evidence." *Regional Science and Urban Economics* 21(4): 565-572.

Holly, S., and N. Jones. (1997). "House Prices Since the 1940s: Cointegration, Demography and Asymmetries." *Economic Modelling* 14(4): 549-566.

Holmans, A. (1990). "House Prices: Changes Through Time at National and Sub-National Level", *Government Economic Service Working Paper 110.*

Holmans, A. (1995). "What Has Happened to the North-South Divide in House Prices and the Housing Market?" *Housing Finance Review 1995/96.* Joseph Rowntree Foundation.

Holmans, A. (1995a). *Housing Demand and Need in England 1991-2011*. Joseph Rowntree Foundation: York.

Holmans, A. (1996). "A Decline in Young Owner-Occupiers in the 1990s." *Housing Finance*, 29: 13-20.

Holmans, A. (1996a). *Housing Demand and Need in Wales 1991-2011*. Joseph Rowntree Foundation: York.

Holzer, H.J. (1991). "The Spatial Mismatch Hypothesis: What Has the Evidence Shown?" *Urban Studies* 28(1):105-122.

Hort, K. (1997). "On Price Formation and Quantity Adjustment in Swedish Housing Markets." *Economic Studies*. 34. Uppsala University: Sweden.

Hort, K. (1998). "The Determinants of Urban House Price Fluctuations in Sweden 1968-1994." *Journal of Housing Economics* 7(2): 93-120.

Hort, K. (2000). "Prices and Turnover in the Market for Owner-Occupied Homes." *Regional Science and Urban Economics* 30: 99-119.

Hosios, A., and J. Pesando. (1991). "Measuring Prices in Resale Housing Markets in Canada: Evidence and Implications." *Journal of Housing Economics* 1(4): 303-317.

Hughes, G.A., and B. McCormick. (1981). "Do Council House Policies Reduce Migration Between Regions?" *Economic Journal* 91(364):919-39.

Hughes, G.A., and B. McCormick. (1985). "Migration Intentions in the UK. Which Households want to Migrate and Which Succeed?" *Economic Journal* 95(Supplement): 113-23.

Hughes, G.A., and B. McCormick. (1987). "Housing Markets, Unemployment and Labour Market Flexibility in the UK." *European Economic Review* 31(3): 615-45.

Hughes, G.A., and B. McCormick. (1990). "Housing and Labour Market Mobility." in J.Ermisch (ed.). *Housing and the National Economy*. Avebury.

Hyclak, T.J., and C. Johnes. (1992). "Regional Wage Inflation and Unemployment Dynamics in Great Britain." *Scottish Journal of Political Economy* 39(2): 188-200.

Ihlanfeldt, K.R., and D.L. Sjoquist. (1998). "The Spatial Mismatch Hypothesis: A Review of Recent Studies and Their Implication for Welfare Reform." *Housing Policy Debate* 9(4): 849-892.

Jackman, R. and S. Savouri. (1992). "Regional Migration in Britain. An Analysis of Gross Flows using NHS Central Register Data." *Economic Journal* 102(415): 1433-1451.

Jones, K., and N. Bullen. (1994). "Contextual Models of Urban House Prices: A Comparison of Fixed and Random-Coefficient Models Developed by Expansion." *Economic Geography* 70(3): 252-270.

Kaldor, N. (1972). "The Irrelevance of Equilibrium Economics." *Economic Journal* 82: 1237-1255.

Kau, J.B., and D. Keenan. (1983). "Inflation, Taxes and Housing: A Theoretical Analysis." *Journal of Public Economics* 21(1): 93-104.

Keenan, P., S. Lowe, and S. Spencer. (1999). "Housing Abandonment in Inner Cities – The Politics of Low Demand for Housing." *Housing Studies*, 14(5): 703-716.

Kennedy, N., and P. Andersen. (1994). "Household Saving and Real House Prices: An International Perspective." *Monetary and Economic Department: Bank for International Settlements. Working Paper 20.*

King, M. (1980). "An Econometric Model of Tenure Choice and Demand for Housing as a Joint Decision." *Journal of Public Economics* 14(2): 137-159.

King, M. (1990). "Discussion of J Muellbauer and A Murphy, Is the UK Balance of Payments Sustainable?" *Economic Policy* 11: 383-387.

King, M. (2000). "Backdoor." *Roof* 25(2): 48.

Koskela, E., and M. Viren. (1992). "Inflation, Capital Markets and Household Saving in the Nordic Countries." *Scandinavian Journal of Economics* 94(2): 215-27.

Kosonen, K. (1997). "House Price Dynamics in Finland: A Time Series Analysis of the Period 1979-95." *ENHR Housing Workshop*, Vienna.

Krugman, P. (1991). *Geography and Trade*. Leuven University Press and The MIT Press.

Lamont, O., and J.C. Stein. (1999). "Leverage and House Price Dynamics in U.S. Cities." *Rand Journal of Economics* 30(3): 498-514.

Leishman, C. (2000). "Estimating Local Housing Market Price Indices Using Land Registry Data." *Housing Finance* 47: 55-60.

Linneman, P., and S. Wachter. (1989). "The Impacts of Borrowing Constraints on Home Ownership." *AREUEA Journal* 17: 389-402.

London Business School. (1979). "Quarterly Econometric Model of the UK Economy."

Long, L. (1992). "Changing Residence: Comparative Perspectives on its Relationship to Age, Sex and Marital Status". *Population Studies* 46: 141-158.

McAvinchey, I.D., and D. Maclennan. (1982). "A Regional Comparison of House Price Inflation Rates in Britain, 1967-76". *Urban Studies* 19(1): 43-57.

McDonald, J.F. (1989). "Econometric Studies of Urban Population Density: A Survey." *Journal of Urban Economics* 26: 361-385.

MacDonald, R., and M.P. Taylor. (1993). "Regional House Prices in Britain: Long-Run Relationships and Short-Run Dynamics." *Scottish Journal of Political Economy* 40(1): 43-55.

McGregor, A., M. Munro., M. Heafey., and P. Symon. (1992) "Moving Job, Moving House: The Impact of House on Long Distance Labour Mobility." *University of Glasgow, Centre for Housing Research Discussion Paper No. 38.*

Maclennan, D., J. Muellbauer, and M. Stephens. (1998). "Asymmetries in Housing and Financial Market Institutions and EMU." *Oxford Review of Economic Policy* 14(3): 54-80.

Maclennan, D., and Y. Tu. (1996). "Economic Perspectives on the Structure of Local Housing Systems." *Housing Studies* 11(3): 387-406.

Malpezzi, S. (1996). "Is Theory Outrunning Measurement in Real Estate Economics? Some Observations from the US." *SHAPE Conference Paper*. London Business School.

Malpezzi, S. (1999). "A Simple Error Correction Model of House Prices." *Journal of Housing Economics* 8(1): 27-62.

Mankiw, N.G., and D.N. Weil. (1989). "Baby Boom, Baby Bust and the Housing Market." *Regional Science and Urban Economics* 19(2): 235-258.

Mark, J., and M. Goldberg. (1984) "Alternative Housing Price Indices: An Evaluation." *AREUEA Journal* 12(1): 30-49.

Marshall, A. (1920). *Principles of Economics*. Macmillan: London.

Mason C., and J.M. Quigley. (1996). "Non-Parametric Hedonic Housing Prices." *Housing Studies* 11(3): 373-344.

Mayes, D.G. (1979). *The Property Boom: The Effects of Building Society Behaviour on House Prices*. Martin Robertson, Oxford.

Mayo, S (1981), "Theory and Estimation in the Economics of Housing Demand." *Journal of Urban Economics* 10(1): 95-116.

Mayo, S., and S. Sheppard. (1992). "Housing Supply and the Effects of Stochastic Development Control". *Oberlin College Discussion Paper*.

Mayo, S. and S. Sheppard. (1996). "Housing Supply Under Rapid Economic Growth and Varying Regulatory Stringency: An International Comparison." *Journal of Housing Economics* 5(3): 274-289.

Meen, G.P. (1989). "The Ending of Mortgage Rationing and its Effects on the Housing Market: A Simulation Study." *Urban Studies* 26(2): 240-252.

Meen, G.P. (1990). "The Removal of Mortgage Market Constraints and the Implications for Econometric Modelling of UK House Prices." *Oxford Bulletin of Economics and Statistics* 52(1): 1-24.

Meen, G.P. (1990a). "The Measurement of Rationing and the Treatment of Structural Change in the UK Mortgage Market." *Journal of Applied Econometrics* 2(2): 167-188.

Meen, G.P. (1995). "Is Housing Good for the Economy?" *Housing Studies* 10(3): 405-424.

Meen, G.P. (1996). "Spatial Aggregation, Spatial Dependence and Predictability in the UK Housing Market." *Housing Studies* 11(3): 345-372.

Meen, G.P. (1996a). "Ten Propositions in UK Housing Macroeconomics: An Overview of the Eighties and Early Nineties." *Urban Studies* 33(3): 425-444.

Meen, G.P. (1998). "Modelling Sustainable Home – Ownership: Demographics or Economics?" *Urban Studies* 35(11): 1919-1934.

Meen, G.P. (1999). "Regional House Prices and the Ripple Effect: A New Interpretation." *Housing Studies* 14(6): 733-753.

Meen, G.P. (2000). "Housing Cycles and Efficiency." *Scottish Journal of Political Economy* 47(2): 114-140.

Meen, G.P., and M. Andrew. (1998). "On the Aggregate Housing Market Implications of Labour Market Change." *Scottish Journal of Political Economy* 45(4): 393-419.

Meen, G.P., and M. Andrew. (1998a) *Modelling Regional House Prices: A Review of the Literature*. Report prepared for the Department of the Environment, Transport and the Regions. The University of Reading.

Meen, G.P., and M. Andrew. (1999). "Spatial Structure and Social Exclusion". *University of Reading Discussion Paper in Urban and Regional Economics No. 140.*

Meese, R.A., and N.E. Wallace. (1994). "Testing the Present Value Relation for Housing Prices: Should I Leave My House in San Francisco?" *Journal of Urban Economics* 35: 245-266.

Meese, R.A., and N.E. Wallace. (1997). "The Construction of Residential House Price Indices: A Comparison of Repeat-Sales, Hedonic-Regression and Hybrid Approaches." *Journal of Real Estate Finance and Economics* 14(1,2): 51-74.

Metcalf, D., and R. Richardson. (1976). "Unemployment in London." in G.D.N. Warwick (ed.), *The Measurement of Involuntary Unemployment.* Allen and Unwin: London.

Miles, D. (1992). "Housing Markets, Consumption and Financial Liberalisation in the Major Economies." *European Economic Review* 36(5): 1093-1136.

Miles, D. (1997). "A Household Level Study of the Determinants of Incomes and Consumption." *Economic Journal* 107(440): 1-25.

Mills, E.S. (1992). "The Measurement and Determinants of Suburbanization." *Journal of Urban Economics* 32: 377-387.

Mills, E.S., and R. Price. (1984). "Metropolitan Suburbanization and Central City Problems." *Journal of Urban Economics* 15: 1-17.

Monk, S. (2000). "The 'Key Worker' Problem: The Link Between Employment and Housing." in S. Monk and C. Whitehead (eds), *Restructuring Housing Systems: From Social to Affordable Housing?* York Publishing Services: York.

Monk, S., B. Pearce., and C. Whitehead. (1991). *Planning, Land Supply and House Prices: A Literature Review.* Monograph 21, Department of Land Economy, University of Cambridge.

Muellbauer, J. (1983). "Surprises in the Consumption Function." *Economic Journal* 93(Supplement): 34-49.

Muellbauer, J. (1990). "The Housing Market and the UK Economy: Problems and Opportunities." in J. Ermisch (ed.) *Housing and the National Economy.* Avebury.

Muellbauer, J. (1994). "Anglo-German Differences in Housing Market Fluctuations: The Role of Institutions and Macroeconomic Policy." *Economic Modelling* 11(2): 238-249.

Muellbauer, J., and A. Murphy. (1990). "Is the UK Balance of Payments Sustainable." *Economic Policy* 11: 347-382.

Muellbauer, J., and A. Murphy. (1994). "Explaining Regional House Prices in the UK." *University College Dublin, Department of Economics Working Paper WP94/21.*

Muellbauer, J., and A. Murphy. (1994a). "Explaining Regional Consumption in the UK." *University College Dublin, Department of Economics Working Paper WP94/29.*

Muellbauer, J., and A. Murphy. (1997). " Booms and Busts in the UK Housing Market." *Economic Journal* 107(445): 1701-1727.

Munro, M., and Y. Tu. (1996). *UK House Price Dynamics: Past and Future Trends.* Council of Mortgage Lenders Research Report.

Munro, M., and Y. Tu. (1996a). "The Dynamics of UK National and Regional House Prices." *Review of Urban and Regional Development Studies* 8(2): 186-201.

Muth, R.F. (1969). *Cities and Housing*. University of Chicago Press: Chicago.

Muth, R.F. (1971). "Migration: Chicken or Egg?" *Southern Economic Journal* 37: 295-306.

Muth, R.F., and A.C. Goodman. (1989) *The Economics of Housing Markets*. Harwood Publishers.

Myrdal, G. (1957). *Economic Theory and Underdeveloped Regions*. Duckworth: London.

Nakagami, Y., and A.M. Pereira. (1991). "Housing Appreciation, Mortgage Interest Rates and Homeowner Mobility." *Journal of Urban Economics* 30: 271-292.

Nakagami, Y., and A.M. Pereira. (1993). "Uptrading and the Macroeconomic Environment." *Journal of Urban Economics* 31: 1-23.

Nellis, J.G., and J.A. Longbottom. (1981), "An Empirical Analysis of the Determination of House Prices in the United Kingdom." *Urban Studies* 18(1): 9-21.

Nordvik, V. (1995). " Prices and Price Expectations in the Market for Owner Occupied Housing." *Housing Studies* 10(3): 365-380.

ONS. (1998). *Focus on London*. Office for National Statistics, London Research Centre, Government Office for London.

Ortalo-Magné, F., and S. Rady. (1999). "Boom In, Bust Out: Young Households and the Housing Price Cycle." *European Economic Review* 43: 755-766.

Ortalo-Magné, F., and S. Rady. (2000). *The Rise and Fall of Residential Transactions in England and Wales*. Council of Mortgage Lenders Research Report.

Oswald, A. (1996). "A Conjecture on the Explanation for High Unemployment in the Industrialised Nations: Part 1". *Warwick University Economic Research Papers No. 475.*

Pain, N., and P. Westaway. (1997). "Modelling Structural Change in the UK Housing Market: A Comparison of Alternative House Price Models." *Economic Modelling* 14(4): 587-610.

Patterson, K. (1993). "The Impact of Credit Constraints, Interest Rates, and Housing Equity Withdrawal on the Intertemporal Pattern of Consumption-A Diagrammatic Analysis." *Scottish Journal of Political Economy* 40(4): 391-407.

Peek, J., and J.A. Wilcox. (1991). "The Measurement and Determinants of Single-Family House Prices." *AREUEA Journal* 19(3): 353-82.

Pennington, G., N. Topham, and R. Ward. (1990). "Aircraft Noise and Residential Property Values Adjacent to Manchester International Airport." *Journal of Transport Economics and Policy* 24(1): 49-60.

Pesaran, M.H., and R. Smith. (1995). "Estimating Long-Run Relationships from Dynamic Heterogeneous Panels." *Journal of Econometrics* 68(1): 79-113.

Pissarides, C.A., and I. McMaster. (1990). "Regional Migration, Wages, Unemployment: Empirical Evidence and Implications for Policy." *Oxford Economic Papers* 42: 812-831.

Pissarides, C.A., and J. Wadsworth. (1989). "Unemployment and the Interregional Mobility of Labour." *Economic Journal* 99(397): 739-755.

Plaut, E. (1987). "The Timing of Housing Tenure Transition." *Journal of Urban Economics* 21: 312-322.

Polinsky, A.M. (1977). "The Demand for Housing: A Study in Specification and Grouping." *Econometrica* 45(2): 447-461.

Polinsky, A.M. (1979). "The Demand for Housing: An Empirical Postscript." *Econometrica* 47(2): 521-523.

Polinsky, A.M., and D.T. Ellwood. (1979). "An Empirical Reconciliation of Micro and Grouped Estimates of the Demand for Housing." *Review of Economics and Statistics* 61(2): 199-205.

Pollakowski, H.O., and T.S. Ray. (1997). "Housing Price Diffusion Patterns at Different Aggregation Levels: An Examination of Housing Market Efficiency." *Journal of Housing Research* 8(1): 107-124.

Porter, M. (1995). "The Comparative Advantage of the Inner City." *Harvard Business Review* 73(3): 55-71.

Poterba, J.M. (1984). "Tax Subsidies to Owner-Occupied Housing: An Asset Market Approach." *Quarterly Journal of Economics* XCIX(4): 729-752.

Poterba, J.M. (1991). "House Price Dynamics: The Role of Tax Policy and Demographics." *Brookings Papers on Economic Activity No. 2*: 143-199.

Power, A. (2000) "From Unlettable Homes to Urban Sprawl: Planning for Housing Need." in R. Bate, R. Best and A. Holmans (eds), *On the Move: The Housing Consequences of Migration*. Joseph Rowntree Foundation: York: 20-34.

Power, A., and K. Mumford. (1999) *The Slow Death of Great Cities?* Joseph Rowntree Foundation: York.

Pryce, G. (1999). "Construction Elasticities and Land Availability: A Two-Stage Least-Squares Model of Housing Supply Using the Variable Elasticity Approach." *Urban Studies* 36(13): 2283-2304.

Quigley, J.M. (1985). "Consumer Choice of Dwellings, Neighborhood and Public Services." *Regional Science and Urban Economics* 41: 41-63.

Ramsey, F.P. (1928). "A Mathematical Theory of Saving." *Economic Journal* 38(152): 543-559.

Reilly, B., and R. Witt. (1994). "Regional House Prices and Possessions in England and Wales: An Empirical Analysis." *Regional Studies* 28(5): 475-82.

Rosen, H.S. (1979). "Housing Decisions and the US Income Tax: An Econometric Analysis." *Journal of Public Economics* 11(1): 1-23.

Rosen, H.S. (1979a). "Owner-Occupied Housing and the Federal Income Tax: Estimates and Simulations." *Journal of Urban Economics* 6(2): 247-266.

Rosen, H.S., and K.T. Rosen. (1980). "Federal Taxes and Home Ownership: Evidence from Time Series." *Journal of Political Economy* 88(1): 69-75.

Rosen, H.S., K.T. Rosen, and D. Holtz-Eakin (1984). "Housing Tenure, Uncertainty and Taxation." *Review of Economics and Statistics* LXVI(5): 405-416.

Rosenthal, L. (1984). "Quarterly Owner-Occupied House Price Indices for the UK 1975-81." *Manchester School* 52(3): 272-283.

Rosenthal, L. (1986). "Regional House Price Interactions in the UK, 1975-1981: A Cross-Spectral Analysis." *Applied Economics* 18(9): 1011-1023.

Rosenthal, L. (1989). "Income and Price Elasticities of Demand for Owner-Occupied Housing in the UK. Evidence from Pooled Cross-Sectional and Time Series Data." *Applied Economics* 21(6): 761-775.

Rothbarth, E. (1941). "The Measurement of Changes in Real Income Under Conditions of Rationing." *Review of Economic Studies* 8: 100-107.

Salant, S.W. (1991). "For Sale by Owner: When to Use a Broker and How to Price the House." *Journal of Real Estate Finance and Economics* 4: 157-173.

Schwab, R.M. (1983). "Real and Nominal Interest Rates and the Demand for Housing." *Journal of Urban Economic* 13(2): 181-95.

Smith, J. (2000). "Attitudes to Home-ownership and Mortgage Choices: 1999 Market Research Findings." *Housing Finance* 45: 20-24.

Steele, M., and R. Goy. (1997). "Short Holds, The Distribution of First and Second Sales, and Bias in the Repeat-Sales Price Index." *Journal of Real Estate Finance and Economics* 14(1,2): 133-154.

Stein, J.C. (1995). "Prices and Trading Volume in the Housing Market: A Model with Downpayment Effects." *The Quarterly Journal of Economics* 110(2): 379-405.

Steinnes, D.N. (1977). "Causality and Intraurban Location." *Journal of Urban Economics* 4: 69-79.

Steinnes, D.N. (1982). "Do People Follow Jobs or Do Jobs Follow People? A Causality Issue in Urban Economics." *Urban Studies* 19(2): 187-192.

Stephens, M. (2000). "Convergence in European Mortgage Systems Before and After EMU." *Journal of Housing and the Built Environment* 15(1): 29-52.

Stern, D. (1992). "Explaining UK House Price Inflation 1971-89." *Applied Economics* 24(12): 1327-1333.

Stigler, G.J. (1961). "The Economics of Information." *Journal of Political Economy* LXIX(3): 213-225.

Stiglitz, J., and A. Weiss. (1981). "Credit Rationing in Markets with Imperfect Information." *American Economic Review* 71(3): 393-410.

Stimson, R.J. (1999). "Concentration and Dispersal, Suburbanization and Reurbanization in Australia." Chapter 10 in K. O'Connor (ed.), *Houses and Jobs in Cities and Regions*. AHURI: University of Queensland Press.

Stuart, A. (1996). "Simple Monetary Policy Rules." *Bank of England Quarterly Bulletin* August: 281-287.

Summers, L.H. (1981). "Inflation, the Stock Market and Owner-Occupied Housing." *American Economic Review, Papers and Proceedings*. 71(2): 429-434.

Swan, C. (1984). "A Model of Rental and Owner-Occupied Housing." *Journal of Urban Economics* 16(3): 297-316.

Taylor, J., and S. Bradley. (1994). "Spatial Disparities in the Impact of the 1990-92 Recession. An Analysis of UK Counties." *Oxford Bulletin of Economics and Statistics* 56(4): 367-382.

Theil, H. (1954). *Linear Aggregation in Economic Relations*. Amsterdam: North Holland.

Thomas, A. (1993). "The Influence of Wages and House Prices on British Interregional Migration Decisions." *Applied Economics* 25(9):1261-1268.

Thurston, L., and A.M.J. Yezer. (1994). "Causality in the Suburbanization of Population and Employment." *Journal of Urban Economics* 35: 105-118.

Tirtiroglu, D. (1992). "Efficiency in Housing Markets: Temporal and Spatial Dimensions." *Journal of Housing Economics* 2(3): 276-292.

Titman, S. (1982). "The Effects of Anticipated Inflation on Housing Market Equilibrium." *Journal of Finance* 37(5): 827-842.

Topel, R., and S. Rosen. (1988). "Housing Investment in the United States." *Journal of Political Economy* 96(4): 718-740.

Tsoukis, C., and P. Westaway. (1994). "A Forward Looking Model of Housing Consumption in the UK." *Economic Modelling* 11(2): 266-279.

Tu, Y. (1999) "The Dynamics of Australian Housing Prices, 1989-1998." in J. Yates and M. Wulff (eds). *Australia's Housing Choices*. AHURI: University of Queensland Press: 53-72.

Tu, Y., and J. Goldfinch. (1996). "A Two Stage Model of Housing Choice." *Urban Studies* 33(3): 517-537.

Turnovsky, S.J., and T. Okuyama. (1994). "Taxes, Housing and Capital Accumulation in a Two-Sector Growing Economy." *Journal of Public Economics* 53: 245-267.

Turok, I., and N. Edge. (1999). *The Jobs Gap in Britain's Cities: Employment Loss and Labour Market Consequences*. The Policy Press.

Wang, F.T., and P.M. Zorn (1997). "Estimating House Price Growth With Respect to Sales Data: What's the Aim of the Game?" *Journal of Housing Economics* 6(2): 93-118.

Weiss, Y. (1978). "Capital Gains, Discriminatory Taxes and the Choice Between Renting and Owning a House." *Journal of Public Economics* 10(4): 45-55.

Wheaton, W.C. (1977). "Income and Urban Residence: An Analysis of Consumer Demand for Location." *American Economic Review* 67(4): 620-631.

Wheaton, W.C. (1990). "Vacancy, Search, and Prices in a Housing Market Matching Model." *Journal of Political Economy* 98: 1270-1292.

White, E., and G. Hewings. (1982). "Space-Time Employment Modelling: Some Results Using Seemingly Unrelated Regression Estimators." *Journal of Regional Science* 22(3): 283-302.

Whitehead, C.M.E. (1971). "A Model of the UK Housing Market." *BOUIES* 33(4): 245-266.

Whitehead, C.M.E. (1974). *The UK Housing Market: An Econometric Model*. Saxon House: Farnborough.

Whitehead, C.M.E. (1975). "Inflation and the New Housing Market." *BOUIES* 35(4): 275-293.

Woodward, S.E. (1991). "Economist's Prejudices: Why the Mankiw-Weil Story is not Credible." *Regional Science and Urban Economics* 21(4): 531-537.

Wulff, M., and S. Evans. (1999). "The Spatial Impacts of Commonwealth Rent Assistant on Australia's Low-Income Households." in J. Yates, and M. Wulff (eds), *Australia's Housing Choices*. AHURI: University of Queensland Press.

Yates, J., and M. Wulff. (1999). "Recent Developments in the Analysis of Australia's Private Rental Market." Chapter 6 in K. O'Connor (ed.), *Houses and Jobs in Cities and Regions*. AHURI: University of Queensland Press.

Yates, J., and M. Wulff. (2000). "W(h)ither Low Cost Private Rental Housing?" *Urban Policy and Research* 18(1): 45-64.

Zorn, P.M. (1989). "Mobility-Tenure Decisions and Financial Credit: Do Mortgage Qualification Requirements Constrain Home Ownership?" *AREUEA Journal*.

Index